Greenfields, Brownfields and Housing Development

D1078805

David Adams

and

Craig Watkins

European Urban and Regional Research Centre
Department of Land Economy
University of Aberdeen

Blackwell
Science

© David Adams and Craig Watkins 2002

Blackwell Science Ltd, a Blackwell
Publishing Company
Editorial Offices:
Osney Mead, Oxford OX2 0EL, UK
  Tel: +44 (0)1865 206206
Blackwell Science, Inc., 350 Main Street,
Malden, MA 02148-5018, USA
  Tel: +1 781 388 8250
Iowa State Press, a Blackwell Publishing
Company, 2121 State Avenue, Ames, Iowa
50014-8300, USA
  Tel: +1 515 292 0140
Blackwell Publishing Asia Pty Ltd,
550 Swanston Street, Carlton South,
Melbourne, Victoria 3053, Australia
  Tel: +61 (0)3 9347 0300
Blackwell Wissenschafts Verlag,
Kurfürstendamm 57, 10707 Berlin, Germany
  Tel: +49 (0)30 32 79 060

First published 2002 by Blackwell Science Ltd

Library of Congress
Cataloging-in-Publication Data
is available

ISBN 0-632-06387-4

A catalogue record for this title is available
from the British Library

Set in 10/13 pt Trump Mediaeval
by Sparks Computer Solutions Ltd, Oxford
http://www.sparks.co.uk
Printed and bound in Great Britain by
MPG Books Ltd, Bodmin, Cornwall

For further information on
Blackwell Science, visit our website:
www.blackwell-science.com

efforts, pointed us to essential reading material and acted as an important exchange for emerging ideas.

Finally, we would want to thank Madeleine Metcalfe, our Senior Commissioning Editor at Blackwell Publishing, for encouraging us to get started, for keeping us on the straight and narrow as we progressed, and for maintaining exactly the right balance between flexibility and persistence as we neared our submission deadline.

About the Authors

David Adams is Professor and Head of the Department of Land Economy at the University of Aberdeen. He has published widely on the relationship between market processes and planning systems, most notably as author of *Urban Planning and the Development Process* (UCL Press, 1994) and as co-author of *Land for Industrial Development* (E & FN Spon, 1994). He has undertaken extensive research for the Economic and Social Research Council on land ownership constraints to urban redevelopment, the market availability of industrial land, access to decision-makers in local planning, and landowner involvement in the local planning process. David Adams is both a Fellow of the Royal Town Planning Institute and a Member of the Royal Institution of Chartered Surveyors.

Craig Watkins is a Senior Lecturer in the Department of Land Economy at the University of Aberdeen. His main research interests are in housing economics and policy. He has published widely in academic and professional journals on the structure and operation of land and property markets and the impact of public policy on property market performance. He is currently undertaking a major Economic and Social Research Council, DTLR and RICS Foundation study measuring performance in the urban regeneration property market.

Abbreviations

ALURE	Alternative Land Use and Rural Economy
AONB	Area of Outstanding Natural Beauty
BEC	Building Employers' Confederation
BES	Business Expansion Scheme
CABE	Commission for Architecture and the Built Environment
CHP	Combined Heat and Power
CLA	Country Landowners' Association
CPO	Compulsory Purchase Order
CPRE	Council for the Protection of Rural England
DETR	Department of the Environment, Transport and the Regions
DOE	Department of the Environment
DOT	Department of Transport
DTLR	Department of Transport, Local Government and the Regions
EZ	Enterprise Zone
FHSA	Family Health Service Association
FMB	Federation of Master Builders
GDP	Gross Domestic Product
GEAR	Glasgow Eastern Area Renewal
GIS	Geographical Information Systems
GOR	Government Offices for the Region
HBF	House Builders' Federation
HMA	Housing Market Area
IPS	International Passenger Survey
LCHO	Low Cost Home Ownership
LEC	Local Enterprise Company
LSVT	Large Scale Voluntary Transfers
LUCS	Land Use Change Statistics
MAFF	Ministry of Agriculture, Fisheries and Food
MIRAS	Mortgage Interest Relief at Source
NFU	National Farmers' Union
NHBC	National House Building Council
NIMBY	'Not In My Back Yard'
NLIS	National Land Information Service
NLUD	National Land Use Database
NPPG	National Planning Policy Guideline
ONS	Office for National Statistics
PES	Price Elasticity of Supply
PPG	Planning Policy Guidance Note
PUR	Polycentric Urban Region
RPC	Regional Planning Conference

RPG	Regional Planning Guidance
RSL	Registered Social Landlord
RTB	Right to Buy
RTPI	Royal Town Planning Institute
ScotLIS	Scottish Land Information Service
SERPLAN	South East Regional Planning Conference
SHG	Social Housing Grant
SLF	Scottish Landowners' Federation
SPZ	Simplified Planning Zones
SVDLS	Scottish Vacant and Derelict Land Survey
TCPA	Town and Country Planning Association
TECs	Training and Enterprise Councils
TIF	Tax and Incremental Financing
TIG	Territorial Interest Group
TTWA	Travel to Work Areas
UCS	Urban Capacity Studies
UDC	Urban Development Corporations
UDP	Unitary Development Plan
UPP	User Pays Principle
UPZ	Urban Partnership Zone
VAT	Value Added Tax
VBSG	Volume Builders' Study Group

Part I

The Policy Context

1

Introduction

Strong growth in household formation rates, a strongly protectionist countryside and environmental lobby, and powerful interests in the private development industry have generated a great deal of controversy around public policy impacting on the provision of land for new housing development. In particular, heated debate has grown up around national and regional estimates of new housing demand, targets for the reuse of previously developed land and what this means for development on brownfield and greenfield sites. The debate has spilled over into disputes about urban sprawl and countryside protection, the role of the green belt, and the establishment of new towns and settlements.

Often the debates surrounding housing development have been presented by the media in emotive terms. One high-profile example is the coverage given to the proposed development of 10 000 new homes in a major urban extension west of Stevenage, described as 'the biggest incursion into the green belt since the war'. While a spokesperson for the House Builders' Federation (HBF) labelled opposition to this proposal as an attempt to 'dictate people's lifestyle or the place they want to live', the Council for the Protection of Rural England (CPRE) describes this and other related development proposals as a choice between '650 miles of freshly concreted countryside or less derelict land, fewer empty homes and an improved quality of life in towns and cities' (quotations from Hetherington & May 1998, p. 15).

Similarly controversial was the content of the Crow Report, produced by the panel appointed to examine the draft Regional Planning Guidance for the South East of England which was published in September 1999 and sought to estimate the levels of development required in the region (Government Office for the South East 1999). The report recommended the development of 1.1 million new homes between 1996 and 2016, of which it considered that only 50% would be on brownfield land. It suggested that major greenfield developments would be required at Stansted, Ashford, Milton Keynes and Crawley. While on the one hand this was heralded by the Town and Country Planning Association (TCPA) and by the HBF as 'common sense' and 'a positive and realistic vision' for the region, individual local authorities, South East Regional Planning Conference (SERPLAN), Friends of the Earth and the CPRE preferred phrases such as 'sheer madness' and 'simply not acceptable' (Grayson 2000).

Against this background, it is clear that decisions about the scale and location of new housing development have a wide range of potential social, economic and political effects. This book provides a comprehensive analysis of the institutional context within which residential development takes place, and examines the economic and political pressures influencing the development of greenfield and brownfield land. In general, housing land policy poses an exemplar test of the extent to which private sector and quasi-independent agencies, operating beyond the immediate control of the state, can be persuaded to deliver government policy objectives. In broader terms, the book examines the extent to which the state is able to influence the operation of land and property markets in partnership with market actors.

Aims and objectives

This book will argue that sustainable compact cities can be achieved only if the process of development is better managed and the products of development are of high quality. This has important implications for private investment and public policy. In particular, excessive reliance should not be placed on the planning system alone as a policy measure. Instead, planning should form part of a broader land policy, if tightened controls on greenfield development are not to prove ultimately self-defeating.

The objectives of the book are thus:

- To examine the institutional and policy context in which residential development takes place.

- To analyse the social, economic and political influences on public policy and private investment in relation to housing development.

- To place current controversies on the location of new housing development within an institutional context.

- To evaluate recent changes in the housebuilding industry and examine the industry's capacity to switch production increasingly to brownfield development.

- To explore how the concept of sustainable development provides both a common and contested discourse for debates on housing development.

- To analyse greenfield and brownfield development potential and recent achievements.

- To examine the financial and economic impact of housing land policies.

- To assess the implications of this analysis for the development of future policy.

The theoretical perspective

In essence, as well as being about greenfield and brownfield development, this book is a case study in changing state–market relations. Although there is no lengthy explicit discussion of the methodological stance of the authors, the approach adopted is broadly that of institutional analysis. This approach infuses the analysis throughout the book and its intellectual antecedents can be found in a range of social science writings, particularly in political economy, political science and sociology and, more generally, in applied policy analysis and evaluation. Indeed, considerable influence has been exerted on our approach by the political economy of 'old' economic institutionalism and the related sociological institutionalism, which focuses on the changing nature of social relations and how these relations are shaped.

The approach adopted is broadly in keeping with the recent resurgence of interest in institutional modes of analysis across a range of social science disciplines. While the breadth of interest is encouraging, however, the distinctive ways in which jargon is used in different research communities introduce the need for some clarification.

We begin this short introduction to our approach by explaining what we mean by an institution and, in turn, by institutional analysis. The economist Walter Hamilton describes an institution as: 'a way of thought or action of some prevalence, which is embedded in the habits of a group or the customs of people.' Hamilton goes on to say 'institutions fix the confines of and impose structure upon the activities of human beings' (Hamilton 1932, p. 84; also cited in Lawson 1997, p. 317; Hodgson 1999, p. 89).

In extending this definition, Hodgson (1997) asserts the social aspects of institutions and the role of habits and emphasises the role of both informal and formal institutions. He states that 'individual habits ... when they are shared and reinforced within a society or group ... assume the form of socio-economic institutions ... not in the narrow sense of formal organisation, but in the broad sense of socially habituated behaviour' (Hodgson 1997, p. 679; also quoted in Guy & Henneberry 2000, p. 2414). Lawson (1997) provides a similar definition. He suggests that the term institution be used to designate those systems, or structured processes of interaction (collecting together rules, relations and positions as well as habits and other practices) that are relatively enduring and can be identified as such. In this context, markets are considered to be inherently social and the market itself is in fact a form of institution (Hodgson 1988).

Although these contributions emphasise the stability of institutions, analysts are careful to explain that institutions are not immutable, and, as we will explore in this book, they themselves can be subject to significant change. To this end, Hodgson (1998) employs a biological metaphor to represent institutional 'evolution'. This encourages analysts to locate studies within their historical context and within a clear understanding of from where and how institutions have emerged.

While the definition of 'institutions' is similar to that employed in sociological, political science and anthropological institutionalism, there are significant differences of emphasis between different schools of institutional thought. For example, within the economics literature, there are important distinctions between the methods and scope of 'old' and 'new' institutionalism. Broadly speaking, 'old' institutionalism covers the contributions of American and European economists writing in the early twentieth century, including John Commons, Wesley Mitchell, Thorstein Veblen and the German Historicists. This school was particularly influential in early land and property market studies. One of its prominent members, Richard T. Ely, helped shape the careers of the US urban land economists Richard Ratcliff and Ernest Fisher. This influence can be further traced to a number of important contributions to land and housing policy debates in the 1960s (see Weiss 1989; Clapp & Myers 2000; McMaster & Watkins 2000). More recently, old institutionalist ideas have again become prominent in the general economics literature (see Hodgson 1993, 1997, 1998, 1999).

More prominent since the 1970s, however, has been the emerging 'new' institutionalism (see Williamson 1975; Eggertson 1990; North 1990; Samuels 1995). This approach differs markedly from 'old' institutionalism (Hodgson *et al.* 1994; Kasper & Streit 1999). Significantly, new institutionalism relies on more mainstream assumptions about the human agents and explains the existence of political, legal and social institutions with reference to the role of individualistic behaviour and its consequences for human interactions. Thus the existence of institutions affects the behaviour of individuals in terms of the choices and constraints they face but does not mould the preferences of the agents in the way 'old' institutionalists would expect. It is this strand of the literature that has most influenced recent housing and commercial property market analyses (van der Krabben & Lambooy 1993; Jaffe 1996; D'Arcy & Keogh 1998; Keogh & D'Arcy 2000) and has also, although to a lesser extent, infused land-use planning studies (Alexander 2001).

Despite their differences, both old and new institutionalists accept the influence of some general market principles but emphasise that the market will also always be shaped by its cultural and institutional substance and content (Hodgson 1989). Institutional economists thus focus on actors and structure. External influences mould the purpose and actions of actors but actions are not entirely determined by them. In the context of land and property market analysis, Keogh and D'Arcy (1999) highlight the role of both formal and informal influences on actors, including actual organisational forms such as professional bodies and deep-seated social attitudes (including the prevailing acceptance of ownership), and emphasise the relative robustness of institutions and the infrequent nature of institutional change. On the other hand, McMaster and Watkins (2000) highlight the dynamic elements of institutional influence and show that the housing market as an institution has been altered by government intervention through a variety of policy initiatives, including the 'right to buy'.

The broad principles of institutional economics find support within other social science disciplines, even though the terminology used can be very different and rather confusing. Within political science, for example, there has been a growth in the prominence of 'new' institutionalist ideas since the 1980s (Hall & Taylor 1996; Lowndes 1996). In this disciplinary context, new institutionalism refers to the political structures that shape political behaviour. Key features of this approach are the acceptance that institutional constraints on behaviour are imposed by political structures that are both historically embedded and, at the same time, also dynamic and contested (Lowndes 2001). Thus, the concern is with formal and informal rules and structures; the way in which institutions embody values and power relationships; and the interactions between individuals and institutions.

This perspective appears closer to the 'old' institutional economics than it is to the new. However, to political scientists, old institutionalism is characterised and criticised as being functional and holistic (focusing on the political system as a whole rather than particular arenas); formalist (rather than also accepting the significance of informal and social norms and influences); and independent (rather than embedded) (Peters 1999; Lowndes 2001). Since the 1990s, the application of new institutionalist analyses has seen urban policy scholars undertake detailed explorations of the role of the informally constituted and dynamic networks, regimes and governing coalitions that have emerged in cities.

These ideas have also influenced the work of anthropologists and sociologists. For instance, in highlighting the routinised thought processes in society, this mode of analysis emphasises that institutions have cultural and cognitive functions that require anthropological investigation (Douglas 1987). Sociologists emphasise the dynamics of social relationships, the formal and informal ways in which these are shaped, and the distribution of power within these (Dyrberg 1997; Vigar *et al.* 2000). It is sociological and anthropological institutionalism, with the emphasis on the social rather than political and economic, that seems to have most influenced planning academics.

Within the planning literature, the evolution of communicative (or collaborative) planning theory, which emphasises how planning work is actually done, is set within a broadly institutionalist framework (see Healey 1997). This draws on the ideas of the American pragmatists and Habermasian critical theory (Vigar *et al.* 2000). This perspective emphasises that actors learn from practice, that they develop an appreciation of the position of other participants in the policy process and the problems they face, and that shared meanings and values provide a basis upon which consensus can be built and conflict can be mediated. The institutional focus is on the capacity within localities and the processes through which institutional capacity is established, shaped and developed.

More recently, Vigar *et al.* (2000) have applied what they describe as a new institutionalist approach to the analysis of planning practice and policy. This approach draws on several strands of institutionalism, including communicative planning theory, the new economic institutionalism of North, and the applied institutional analysis of economic geography (see, for example, Amin & Thrift 1995; Lambooy & Moulaert 1996).

Vigar *et al.* (2000) suggest that this approach has five strengths. First, the institutional approach offers a dynamic and relational view of the world. The approach focuses on the process through which actions are accomplished and how norms are established rather than on the outcomes themselves. Second, the approach places the actors at the centre of the analysis and recognises their role in shaping and stimulating change. It acknowledges the power of agency as well as the influence of wider forces. Third, the analysis accepts that the social worlds of actors are intertwined with their formal roles. It emphasises that actions are embedded within economic activity and civil society. Fourth, there is recognition that policy ideas have been influenced by institutional structures, including political and social influences. Importantly, this means that policy change requires not just a change in legislation but also a change in discourse. Fifth, the approach provides a framework for empirical analysis and provides a basis for understanding where external forces have influenced rules and frames of reference within contested policy areas. Critically, the implication is that the institution is a more useful unit of analysis than the individual (Hodgson *et al.* 1994).

The application of institutional analysis to the study of property and planning, of course, has not been without controversy. Hooper (1992), for example, sets out a detailed critique of Healey's earlier institutional work (see Healey 1991, 1992). In particular, critical comment highlights the fact that institutional analysis can offer only a lower-level theory (see also Guy & Henneberry 2000). There is considerable difficulty in substantiating precise connections between events and wider forces. Indeed, the institutionalists Keogh and D'Arcy (1999) concede that it is extremely hard to pin down informal institutional constraints.

Elsewhere, Ball (1998) expresses concerns at the way in which the institutional analyses of property markets and planning and development have underemphasised the influence of economic structural factors in favour of actor-orientated analyses. These concerns are shared by a number of planning analysts (Richardson 1996; Tewdwr-Jones & Allmendinger 1998). In more recent work, this limitation has been acknowledged. It is argued that an institutional framework brings together the structuralist and agency approaches (Vigar *et al.* 2000). Guy and Henneberry (2000) make similar advances. In their analysis of the property development process, they adopt a relational approach in which economic and social influences on the wider process of urban change are inter-related and within which structure and action are recursively linked.

In line with these broad influences, we focus on institutional dimensions of the greenfield/brownfield housing development debate. We consider the nature and dynamics of the specific institutions involved. This analysis encompasses the strategies and interests of the production side in the development process, as well as consumer interests and the role of the state. We are able to examine the ways in which economic and political arguments, and social changes, impact on the policy arena in formal and informal ways.

This provides a framework within which the principal actors' decisions are embedded and which is sensitive to the institutional changes (and, in particular, policy changes and changes in the economic and political climate) that provide the context for individual land-use decisions. This framework allows us to investigate the nature of power relations, the distribution of power and influence, and the ways in which this distribution is influenced by the available resources, rules and social processes that shape interaction. As we next discuss, key themes emerge in the book from adopting this mode of analysis. In particular we seek to give prominence to economic, social and political 'institutions' and institutional change throughout the book.

Key themes of the book

From this strong but implicit theoretical basis for the book, we emphasise three key themes. Each of these can be seen to shape the actions of those operating within, and seeking to influence the nature and direction of, housing development (including the quantity and location of new development) and its policy context.

The first theme focuses on the policy context of the debate. This encapsulates a relational view of state–market relations, and highlights the fragmented polity, the increasing involvement of a large number of agents, and the growth of inter-agency partnerships and policy integration.

The second theme explores the changing market (or economic) and political context within which housing development takes place. This strand of analysis highlights the way in which consumer demand has changed, with the growing preference for owner-occupation. On the supply side we consider the nature of change in the housebuilding industry. This analysis is located within an examination of the social and political influences on development. This explores the voter-centric positions of the major political parties, the rise in stakeholder participation and the growth in environmentalist and urbanist movements and the extent to which these have sought to exert power over the direction of policy and political decisions, and over the behaviour of private sector actors.

The third theme of the book is the detailed evaluation of policies relating to the development of brownfield and greenfield land. Our evaluation is embedded within, and draws on, the influences upon policy of the social, political and market context within which development takes place.

Structure of the book

These themes inform the structure of the book, which is developed in three main parts. The first part of the book, encompassing Chapters 2 to 4, considers the policy context within which debates about the location of new housing development have been conducted. In the second part, Chapter 5 examines the market context, before Chapter 6 explores the influence of the social and political sphere. This provides the context for the final part, Chapters 7 to 10, in which a more detailed and integrated analysis of past and future policy initiatives is undertaken. The way in which these issues are teased out and developed is elaborated below.

Part I: The policy context

The next chapter provides a fairly broad overview of the historical, institutional and policy context of the book. This account stresses the interwoven nature of changes in population and household location and spatial patterns of business activity and employment. The chapter also explores the nature of change in the housing system and, in particular, outlines the post-1945 rise in owner-occupation and the related decline in the rented sectors. The review considers the impact of policy shifts on the changing roles for, and relationships between, the public and private sectors in developing new housing for sale and rent.

These themes run through an account of the main phases in housing policy and an examination of the wider policy context within which housing development takes place. This includes a review of influential changes in the direction and content of urban regeneration and planning policy. Again the changing relations between state and market emerge strongly from the review. The chapter also highlights the increasingly fragmented polity within which housing development takes place, and the broader range of agencies and strands of government policy that exert an influence on the housing sector and development activity.

Against this background, Chapter 3 provides a more in-depth examination of the emergence and influence of the sustainable development policy agenda. It explores the extent to which the concept of sustainable development provides both a common and contested discourse around which controversial debates on the form and location of new housing development now take place. It considers how, at least in terms of public policy, sustainable development has become associated more with the overall quality of life than with mere resource conservation. This provides the basis to examine the characteristics of a sustainable residential development and to assess the relative importance of residential location within those characteristics. From this, we investigate why many favour urban compaction as a means to secure sustainable urban development. This is complemented by an evaluation of how different patterns of development requiring greenfield land, such as major urban extensions and new settlements, can be designed to be both compact and sustainable.

The chapter also explores how the reuse of brownfield land for housing development has become increasingly paramount within official interpretations of sustainable development in the UK and identifies three important issues, which reach to the heart of the analysis in later chapters of the book. These are the origins and rationale for the emphasis on brownfield rather than greenfield residential development in public policy; the extent to which existing planning and development processes are capable of delivering brownfield development; and the identity of the interests most likely to gain and to lose from this policy emphasis.

In Chapter 4, the last of the three chapters examining the policy context, the focus is on the way in which the planning system is used as a means of securing the government's broad policy objectives. The chapter sets out to evaluate how and why the state has used the levers available through the planning system in responding to pressure for new housing development. It provides a critical analysis of the approach used to estimate housing demand, housing need and in the delivery of affordable housing. Despite the abandonment of the 'predict and provide' approach to planning for housing, our analysis of the system leads us to conclude that the focus is still primarily on an essentially technical approach to land allocation and not on the delivery of a strategic vision. The suggestion emerges that, although recent policy changes may herald a rise of planning as place-making, there are still considerable challenges to be faced in facilitating the effective resolution of controversies involving actors in the housing development arena.

Part II: Market, economic and political context

A major feature of the challenge for policy-makers relates to the extent to which the limited levers available through planning and urban policy circumscribe the ability of the state directly to influence the actors and agencies involved in the land and property market. Thus, Chapter 5 examines the way in which the current structure of the speculative housebuilding industry influences market outcomes. The analysis shows how capital in the industry has become increasingly concentrated and how strategies such as internal regional competition are adopted by the larger housebuilders to enhance corporate profitability. In this context, it becomes clear that the government's desire to switch the balance of residential development to brownfield sites requires a change in the prevalent behavioural patterns and attitudes of much of the industry.

We therefore examine the speculative housing development process, with a view to pinpointing how any redirection of emphasis towards brownfield land may call for different skills, strategies and an extension of the industry's product range to include individually tailored products for specific locations. The final part of the chapter considers the distinctions between brownfield and greenfield development and seeks to evaluate whether speculative housebuilders are capable of making a significant change in their product range and locations over the next few years.

Chapter 6 investigates the political context of planning and housing development. Here, the intellectual and theoretical basis for conflict over new housing development and planning intervention is examined. The chapter begins by considering ideological views on the role of the state versus the market and examines private property rights arguments for a market-based allocation of development rights. Rather than being ideological or party political, it is clear that conflict surrounding planning and housing development is best understood by examining stakeholder interests and the nature of their involvement. The chapter goes on to look at the key groups involved in the housing development arena and summarises the basis for their involvement and their policy preferences.

The chapter then considers a number of theoretical perspectives on interest group involvement in the policy process, including public-choice, corporatist and Marxist views. These theoretical explanations provide some insights into how we might expect political decisions concerning housing development and land allocation to be made. This is contrasted with evidence of how decisions are made in practice and provides insights into the winners and losers from the process.

Part III: Policy evaluation

In Chapters 7 and 8, the book starts to focus in detail on specific issues relating to greenfield and brownfield development. Chapter 7 begins by reflecting on the supply and demand factors that create market preferences for greenfield development. It goes on to compare three policy responses:

management, resistance or accommodation. The chapter critically examines whether current policy mechanisms will be able to contain future greenfield development or whether more radical proposals, such as the introduction of a greenfield development tax, would be beneficial in reinforcing planning restrictions. More fundamentally, we question whether, as a result of the prevalent determination of politicians to protect greenfield land, the planning system has focused too much on limiting the quantity and impact of greenfield development, and not enough on raising the quality and sustainability of such development, when it actually takes place.

Chapter 8 starts with a quantitative assessment of brownfield development potential. This leads on to an investigation of how the brownfield redevelopment process is impeded by specific constraints, such as planning, physical and ownership difficulties. These constraints mean that, while towns and cities can appear to the general public to contain numerous brownfield sites capable of residential development, the practical suitability of brownfield land for development may well be limited, unless the state acts to ensure that such supply-side constraints are overcome. However, even in these circumstances, housebuilders will not be persuaded to switch their activities increasingly to brownfield sites, unless they also perceive a demand for their products. The chapter therefore considers the nature of recent demand for new housing at brownfield locations and examines how it might be broadened. It is suggested that, in contrast to greenfield locations, successful marketing of brownfield development is likely to be less dependent on the images created by housebuilders and more dependent on the capacity of urban policy-makers to promote and create thriving towns and cities.

Chapter 9 takes a step back from the assessment of specific policy options. The chapter serves two purposes. First, it offers a critical evaluation of excessive reliance on the planning system as the main mechanism with which to influence the operation of land and property markets in pursuit of broad housing objectives. Secondly, the chapter explores the impact of the planning system on land and housing markets. In doing this, it focuses on the economic analysis of two specific issues central to the debates about the location of housing development and the role of the planning system in the housing market.

The opening section considers the impact of planning on the housing system in terms of price effects, quantity effects and the influence on densities and house types. The way in which these outcomes might impact on different groups of actors, including developers, existing owners and new purchasers is also considered. The section concludes with reflections on the extent to which planning intervention contributes to societal and environmental goals by steering market activity.

The next part of the chapter focuses on the economics of planning gain. Using a textbook economic framework, we assess the case for using planning gain as a means of requiring developers to provide an element of affordable housing within development sites and try to determine the extent to which the cost of planning gain will impact on different groups, including landowners, developers and house purchasers. The analysis suggests that the distribution of these impacts will inevitably have an effect on the ability of planners to negotiate the development of adequate levels of social and affordable housing through the market.

Finally, as both parts of the chapter are based largely on the analytical framework characteristic of the neo-classical school of economics, we consider the limitations of this mode of analysis and reflect on the potential value of applying the tools of behavioural social science, and institutional economics. Some areas for further research are identified.

The final chapter summarises the main findings of the book and explores the implications of these findings for policy. Specifically, we focus on three key areas. These are the relationship between housing development and environmental sustainability; the requirement for greater flexibility in the housebuilding industry in order to establish the institutional capacity to meet housing demand and need in a sustainable manner; and the case for extending policy levers, in the form of a broader land policy, in order to have any chance of achieving brownfield land targets of the magnitude set by the current government, other than for a short period.

A matter of definition

At the start of this book, it is important to define what we mean by brownfield and greenfield land. It is commonly accepted in the UK that brownfield land can be either derelict or vacant (Syms 1994; Urban Task Force 1999; Alker *et al.* 2000), although some have also argued that brownfield land must be capable of redevelopment in accordance with planning policies or urban renewal objectives (Syms 2001).

Derelict land is defined in England as 'land so damaged by previous industrial or other development that it is incapable of beneficial use without treatment' (NLUD 2000). Excluded from this definition, however, is land damaged by development that, over time, has blended into its natural surroundings or has been put to some use that no longer constitutes a problem. Where sites are only partly derelict, guidance suggests they should be split if possible (DTLR 2001a). There is considerable scope left for different interpretations of what makes for acceptable blending with natural surroundings, or what might allow land parcels to be split, or even what makes for a notional maintenance regime.

In Scotland, where a broader definition applies, derelict land is considered to be:

> land which has been so damaged by development or use that it is incapable of development for beneficial use without rehabilitation and which is not being used for the purpose for which it is held or for use acceptable in the local plan or land which is not being used and where contamination is known or suspected (even if treatment is required only for the buildings thereon).
>
> (SVDLS 2000)

Whereas in the USA brownfield land is generally interpreted as being either contaminated or polluted, in the UK it is well understood that such land can be merely vacant rather than derelict. Vacant land is defined in England as 'land that was previously developed and is now vacant which could be developed without treatment' (NLUD 2000). In this case, treatment can include demolition and levelling. The definition excludes land previously used for mineral extraction or waste disposal, which has been or is being restored for agriculture, forestry, woodland or other open countryside use. According to this definition, vacant land need not be confined to urban areas but may also be found in areas that are predominantly rural.

In Scotland, a different definition again applies in which vacant land is considered to be:

> land in urban settlements (with a population of 2000 or more) or land within one kilometre of the edge of such settlements, which would commonly be considered as having the characteristics of urban vacant land (e.g. some combination of factors generally including being unused or unsightly or land which would benefit from development or improvement, etc.).
>
> (SVDLS 2000)

How far should the concept of brownfield land be extended to include vacant buildings that could soon be turned into vacant land? In England, vacant buildings are categorised separately by NLUD (2000) under the definition of 'unoccupied buildings that are structurally sound and in a reasonable state of repair (i.e. capable of being occupied in their present state).' This definition includes buildings that have been declared redundant or where re-letting for their former use is not expected (where long-term vacancy is an issue) but excludes vacant buildings expected to be subject to re-letting for their former use in the short to medium term as a result of the normal market cycle of sale and transfer. Information on vacant buildings is not collected on a comprehensive basis in Scotland.

Although it would be possible to produce a detailed definition of the term brownfield from a synthesis of the above sources, the central importance of policy evaluation to the themes of this book makes us rely on the official concept of 'previously developed land' in Policy Planning Guidance note 3 (PPG 3), for which we use the term 'brownfield' as shorthand. According to the DETR (2000a), previously developed land:

- Is or was occupied by a permanent structure (excluding agricultural or forestry buildings), and associated fixed surface infrastructure.

- Occurs in both built-up and rural settings.

- Includes defence buildings and land used for mineral extraction and waste disposal where provision for restoration has not been made through development control procedures.

- Excludes land and buildings that are currently in use for agricultural or forestry purposes, and land in built-up areas which has not been developed previously (e.g. parks, recreation grounds and allotments, even though these areas may contain certain urban features such as paths, pavilions and other buildings).

- Excludes land that was previously developed but where the remains of any structure or activity have blended into the landscape in the process of time (to the extent that it can reasonably be considered as part of the natural surroundings), and where there is a clear reason that could outweigh the reuse of the site (such as its contribution to nature conservation) or where it has subsequently been put to an amenity use and cannot be regarded as requiring redevelopment.

Although, again for the purposes of shorthand, we regard any land not falling into the above definition as greenfield, it is important to acknowledge that, often, land may be of a quality somewhere between the common perception of the two. Some greenfield sites, for example, may require extensive commitment to the provision of infrastructure and have characteristics that make them complex to develop and render their development dependent on considerable building skill or on the remediation of difficult site conditions. Conversely some brownfield sites may be straightforward by comparison with the required infrastructure in place. Although greenfield sites are generally considered less costly to develop, this will not always be the case.

Moreover, as the book proceeds our analysis will reveal the many ways in which the greenfield/brownfield dichotomy is not an entirely useful basis from which to begin the search for a sustainable solution to the question of where to locate new housing development. For, by couching the debate in these terms, there is a tendency to over-simplify the issues and to adopt the view that brownfield development is by definition the sustainable option. This ignores many of the key principles of sustainability, including compactness, mix of uses, links with transport and other services, and the fact that by embodying these principles, greenfield development might also be sustainable. It also denies the underlying heterogeneity of land parcels, whether within the brownfield or greenfield categories.

Although we thus use, as shorthand, the term 'brownfield' to refer to previously developed land as defined by the DETR (2000a) and 'greenfield' to refer to land that has not been previously developed, we are conscious that even these definitions are not wholly accepted by all UK experts (let alone those based in the USA). More importantly, however, we seek throughout the text to avoid the assumption that greenfield development will always be cheap but unsustainable, and that brownfield development will always be expensive but sustainable. Since the heterogeneity of urban land clearly makes such assumptions invalid, by extension it circumscribes the usefulness of any policy measures predicated on such simplifications.

2

The Changing Policy Context of Housing Development

In November 2000, the Blair Administration launched its Urban and Rural White Papers (DETR 2000b; DETR/MAFF 2000). Supporters of the White Papers heralded their publication as a significant statement of 'joined up' thinking on policy issues. Together these documents place contemporary debates about housing development and planning policy at the centre of concerns about quality of life and locate issues associated with new housing development within the wider policy context. As Tony Burton (2001, p. 14), the former Deputy Director of the CPRE, explains 'the roots of the Urban White Paper lie in conflicts over new housing development on greenfield sites which the government sparked in late 1997 and early 1998 through controversial planning decisions'. The documents stress the importance of housing across the policy spectrum, highlight the need for policy integration and announce plans for a range of policies that seek to reform institutions, legislation and policy guidance related to planning for new housing.

These documents are illustrative of the background to this book. The scale of housing development and the balance between greenfield and brownfield land are influenced not just by housing land policy but by a much broader range of policies. This chapter seeks to tease out the way in which public policy has directly and indirectly influenced development. The three main objectives of this review are:

- To provide an overview and explanation of the processes of decentralisation, with particular reference to the dispersal of housing, employment and industry and the linkages between household and business locations.

- To provide an overview of the nature of change in the housing system, with emphasis on the rise of owner-occupation at the expense of rented housing.

- To explore the wider context of housing development by reviewing changes in urban regeneration and planning policy.

Throughout this review of social, economic and policy change since 1945, the way in which relations between state and market have altered over time emerges as a central theme. The concluding section draws out some of the implication of these changing relations for greenfield and brownfield housing development. It also highlights the potential importance of increased policy integration and of the growing diversity in the range of actors now involved in the formulation and implementation of housing land and planning policy. Overall, the chapter covers both the historical and current context within which our more detailed discussion of the specific policy initiatives seeking to influence brownfield and greenfield housing development is set.

Urban growth and change

Population growth and demographic change

The growth of British cities was a product of the population increase and changing economic structure in the nineteenth century. During this period, the population grew from 10.5 million to 37 million and the economic base switched from agrarian to industrial production. Britain changed to an urban society, with its transformation characterised by the concentration of growth in manufacturing towns in the north and in cities such as London, Glasgow, Birmingham and Bristol. During this process, the population of Glasgow, for example, grew from a mere 77 000 in 1801 to over 300 000 at the turn of the twentieth century (Keating 1988), while the population of London doubled from around 1 million to 2 million between 1801 to 1851, doubled again to 4 million at 1881 and reached 6.5 million by 1911 (Hall 1993).

This rapid, large-scale urban growth was underpinned by both a general increase in the population and the redistribution of the existing population from rural to urban areas. Although the rate of population increase has slowed down, changing demographic trends and the changing structure of households means that increasing demand for housing remains at the centre of policy concerns. Since the 1960s, the rate of new household formation has never dropped below 100 000 per annum and has reached almost double that figure at times. As well as population growth and demographic change, however, population redistribution too remains a central issue in policy debates. This redistribution now takes the form of a flight *from* rather than *to* the cities.

Population decentralisation

Since the 1930s, there has been a significant redistribution of the population and of economic activity. Although the major cities continued to grow
between the wars, the population peaked around 1940 and evidence began to
emerge of a slowdown or reversal of the urban growth process. Many of the
major cities, including London, showed a decrease in population in the period
between 1931 and 1951. By 1951 this trend was common to all major cities.
From then to 1961, the decline in population was being driven by moves from
the urban core to suburban locations. The overall size of conurbations continued to rise, until after 1961, from which point they too began to decline as
population expansion became concentrated in free-standing urban towns.

This general pattern of urban change reflected the process of industrial restructuring and the related alteration in the pattern of industrial location.
The process of de-industrialisation in the UK has been relentless since the
1940s. This has been more pronounced than in other countries and began
with a fairly gentle decline in the 1960s, followed by rapid acceleration in the
1970s since when the pace has steadied (Hadjimatheou & Sarantis 1998).

Decentralisation is clearly reflected in the rate of employment loss from
cities. For example, employment declined in London by almost 253 000 jobs
between 1971 and 1978 and by almost 400 000 by 1981 (Green *at al.* 1986;
Champion *et al.* 1987). This trend was mirrored in Liverpool, Glasgow, Birmingham and Manchester. On the other hand, over 20 000 new jobs were
created in free-standing settlements, such as Aberdeen and Reading, where
there had been less reliance on traditional industries. Between 1981 and
1996, the largest proportionate falls were in Liverpool, Glasgow and Birmingham (Turok & Edge 1999).

This redistribution of the population was reinforced by changes to the
transport network and by housing and planning policies. As Jones (1979)
explains, the process of suburbanisation can be traced back to the opening
of the tramways in the 1870s. The expansion of free-standing towns in the
1960s was aided by major improvements in the inter-urban road network.
The planning system supported this by promoting urban containment and
the development of new and expanded towns.

Overall population redistribution is reflected in two general migration patterns, the flow from the north to the south, and movements from urban to
rural areas. Both of these trends have brought with them policy challenges
in the form of uneven urban and regional economic development but it is the
urban to rural flow that now dominates.

Table 2.1 Population distribution and change in Great Britain, 1981–91, by region

Region	1981 (000s)	1991 (000s)	1981–91 (%) change
East Anglia	1 895	2 091	10.4
South West	4 381	4 723	7.8
East Midlands	3 853	4 026	4.5
South East	17 011	17 558	3.2
Wales	2 814	2 886	2.6
West Midlands	5 187	5 255	1.3
Yorkshire & Humberside	4 918	4 952	0.7
North	3 117	3 084	−1.1
North West	6 459	6 377	−1.3
Scotland	5 180	5 100	−1.5
Great Britain	54 815	56 055	2.3

Source: Office of Population Censuses and Surveys and Registrar General Scotland; adapted from Champion (1993).

Table 2.1 shows evidence of population distribution and change for standard regions between 1981 and 1991. The data show that almost one-third of the population of Britain lives in the South East, an area that accounts for less than one-eighth of the land mass. This area has a density of 645 persons per square kilometre, which is well over twice the national average. Although this is less dense than the 868 persons per square kilometre in the North West, the most densely populated region, it massively outstrips the 66 persons per square kilometre in Scotland (Champion 1993). Despite this, the figures continue to show evidence of a population drift from the north to the south. Three northern regions show population losses of greater than 1% in the 10-year period, while in the South, the East Anglia region grew by around 10%.

More recent evidence shows a continuation of these trends. An analysis of UK cities and conurbations shows that between 1981 and 1999, the population of Greater London grew by a further 7%, while Liverpool fell by almost 9%, Glasgow by more than 5% and Manchester by just under 2% (Gibb *et al.* 2001). The spatial impact of growth, however, is shaped not just by demographic factors but also by migration. Table 2.2 shows the population changes by different type of district and demonstrates the challenge presented to policy-makers by the urban to rural drift.

The migration flows, in the majority of regions, have become a more important source population change than births and deaths. In the South East, Cox (2000) reports urban–rural shifts amounting to a net flow of around 90 000 people per year from the six metropolitan counties and London. Those leaving for the countryside tend to be wealthier families and retirement couples (Champion *et al.* 1998).

Table 2.2 Population changes resulting from within-Britain migration, 1990–1991, by district types.

District type	Net migration	As percentage of total population
Inner London	−31 009	−1.24
Outer London	−21 159	−0.51
Principal metropolitan cities	−26 311	−0.67
Other metropolitan cities	−6 900	−0.08
Large non-metropolitan cities	−14 040	−0.40
Small non-metropolitan cities	−7 812	−0.42
Industrial districts	7 194	0.10
Districts with new towns	2 627	0.09
Resort, port and retirement	17 736	0.49
Urban/rural mixed	19 537	0.25
Remote urban/rural	13 665	0.59
Remote rural	10 022	0.61
Most remote rural	36 450	0.77

Source: Adapted from Champion (2000); calculated from 1991 census.

The evidence suggests that a 'counter-urbanisation cascade', shown in Fig. 2.1, applies widely and the proportionate impact of migration flows increases as we move down the urban hierarchy. The more densely populated an area, the greater the level of out-migration, while the more remote, the greater the relative level of in-migration. Thus, as Champion (2000) explains, even when 'shire Britain' gained 85 000 in-migrants from the large conurbations, the cities also lost people to the most remote rural districts which, in turn, is where the largest net gain in absolute number and relative terms has been recorded.

This phenomenon has persisted over a fairly long time period. Roberts and Randolph (1983) show that the seven largest cities contracted by two million people during the 1960s. At that time they interpreted the evidence as being indicative of the disappearance of the last vestiges of rural depopulation. Jones and Armitage (1990) also note that remoter largely rural areas

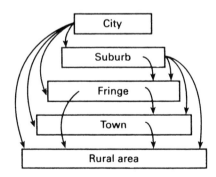

Fig. 2.1 The counter-urbanisation cascade (source: Champion 2000).

experienced remarkably high rates of population growth during the 1970s, and although the rate of net in-migration fell during the late 1970s and early 1980s, it increased again from 1988.

Champion (2000) goes on to suggest three possible explanations for the re-location of households away from the cities. The explanations are based on flight from the ills of the city; the lure of the countryside; and the inability of the cities to accommodate further growth. The first of these implies that the shift to rural living is caused by push factors including negative views of the physical, environmental conditions in cities or other perceived problems including crime rates, and quality-of-life issues. The second reflects a posi-tive expression of the preference for a more rural lifestyle. The third implies that there is simply not enough room in the city, and that this leads to an overspill. He concludes that, in reality, none of these explanations, on its own, stands up to close scrutiny. Rather, a combination of influences would seem to be important.

As Bramley (2000) notes this observed pattern of urban to rural migration is often conceived as a planning problem. This explanation implies the failure of urban regeneration and waste of the potential of cities, increased pressure on environmental resources, greater infrastructure costs, greater car depend-ence and longer commuting distances. In addition, the selective nature of out-migration, which tends to be dominated by members of higher-income groups, can worsen the cycle of cumulative decline. On the other hand, migration is clearly supporting choices about quality of life, type of environ-ment, and housing space preferences and standards.

It is clear that the issue of brownfield development has appeared on the policy agenda only as the effects of urban population decline have become ever more apparent. The postwar philosophy implicitly welcomed planned greenfield development. Many local authority housing estates were built on greenfield sites within city boundaries. It was only when attention turned to slum clearance that major brownfield opportunities started to emerge. The migration patterns outlined above were dominated by moves to smaller settlements, and with only limited brownfield opportunities in these towns, these also implicitly supported mainly greenfield housing development. It seems that the current patterns continue to imply stronger demand for greenfield development than for brownfield sites (see Chapters 7 and 8).

Changing land-use patterns

Although urban sprawl and containment have been of policy interest since the beginning of the twentieth century, until recently there has been little evidence of the extent to which land has changed from rural to urban uses (DOE 1990). In the 1970s and 1980s, commentators highlighted both the tendency of households to move further from major cities and the decentralisation of employment in support of the assertion that significant tracts of the countryside were becoming urbanised.

This argument was further buttressed by the projected increases in household numbers, and it was widely held that the rate of urban encroachment would continue to increase. The factual basis for this argument, however, has been described as being 'extremely weak' (DOE 1990, p. i). Indeed, the impact of urbanisation has been such that even at the relatively high 1980s building rate of 200 000 dwellings per annum (assuming the prevailing density of 24 dwellings to the hectare) only around 8400 hectares were being developed each year (King 1993).

A large amount of land is subject to restrictions that prevents housing development. This includes land protected by green belt coverage, National Parks and high-quality land designated for agricultural use. Official estimates suggest an overall change to urban use between 1980 and 2001 of a fairly modest 105 000 hectares (which represents approximately 0.8% of the land area in England (DOE 1990). However, these estimates may slightly understate the rate of change. Between 1991 and 1996, an annual average of nearly 14 000 hectares of land changed to urban use (0.1% of the total land area) (DTLR 2001a). Yet, as we discuss in Chapter 8, contrary to much political wisdom, there is little evidence to suggest a significant increase in the absolute amount of previously developed land which has been recycled for housing in recent years.

Changing spatial economic structures

These changes in household and employment location and land use are clearly impacting on the spatial economic structures of British regions. Using spatial modelling techniques, Batty (2001) explores changes in British settlement patterns and shows that state and market agents have created a polycentric spatial structure. Champion (2001) also notes that in the last three or four decades, polycentric urban regions (PURs) have emerged from significant change to settlement systems.

Specific features of the changing systems have been the switch from urbanisation to counter-urbanisation; the emergence of multi-nodal regions from separate urban centres; and the reduction in influence of the traditional central business district with the growth of centres in suburban and peripheral locations. The new form of settlement provides a different spatial context within which the population must arrange itself and undertake its economic and social activities. Changing spatial patterns are illustrated by the exodus of relatively wealthy urban residents to smaller settlements and rural areas (described above), and relate to changes in travel to work distances. These have been accompanied by a strong urban–rural shift in employment (Turok & Edge 1999).

These trends have challenged the conventional notion of monocentric patterns of economic organisation. The de-concentration of economic activity, facilitated by technological change, undermined the notion of the negative rent gradient (i.e. the view that land and property prices decline with distance from the city centre) as an explanation for residential location. It also challenged the belief that people would commute from suburbs and out-of-town locations for all forms of economic activity (Anas *et al.* 1998). The displacement of single-earner households by dual-income households as the typical household type means that the selection of an optimal residential location is more complicated than the picture captured in traditional urban economic analysis (Kloosterman & Musterd 2001).

Recent research indicates that business location is not a given factor to which population movements respond but that there are interactions between the two. DTZ Pieda (2000) argues that a household will now tend to select a home location and then choose jobs that are commutable from that home. This is consistent with rising commuting distances and, of course, has important implications for the location of housing development. Breheny (1999), for example, contends that the pressure for brownfield development has not taken account of the suburbanisation of jobs. He suggests that the need to relocate jobs within cities will not be easy to achieve.

The changing nature of the housing system

Phases in postwar housing policy

Williams (1997) notes that, for the past 70 years or more, the UK has been struggling to identify and implement a coherent set of housing policies that might be sustained across political persuasions and in a range of different social and economic conditions. Although there have been periods of consensus around relatively narrow goals, notably in the immediate postwar period when the objective was to increase supply, housing policy has been characterised by major changes in emphasis as new governments have been elected and as economic conditions have changed.

There have (arguably) been five important periods in the evolution of housing policy since the start of the last century. The first was the 1914 to 1939 period that sought to address the Victorian legacy of poor-quality housing, high levels of poverty and rising rents (see Spicker 1998 for an account of the social problems). The central themes in policy were thus rent control and slum clearance. An overarching policy framework was developed that was based on a variety of forms of state intervention, including direct involvement in housing development (Malpass & Murie 1999).

The second identifiable period in housing policy relates to the development of the post-Keynesian welfare state between 1945 and 1968. This encompassed three phases of high housing output. From 1945 to 1953, under Labour, the clear objective was to increase the supply of homes through state provision. After 1954, although output remained high and retained its place at the centre of the Conservatives' policy concerns, the relative levels of private and public sector provision changed. Between 1964 and 1968, high output was again maintained by Wilson's Labour Administration. Significantly, however, this was not based on a return to predominantly public sector provision but instead saw the maintenance of broad parity with the private sector (Malpass & Murie 1999). Throughout this period, there was a degree of policy continuity with the focus on addressing the housing shortage, and clearing and replacing slums.

The third distinct period in housing policy followed the 1969 Housing Act. This Act emphasised housing improvement over redevelopment. This was subsequently reinforced by the 1974 Housing Act which, in seeking to avoid the need for demolition and replacement, added action areas within which systematic rehabilitation and environmental improvement were to be supported by higher levels of grant aid. This apparent abandonment of the high output policy was, in large part, explained by wider economic problems (Malpass & Murie 1999). Issues relating to finance had also become more prominent in the politics of housing and there were emerging concerns about the possible impact of large-scale development on urban communities.

The fourth and fifth distinctive periods in housing policy can be traced respectively to the first election victories of Prime Ministers Thatcher and Blair. Both of these periods have been characterised by greater emphasis on the market and by two different large-scale privatisation programmes, the Right to Buy (RTB) and Large Scale Voluntary Transfer (LSVT). The Thatcher period marked a rapid transformation in the tenure structure of the British housing system.

Maclennan and Pryce (1998) argue that the Thatcher and Major Administrations brought several improvements to the housing system including greater efficiency in the use of public resources, greater use of private finance and greater choice in terms of tenure and housing management. They also acknowledge a range of failures including the contribution of policies to the erosion of communities. In early policy statements, Hilary Armstrong, then Labour's Housing Minister, was also critical of the boom–bust market inherited from the previous Conservative Administration and the problems associated with the dysfunctional features of high levels of home ownership. She also highlighted the inefficiency caused by deregulating the private rented sector (see, for example, Armstrong 1999). Despite this rhetoric, to date, the impact of the Blair Government, while much less radical, has continued to be based on general support for owner-occupation as the principal tenure.

Although this might be interpreted as a new consensus surrounding housing policy, some commentators suggest that this period may in fact represent the end of a distinctive, meaningful housing policy (Bramley 1997; Malpass 1999). The decision to restrict and to remove most of the tax advantages and mechanisms for supporting owner-occupiers means that a large proportion of housing consumers are not directly affected by active housing policies (Cowan & Marsh 2001). More important, however, are the links being made between housing and other policy sectors, including sustainable development, planning and regeneration initiatives.

Table 2.3 summarises the changes in the housing tenure structure at key points in the development of housing policy in the twentieth century. From the short account above, it is clear that many of the important changes in

Table 2.3   Housing tenure in Great Britain in the twentieth century (as percentages of all households).

	Public rented	Owner-occupied	Private rented
1914	0	10	90
1945	12	26	62
1951	18	29	53
1961	27	43	31
1969	30	49	21
1971	30.8	52.7	16.5
1979	31.9	54.6	13.5
1985	29.1	60.5	10.4
1990	24.9	65.8	9.3
1995	23.2	66.7	10.0
1999	22	69	9

Sources: Adapted from Malpass and Murie (1999); *Social Trends* (2001); Wilcox (2000).
Note: For convenience we report local authority and housing association figures together. This ignores the growing importance of the housing association sector since 1974 (see Malpass 1999 for details).

policy have related to changing attitudes towards different tenures and are thus reflected in significant changes in the tenure structure.

The growth of home ownership

The tenure structure of the UK housing system is now dominated by owner-occupation. The growth in home ownership, shown above, was a result of the action of successive postwar governments, whose policies actively promoted ownership. This rise in fortunes was implicitly supported by the development of a tax and subsidy system favourable to owner-occupation. The rate of growth, however, has been uneven over time, with the most rapid acceleration occurring in the last two decades. At 1945, the majority of households in the UK were renters and home ownership accounted for only 26% of households. By the time the first Thatcher Administration was elected home ownership had risen to 59%. At the time of writing the best estimate suggests that the 69% of all households are owners (*Social Trends* 2001).

It is debatable whether the growth of home ownership is a demand-side process, driven by consumer preferences, or a supply-side process, which is driven by producer concerns (see, respectively, Saunders 1990; or Ball 1986; or Malpass & Murie 1999, for a summary). The demand-side argument is arguably reflected in the aspirations of most households. In 1975, 69% of individuals over the age of 16 aspired to be owner-occupiers within the next two years, even though only 62% of the sample expected to achieve this within 10 years (Whitehead 1997). By 1993, 69% of the sample had achieved home ownership, although by that time the proportion aspiring to owner-occupation had risen to 81%. Estimates of those aspiring to home ownership have remained stable, even in the poorer economic conditions that subsequently prevailed (see Coles & Taylor 1993 for details). The widespread appeal and rise in access to home ownership has brought about a change in the social basis of the tenure (Hamnett 1999).

During the 1970s and much of the 1980s housing appeared to be a good investment, with potentially high capital gains and relatively high levels of price inflation that took much of the risk out of house purchase (Boleat 1997). By 1974 the average house price in the UK had more than doubled to £11 000 from the 1970 figure of around £5000. By 1980 and 1990, the average price reached £24 000 and £60 000 respectively (Meen & Andrew 1998).

Further impetus came from Margaret Thatcher's vision of 'a property-owning democracy' that was underpinned by a number of policy developments, many of which lend support to the notion that expansion of ownership was largely a supply-side issue. The most visible was the privatisation of council homes through the introduction of the *Right to Buy* (RTB) in the 1980 Housing Act for England and Wales and the equivalent legislation for Scotland. This legislation gave tenants the mandatory right to purchase their home at a discount of up to 60% (or 70% in the case of flats) of the valuation of the property depending on the length of their period as a renter. Most recent estimates suggest that the RTB has led to the transfer of approximately 1.85 million homes from social rented to owner-occupied tenure (Wilcox 2000).

This policy programme was supported by a proliferation of low-cost home ownership initiatives, including *Cash (and Tenants) Incentive Schemes, Rent to Mortgage*, and *Shared Ownership* and *Shared Equity Schemes* (see Bramley & Morgan 1998 for a review). The impact of these schemes, however, has been minimal and, in the mid-1990s, affected around 15 000 units per annum (Wilcox 1997). Bramley and Dunmore (1996) estimated that the total stock of shared ownership homes in England was around only 70 000.

Further support was available in the form of grants, subsidies and tax advantages. These advantages include, *inter alia*, favourable taxation treatment of income from capital gains and inheritance. More significant, however, has been the advantage given by mortgage interest tax relief (or mortgage interest relief at source, MIRAS), which reached its peak at 38% of total mortgage interest (Holmans 1997). This policy was subject to considerable criticism, particularly as it was ineffective at meeting its main aim, which was to help first-time buyers over the phase in their life cycle when households are most cash constrained (Muellbauer 1990).

As Maclennan (1994) argued, the failure to target the incentive properly meant that it was ultimately wasteful, inequitable and inefficient. It also helped fuel house-price inflation in the late 1980s' boom. This influence was particularly prominent when, in 1987, the Chancellor gave three months' notice that 'double MIRAS' (which had allowed two unrelated adults interest tax relief of up to £30 000 on a jointly purchased property) was to be removed, causing an additional burst of demand. MIRAS was progressively eroded by successive administrations, with a reduction to 20% and then 15% in the 1990s, before being abolished completely in April 2000.

Financial deregulation also played a significant part in the growth of home ownership. As part of a wider package of proposals, the Conservative Government deregulated the credit market through the 1985 Financial Services Act and the 1986 Building Societies Act and encouraged the emergence of new credit providers (Ford *et al.* 2001). The changes heralded a phase of intensive competition in the mortgage market that resulted in an expansion in the availability of home loans. This also marked a significant departure from the redlining policies that had been used to limit loans to households from poorer neighbourhoods (Jones & Maclennan 1987).

In addition, a rise in both the loan to house price and loan to income ratios meant that the size of individual loans also increased. The average advance to first-time house buyers rose from 74% of the house price in 1980 to 89% in 1995, before falling to 80% in 1999. The advance to owners re-entering the market rose continually over this period, from 46% in 1980 to a high of 64% in 1999 (Wilcox 2000). The number of mortgagors rose from 6.2 million in 1980 to almost 11 million in 2001, with approximately 593 000 of the 1.2 million new loans advanced in 1999 going to first-time buyers (Wilcox 2000). Loan to income ratios also increased and, in 1991, households were purchasing homes at prices more than four times their income level compared with the historical long-term relationship of nearer 3.25 (Council of Mortgage Lenders, various).

Having achieved a 17% rise in owner-occupation in the two decades to 1995, the rapid growth in home ownership was halted by the impact of the recession on the housing market. As Forrest and Murie (1994) note, the inflationary discourse of gentrification, gazumping and equity gain disappeared. Instead, housing analysts focused on the rise in negative equity and its consequences, and issues of debt overhang, arrears and repossessions.

The severity of the 1989 to 1992 housing market slump had wide-reaching implications. The adverse circumstances created for some groups had still not unwound by the late 1990s (Maclennan 1997). This period saw the first sustained fall in nominal house prices since the 1950s (Meen & Andrew 1998). This caused highly concentrated negative equity problems that, in many places, have been only slowly eroded. Mortgage arrears of more than 12 months increased from only 5540 in 1982 to a peak of 151 810 in 1993 and were still in excess of 60 000 by 1996, while repossessions, which had risen from just over 6000 to a peak of 68 540 at 1992, still exceeded 30 000 in 1999 (Ford *et al.* 2001).

Importantly, the previously held views of owner-occupation as a secure tenure were tarnished and replaced with the realisation that home ownership was, in fact, a potentially risky commitment. This risk was largely introduced by significant structural changes in the labour market, including the rise in part-time employment, the impact of technological innovation and change on production processes, labour market deregulation, globalisation and a reduction in longer-term job security as an accompaniment to greater market flexibility (Maclennan 1997; Ford *et al.* 2001). In keeping with the regional differences in the tenure structure, the effects of the slump also had an uneven geographical impact. While Maclennan (1994) notes that additional borrowing and new additional loans were most prevalent in southern Britain, Ford *et al.* (2001) present a similar pattern of incidence of mortgage arrears and repossessions.

Against this background, recent studies suggest that the level of home ownership is reaching social and economic capacity. The DOE (1995a) has forecast that owner-occupation will reach 70% by 2005. More recently, Meen *et al.* (1997) estimate that home ownership will grow at only 0.3% per annum to around 72% by 2016. Similarly Radley (1996) suggests that the sustainable limit is around 72% and that almost all of the increase from current levels will come from the ageing of existing owner-occupiers. He argues that a range of factors including the effects of low inflation, increasing job insecurity, the reduction in the financially advantageous status of ownership, and a general rise in economic insecurity will limit the rate of new entry to the tenure. The absence of first-time buyers from the market seems to be supported by empirical evidence (Holmans 2001a). While new flexible lending and stronger mortgage protection packages might help, their impact seems likely to be relatively small.

As Andrew (2001) explains, while home ownership continues to be the tenure of preference in the long term, it may have become less attractive in the short term. This will be partly influenced by the difficulties faced by many owners during the collapse. In addition, however, as a result of structural economic change, labour market flexibility and consequent changes in the way younger age groups formulate their life-cycle plans, there has been growth in the number of young people living in the parental home. As such, a more important influence on the future levels of ownership will be the availability of suitable dwellings in the social and private rented sectors and also, possibly, the emergence of new flexible tenures. There will still be a need for the state to provide assistance in securing the provision of affordable homes.

Overall, the promotion of home ownership has had some important, and largely unintended, effects on the nature and location of new housing development. For example, the expansion of home ownership has been largely greenfield-based. The classic studies of the negative effects of the housing market slump tended to focus on new owners on newbuild estates, such as Bradley Stoke on the outskirts of Bristol (Memery *et al.* 1995). To some extent, the households in these estates were engaging in behaviour shaped by policy. The implicit incentive for households to maximise the benefits from the tax advantages available often led to homeowners purchasing as expensively as possible. For a great many, this meant buying in a new, private, greenfield development.

Although, arguably, some other policy measures, including the end of building society redlining and the promotion of low-cost home ownership (LCHO) schemes, might have supported the demand for brownfield development, the scale of this has been comparatively small. These unintended effects of housing policy, however, raise some interesting questions. For instance, if policy had been more selective, say through targeted taxation, would it have delivered more brownfield development in cities?

The decline in private rented housing

As the tenure figures show, in 1914 around 90% of all households rented privately. The most recent figures put the proportion renting at less than 10%. This decline in the fortunes of the sector has been accompanied by a significant change in its role. At one time, the sector housed a wide range of social and economic groups and household types (Kemp 1997a). Now, however, it plays a much more specialised role in the housing system and houses either mainly low-income, non-family households in furnished accommodation or elderly households, with contracted long-term tenancies, who occupy unfurnished homes (Crook & Kemp 1996).

Although the decline in the sector can be traced to numerous social and economic changes, public policy has also played an important role (Kleinman & Whitehead 1996). Key policy influences include the role played by rent control in reducing returns, and the additional risk and illiquidity introduced by security of tenure. This was reinforced by the unfavourable tax treatment of private landlords compared with owners. Private landlords are taxed on both rental income and capital gains.

The net effect has been that households who could afford to buy were better off doing so, while households who could not were better off benefiting from the subsidised housing and greater security of tenure provided by the public sector. This left only low-income non-family households, who failed to qualify for social housing, in the sector. These households were generally unable to pay the level of rents required to provide a competitive return to any private landlord providing a well-managed property in good condition. The result was a tendency for private rented accommodation to be in poor condition and to be poorly managed and maintained. This, of course, has had an adverse effect on the image of a sector already tarnished by the picture of slum landlordism, given additional public visibility by the Rachman scandal (see Kemp 1997a, b).

In the late 1980s, the Conservative Government sought to revive the sector. This was given impetus by the clear recognition that the private rented sector could support household mobility and was required to enhance labour market flexibility (Maclennan 1994). There was also a desire to see a modern form of landlordism based around an increase in ownership by private property companies funded by financial institutions (Crook & Kemp 1996).

In keeping with general efforts to develop a more pluralist and market-oriented system, the new policy measures centred on the use of market processes to revive the sector. Specifically this included the deregulation of all new lets (under the 1988 Housing Act). This enabled landlords to set new lettings at market rents but left the position of existing tenants largely unchanged. It also simplified the process of repossession and provided some temporary tax incentives. The *Business Expansion Scheme* (BES), which had been established to help new manufacturing companies, was extended to cover unquoted companies letting assured tenancies and gave individuals tax relief on acquiring shares in property companies and on gains generated in trading these shares.

Despite this package of changes, attempts to revive the sector cannot be considered wholly successful. Although there appear to have been an increase in lettings and an expansion of the supply of rented properties, much of this was attributed to the property slump and highlighted the inter-dependencies between the sectors (Crook & Kemp 1996). As Crook *et al.* (1995) explain, rental levels failed to reach competitive levels. In addition, the corporate structure of residential property companies had not developed to the extent to which investment from major financial institutions could be attracted. While over £3000 million was invested in the 903 assured tenancy companies set up under BES, this investment was concentrated in the South East. It also failed to have an enduring impact as most companies were wound up at the end of the qualifying period. At the same time, reductions in entitlement to housing benefit reduced demand for private rented housing from lower-income groups (Bailey 1998). This, however, has been counter-balanced by the rising numbers of skilled and economically active young people entering the private rented sector since the early 1990s (Kemp 1997a).

Changes in the social rented sector

Before 1914, local authorities built only 24 000 dwellings, mainly in London, and were generally resistant to adopting the role of residential landlord (Merrett 1979; Malpass 2001). Between 1919 and 1939, however, they built over 1 million houses. In quantitative terms, this outstripped the contribution of the combined development activity of the philanthropists, voluntary organisations and other non-municipal providers who had contributed to the earliest attempts to house lower-income social groups (Malpass 2001). This was partly a consequence of the difficulties faced by private sector providers in raising capital and the failure to realise the expectation that employers might provide capital to house workers.

In this context, the subsidy system played a significant part in the rise of the social rented sector in Britain (Lowe 1998). The system, from which private landlords were excluded, offered local authorities a 'bricks and mortar' subsidy that was paid annually into the authority's housing revenue account. Thus, dating from the 1930 Housing Act, each dwelling would attract a stream of revenue in subsidy payment, which in some cases would last for 40 years or more, as well as rental income. Without access to the subsidy, the private sector was unable to compete.

By 1939, council housing was established as an important form of housing provision, but accounted for only 10% of the total stock. The sector grew at a more rapid rate after 1945 and, in fact, continued to grow in almost every year until the 1980s. This growth was underpinned by political support from all parties. Such support was offered for a variety of reasons which included the desire to provide a safety net for the poor; the desire to provide a means of re-housing people after slum clearance programmes; the commitment to finding a means by which new homes could be built quickly; the wish to see the development of a normal tenure for the working classes; and, more briefly, the desire to establish council housing as a tenure for all (English 1998).

In the immediate postwar period, the Labour Party's pro-public sector ideological position was aided by rhetoric about social mixing and the creation of 'one class' of housing. A pre-election manifesto commitment to improving subsidies meant that the volume of council housing development further increased after the Conservatives' election victory in 1951. Although this commitment was displaced by a commitment to promoting owner-occupation, the last few years of Conservative Government up to 1964 were marked with a revival in council building. Under Harold Wilson, the numbers game continued and Labour announced a target of 500 000 houses per year up to 1970. Although this was never achieved and was subsequently replaced by a commitment to a more balanced approach to tenure, building remained strong. By the 1970s, however, the Conservatives began to explore the possibility of selling council homes.

Despite a slight revival in fortunes during the 1970s, the competitive advantage of council housing was finally challenged by the policy decisions of successive governments. Most significant among these were the drive to restore rents to market levels, the RTB and the low levels of new building. As we note above, these measures had the effect of promoting home ownership and reviving the private rented sector as attractive alternatives. Public sector housing development fell from 170 000 units in 1970 to only 2000 units in 1995 (Goodchild & Karn 1997).

At the same time, Housing Associations (or, since the introduction of the term in the 1996 Housing Act, Registered Social Landlords, RSLs) have become much more significant players. In addition, in line with more general attempts to promote a 'holistic' approach to public policy, the planning system and regeneration agencies have become more closely involved in provision of affordable homes. For example, as we discuss more fully in Chapter 4, where traditionally social housing would be directly provided by the local authority, the Government now places the need to secure the provision of affordable housing with the planning system (DETR 2000a). In asking developers to provide affordable housing within largely private schemes, and in effect to use the market to subsidise private provision, the burden has been removed from local councils and the decline in council housing seems set to continue. This is a reflection of the end of the implicit separation of planning and housing policy that had persisted until the late 1980s (Hull 1997; Crook 1998).

Although better linkage between planning and housing is to be welcomed, it remains to be seen whether it has gone far enough. The supply of new development by RSLs and the number of affordable homes secured through the planning system have been nowhere near matching the decline in public sector development. Indeed, with the very low levels of development activity in the rented sector, it is difficult to see much of a role for the sector in meeting brownfield development targets. As we suggest in Chapter 8, it is likely that rented housing will increasingly serve specialist niche markets for student or 'executive' housing.

Housing development and wider policy change

Housing and the changing planning system

The planning system has been defined as a set of instruments and institutional arrangements that constitute a framework for the management of land-use change (Healey *et al.* 1988). It was widely assumed that the central concern of the postwar planning system would be the redistribution of household and business location (Cullingworth 1999). This was underpinned by the implicit expectation that the social and economic system would remain stable and that there would be little in the way of demographic change. As a consequence, policy developed around attempts to restrain urban growth and the desire to channel new development into new and expanded towns. As the most recent set of population and households estimates demonstrates, demographic change has in fact led to growing demand for housing and housing land. The need to meet this demand continues to present the single most difficult challenge for the planning system.

There have been several important phases of change impacting on housing development since the 1940s. These phases relate to the early use of the 1947 Town and Country Planning Act, the reorganisation of the planning system and local government in the 1960s and 1970s, the anti-interventionist New Right agenda in the 1980s and 1990s, and (perhaps) the reforms taking place at present.

The 1947 Act set out a framework for planning that was influenced at a general level by visions of a centrally planned economy and the emerging outline of the welfare state (Healey *et al.* 1988). The system sought to address the legacy of urban sprawl, poor urban housing conditions and postwar bomb damage. This required that an element of countryside protection should sit alongside the desire to achieve the reconstruction of major cities. As a result, the Act moved away from the zoning approach that characterised prewar planning legislation. It had six main parts which outlined the effective nationalisation of development rights, powers of compulsory purchase of land by local authorities, the introduction of betterment tax on transactions over and above existing use value, arrangements for policies to be set out in development plans, rules defining the circumstances in which proposed changes to land would be seen as development and the decentralisation of powers to counties and boroughs.

The system that emerged was comprehensive and gave all local authorities the responsibility for the production of policies for the use of land and development control. The main attributes of the system were its flexibility and discretionary nature. The system combined centrally controlled powers of direction with local responsibility for implementation. Central and local government had responsibility for determining the public interest in development proposals. Development effort was to be directed towards new towns and development control was exercised as a tool for urban containment.

The first significant change to the system was the removal of the development land charge in 1952. This effectively allowed market value to be asserted in all transactions and reduced the potential for the state to act as major developer. The removal of the provision for local authorities to purchase land at existing use value in 1959 further supported the expansion of private sector housing development (Healey *et al.* 1988). By the 1960s, the intended redistribution of population and business to new and expanding towns had begun to be overtaken by market-driven decentralisation based on increasing economic prosperity and personal wealth and underpinned by demographic change (Hall *et al.* 1973). The urban periphery was becoming the focus for new development activity and green belt policies were being used to resist this.

This tension ultimately led to debates about regional and spatial policy. In the late 1960s, the introduction of structure and local plans signalled the second significant change to the system. These changes were aimed at ensuring that the system had the flexibility demanded by the need to react to the dynamic process of urban change. The 1968 Town and Country Planning Act's proposals sought to reinforce the effectiveness of central policy directions, while allowing greater discretion over local matters. The change saw an increased emphasis on plan preparation, on technical survey and analysis methods, and in the promotion of public participation in the planning system. Although the intention was that structure plans and local plans would fall within the remit of a unitary authority, the reorganisation of local government in 1974 complicated matters by dividing the planning function between two levels of government, district and county. The divided function, of course, gave rise to the possibility of political county–district conflict. At the same time, central–local relations became increasingly uneasy (Rydin 1986; Healey *et al.* 1988). From the 1970s the national government regularly asserted that the planning system should focus on land-use matters rather than strategic policy issues (Vigar *et al.* 2000).

The important implication for those involved in planning for housing development was that opposition to growth around major conurbations intensified. The policy response was based on the identification of major growth areas into which investment could be channelled. This was accompanied by a focus on city centre and inner city redevelopment. As discussed above, the programmes of slum clearances and major road schemes connecting inner areas to motorway networks during this period brought about large-scale spatial change in cities.

The emergence of inner city problems, including the erosion of neighbourhood communities and concentration of poverty, led to a rethink on decentralisation and a challenge to the long-standing policy of redistributing people and jobs and to the emergence of housing renewal as an important plank of planning policy (Healey *et al.* 1988). This rethink culminated in the White Paper *'Policy for the Inner Cities'* in 1977. The White Paper provided a strong commitment to the problems of inner urban areas and advocated a strategy of urban regeneration with a significant economic element (DOE 1977). These policies sought to operate against the forces for decentralisation, including the effects of economic restructuring and de-industrialisation, the improved road and high-speed rail networks, and took the form of urban containment through restraint.

This position persisted until the election of the Thatcher Government. This election victory introduced a sustained period of New Right government during which planning for housing was reoriented through the commodification of the system (Rydin 1986; Goodchild 1992; Thornley 1996). Circulars in the early 1980s emphasised that there should be a general presumption towards development (DOE 1980a). There was also a requirement that a five-year supply of land should be available for housebuilding (DOE 1980b). Together these facilitated a system of 'planning by appeal' in which developers brought forward sites that they considered reasonable in planning terms, even though they did not fit with the local planning authorities' plans.

The changing attitudes of the New Right to planning are often analysed in terms of two distinct phases (Allmendinger & Thomas 1998). The period from 1979 to 1989 has been characterised as the 'project-led' phase, while the period from 1989 to 1997 is generally described as the 'plan-led' phase. 'Project-led' planning was strongly pro-development and featured the introduction of Simplified Planning Zones (SPZs) and accompanying urban policy initiatives including promotion of the Urban Development Corporations and Enterprise Zones. This position changed in response to pressure from Conservative voters in the shires who were generally suspicious of attempts to deregulate planning controls. The change, however, was not substantive but rather represented a change in the order of priority given to the three main tenets of planning policy, namely, centralisation, rule of law and market orientation. After 1989, market orientation thus became of less importance than centralisation and rule of law in guiding the trajectory of policy.

Despite this slight alteration in the Conservatives' strong pro-development stance, the primacy awarded to the market remained a feature. Although New Labour's attitude towards planning has been confused and at times statements have been conflicting and contradictory, the market orientation of the system has survived the 1997 election (Allmendinger *et al.* 2002). Much of this analysis, however, relates to rhetoric and discourse. In the first five years in government, the Labour Party did little more than tinker with the system. The most significant change related to the reduction in weight given to estimates of housing numbers. Indeed, as we discuss in more detail in Chapters 4 and 6, the old 'predict and provide' approach to housing need was abandoned and replaced with a new policy of 'plan, monitor and manage'. Under this new system greater weight is placed upon the need for local planning authorities to work together in order to come to agreements (and to resolve disagreements) about how best to meet local requirements. This is based on a more transparent approach to agreeing regional guidance and to testing evidence in public (DETR 1999a).

Potentially more radical are the proposed changes floated in the Green Paper, '*Planning: Delivering a Fundamental Change*' published in late 2001 (DTLR 2001b). The main proposals include the replacement of the existing multi-layered plan hierarchy with a simplified two-level system principally of local development frameworks and regional spatial strategies produced to be consistent with the national planning framework. The impetus for change came from the desire to make the system simpler and more responsive. The paper also contains proposals for 'Business Planning Zones', similar to the old SPZs, where there will be minimal development controls.

Overall, these changes have been characterised by the Government as being 'people-led' rather than 'plan-led'. In the official DTLR press release, the Secretary of State was quoted as saying that this:

> is a radical change in the way we look at planning. Instead of being led by plans we will be led by people. We want a planning system in which the values of the whole community are allowed to prosper and develop. The current system does not allow that. It is slow ponderous and uncertain.
>
> (DTLR 2001c, p. 1)

Importantly, the proposals seem to address some of the major criticisms levelled at the previous system of dealing with proposed new developments. For instance, critics had suggested that, in effect, housing planning decisions about major housing developments have inevitably become issues of local choice rather than strategy. These choices tended to be heavily influenced by local political sensitivities when they should be issues of national or regional strategy. Cullingworth (1999), for example, notes that despite attempts to consider the relative merits of alternative patterns of development, local public opposition has tended to defeat proposals for new settlements.

By implication, under the current planning system, local political interests appear to be able to overpower national strategic decisions, even if those have been based on a sound understanding of the social and economic needs of local urban and rural communities and have been based on the principles of sustainability and a 'holistic' view of policy. For this reason, Cullingworth (1999) describes the British system and its elements of local opposition, public inquiries and ministerial intervention as a 'non-planning' approach.

Although providing the rationale for making provision for regional-level strategic decision-making on the location of major new housing development proposals, it is possible to question the validity of the Secretary of State's attempts to emphasise that the new 'people-led' system will promote community interests. For instance as the Director of the CPRE, Kate Parminter, asserts, in proposing that strategic decisions over the scale and location of development should be taken at regional level, the Government may in effect be 'taking away people's right to get involved' and is 'taking away key opportunities to influence crucial decisions' (CPRE 2001, p. 1). She goes on to stress that abolishing the county structure plan system 'would leave a gaping hole where democratic, strategic planning used to be'.

Even though, at the time of writing, the ramifications of the latest proposals for change are not known, it is a widely held view that the planning system is ripe for reform (Cullingworth 1997; Hall 1998; DTLR 2001b). There is less consensus about the nature and extent of this reform. This stems, in part, from disagreements about the extent to which the system has, in fact, changed in the last 50 years. Although there have been significant institutional changes, notably in the Conservatives' changes to the structures supporting the welfare state, a number of writers highlight that the planning system has exhibited a relatively high degree of continuity (Brindley *et al.* 1996; Tewdwr-Jones 1996).

Cullingworth (1997) observes that the planning system is very recognisably the same as it was when introduced. This he attributes to the strength of public support for the protection the system provides. This support represents an alliance of old-style preservationists and new-style environmentalists who both have a stake in resisting change to the system. While accepting that the system has largely remained unaltered, Allmendinger (1999) explains that important policy changes have been directed at the processes of planning. This finds support from Vigar *et al.* (2000) who note that significant changes in policy communities, policy arenas and discourse mean that the tools and competencies of the system are being used differently.

Others point to changing state–market relations as evidence of substantive alterations within the system (Tewdwr-Jones 1996; Thornley 1996). These changes relate to the two-way interactions between state and market. In one direction planning is often criticised for being insufficiently aware of the impact of policy on the market (Healey 1992). In the other direction, the increased influence awarded to the market in matters of resource allocation has changed the relationship between planners and private sector actors.

In this context, Brindley *et al.* (1996) demonstrate the way in which these interactions can lead to different planning styles. Healey's discussion of development plans helps highlight the extent to which key relationships have changed over time (Healey 1992). She identifies three approaches to planning: following the market, managing the market and creating the market. The relationship between state and market is dependent on political and economic conditions (Thornley 1996). Thus, the period of economic growth during the 1960s and early 1970s was distinctive in creating the market. The 1980s recession represented a period of following the market. As Thornley (1996) notes, this also incorporated a period when planning was subservient to other areas of public policy, notably project-led urban regeneration.

It is clear that, since the war, the institutional context and, in particular, the relations between state and market, within which the planning system operates, have undergone dramatic change. Local government has been reorganised (more than once), the private sector has become the dominant force in development, the role of the public sector is now limited and fragmented, and the relatively steady economic expansion of the 1950s and 1960s has been replaced at first by severe cycles and then more recently by relative stability. Population expansion has increasingly placed demands on land use.

The tools of planning have also changed, with planning gain prominent on the agenda. Procedures have been altered significantly in order to allow greater access to decision-making through higher levels of public participation. Importantly, the planning system has responded to greater levels of policy integration and is now necessarily more responsive to changes in *inter alia* the transport, housing, social, urban and rural policy arenas. In fact, the demarcations between sectional policy interests have to a large extent become blurred and, as we note in the introduction to this chapter, issues relating to planning for housing development are at the heart of contemporary urban (and rural) policy debates.

It is only very recently that the changes to the system have started to challenge the implicit support for development on mainly greenfield locations. This review of changes to planning policy is dominated by measures that have been underpinned by a general presumption that greenfield development was desirable and was seen as a chance to develop at lower densities. The removal of aspects of the 1947 planning system acted as a spur to green-

field development. Conversely, the abolition, in 1959, of the ability to purchase land at existing use value acts as a real barrier to brownfield housing
development in many locations. These, of course, are only a few illustrative
examples of the implicit preference for greenfield development.

Housing development and urban regeneration policy

As we note above, specific planning policies introduced in the 1960s contributed to the relocation of households from the urban core to peripheral
housing estates. In addition, since 1946, planning policy has supported the
creation of 28 new towns, housing 1.1 million people (Potter 1987). It is
possible, thus, to make a distinction between the planned and unplanned
elements of decentralisation (Lawless 1989). These planned elements made
up only 10% of those leaving cities. This also had the unintended effect of
inducing many wealthy suburbanites to leave urban areas. There was also
an additional significant outflow of migrants who sought to take advantage
of the more attractively located and cheaper owner-occupied homes outside
cities (Kennett & Hall 1981). The scale and selective nature of decentralisation after 1961 meant that those remaining in the urban core included
disproportionately high numbers of unemployed, elderly and lower socio-
economic groups. The concentration of these more disadvantaged groups
within the cities gave impetus to the development of an urban policy distinct
from existing housing and planning policy initiatives.

Thus, the emergence of a comprehensive urban policy in the UK can be
traced to a number of urban experiments undertaken in the 1960s and the
introduction of the Urban Programme in 1968 (Atkinson & Moon 1994).
Since this point, however, the nature of policy has changed direction several
times. In particular the extent to which public sector intervention has been
perceived to be central to urban regeneration has changed markedly. This
is reflected in the more gradual shifts in emphasis regarding the nature and
form that this involvement should take. The general influences on these
broadly follow those impacting on the direction of housing and planning
policy, namely the early evolution of the welfare state, local government reorganisation in the 1960s, and the more recent influences of New Right and
New Left (or Third Way) projects. The temporal evolution of regeneration
policy initiatives is summarised in Fig. 2.2.

During the 1970s urban policy rested on two assumptions shared by both
main parties (Parkinson 1998). First, policy should provide social and welfare
support for those adversely affected by economic restructuring in the inner
cities and wealth should be created in these areas. Second, since selective

investment by the private sector was seen as one of the causes of urban problems, the public sector should have a natural role in promoting urban regeneration. These principles underpinned initiatives such as the Urban Programme, the GEAR (Glasgow Eastern Area Renewal) programme, and the Comprehensive Community Programme experiments.

	SCOTLAND	ENGLAND	WALES
1964	Labour Government elected under Harold Wilson		
1967	*Educational Priority Areas* advocated in Plowden report	*Educational Priority Areas* advocated in Plowden report	*Educational Priority Areas* advocated in Plowden report
1968	*Urban Programme* proposed for areas of special social need	*Urban Programme* proposed for areas of special social need	*Urban Programme* proposed for areas of special social need
1969	*Urban Programme* began, *Community Development Projects* initiated *General Improvement Areas* introduced	*Urban Programme* began, *Community Development Projects* initiated *General Improvement Areas* introduced	*Urban Programme* began, *Community Development Projects* initiated *General Improvement Areas* introduced
1970	Conservative Government elected under Edward Heath		
1974	*Housing Action Areas* introduced	*Housing Action Areas* introduced *Comprehensive Community Programme* experiments. *Inner Area Studies* commissioned for London, Birmingham and Liverpool	*Housing Action Areas* introduced
1974	Labour Government elected under Harold Wilson		
1975	*Scottish Development Agency* formed		*Land Authority for Wales* and *Welsh Development Agency* formed
1976	*Glasgow Eastern Area Renewal* (GEAR) Programme initiated		
1977	White Paper on *Policy for the Inner Cities*	White Paper on *Policy for the Inner Cities*	White Paper on *Policy for the Inner Cities*
1978	*Inner Urban Areas Act.* *Urban Programme* recast to meet economic and environmental as well as social need	*Inner Urban Areas Act.* *Urban Programme* recast to meet economic and environmental as well as social need	*Inner Urban Areas Act.* *Urban Programme* recast to meet economic and environmental as well as social need
1979	Conservative Government elected under Margaret Thatcher		
1981	*Enterprise Zones* introduced (eventually 4 in Scotland) *Public Land Registers* established for vacant land in public ownership	*UDCs* set up in London Docklands and Merseyside *Enterprise Zones* introduced (eventually 20 in England) *Public Land Registers* established for vacant land in public ownership	*Enterprise Zones* introduced (eventually 4 in Wales) *Public Land Registers* established for vacant land in public ownership
1982		*Urban Development Grant* (UDG) launched	
1983	*Local Enterprise Grants for Urban Projects* (LEG-UP) launched		
1984		Liverpool *Garden Festival*	
1985		*City Action Teams* set up to coordinate government initiatives and encourage local partnerships *Estate Action* established	
1986		Stoke on Trent *Garden Festival.* Government *Task Forces* established to coordinate local renewal	
1987		*Urban Regeneration Grant* (URG) launched *UDCs* set up in Black Country, Teesside, Trafford Park and Tyne & Wear	Cardiff Bay *UDC* set up

Fig. 2.2   Almost 35 years of urban regeneration policy.

1988	Glasgow *Garden Festival* *New Life for Urban Scotland* initiated for peripheral housing estates at Whitfield in Dundee, Wester Hailes in Edinburgh, Castlemilk in Glasgow and Ferguslie Park in Paisley	*Action for Cities* initiative including UDCs in Bristol, Leeds, Manchester and Sheffield *City Grant* introduced to replace UDG, URG and private sector derelict land grant *Safer Cities Programme* (first phase) initiated	*Programme for the Valleys* (first phase to 1993)
1989	*Scottish Homes* formed *Scottish Safer Cities Programme* initiated		
1990	*Smaller Urban Renewal Initiatives* started (renewal of smaller housing estates)	Gateshead *Garden Festival*	
1991	*Scottish Enterprise* formed by merger between SDA and Training Agency for Scotland. Now works through 22 *Local Enterprise Companies*	*Training and Enterprise Councils* set up to involve local business leaders in training and business support *City Challenge* introduced	*Training and Enterprise Councils* set up to involve local business leaders in training and business support
1992		Announcement of end to Urban Programme *UDC* set up in Birmingham Heartlands	Ebbw Vale *Garden Festival*
1993	*Progress in Partnership* consultation paper issued	*Government Regional Offices* established (subsume CATs) *UDC* set up in Plymouth *City Pride* initiated for London, Birmingham and Manchester	*Programme for the Valleys* (second phase to 1998)
1994		*English Partnerships* set up *Single Regeneration Budget* introduced to replace 20 separate programmes *Safer Cities Programme* (second phase) initiated	*Strategic Development Scheme* to replace *Urban Programme* *Urban Investment Grant* introduced
1996	Introduction of *Priority Partnership Areas* and *Regeneration Programmes*	*Estate Renewal Challenge Fund* introduced	*Welsh Capital Challenge* introduced to replace *Strategic Development Scheme*
1997	Labour Government elected under Tony Blair		
1997		*Social Exclusion Unit* established in Cabinet Office Discussion Paper *Regeneration Programmes – The Way Forward* published	
1998	*Working for Communities* launched on pilot basis	*Urban Task Force* begins work *New Deal for Communities* announced *Policy Action Teams* established *Single Regeneration Budget* redirected to areas of need	*People in Communities* launched
1999	Scottish Parliament established *Social Inclusion Partnerships* replace Priority Partnership Areas, Regeneration Programmes and the Urban Programme. To be integrated with *Rough Sleepers Initiative, Drug Action Teams* and *Local Health Care Cooperatives* Glasgow *Employment Zone* established and *Working for Communities* extended *Community Planning Strategies* introduced for all local government areas	*Regional Development Agencies* commence work *Urban Task Force Report:* 'Towards an Urban Renaissance' published *Urban Regeneration Companies* launched in Liverpool, Manchester and Sheffield New area-based initiatives launched including *Community Legal Service Partnerships, Crime Reduction Programmes, Education Action Zones, Employment Zones, Health Action Zones* and *Sure Start*	National Assembly for Wales established
2000		Urban White Paper '*Our Towns and Cities: The Future – Delivering an Urban Renaissance*' published Social Exclusion Unit set out '*National Strategy for Neighbourhood Renewal*' More *Urban Regeneration Companies* established	*People in Communities* expanded and *Communities First* launched
2001	*Communities Scotland* supersedes Scottish Homes and assumes responsibility for delivery of regeneration and housing modernisation programmes	*Local Strategic Partnerships* established to develop community strategies. *Neighbourhood Renewal Unit and Fund* set up	
N.B.	This table concentrates on national urban policy and does not specifically identify the Structural Funds of the European Union or the numerous initiatives of local authorities or local authority associations.		

Fig. 2.2   *(Continued.)*

These assumptions were fundamentally challenged after 1979. Since that point there has been a general assumption that the private sector has lacked the confidence to invest in inner cities (Jones & Watkins 1996). The rationale for urban regeneration policy is still provided by the need to reverse the economic, social and physical decay in towns and cities, especially where it has reached that stage when market forces alone will not suffice (Adair *et al.* 1998). However, the natural mechanism for intervention is no longer the public sector. The role for policy is to restore private sector confidence in investing in urban areas. Generally, under the successive Conservative administrations, the policies introduced were based on an approach that was top-down and geographically focused in character (see *inter alia* Healey *et al.* 1992; Turok 1992; Imrie & Thomas 1993).

By the early 1980s, regeneration policy mainly took the form of property development led by the private sector. This emphasis on physical property-led projects coincided with the property market boom and a general increase in the level of finance supporting speculative development. A range of policy initiatives and instruments were developed to support this activity including Enterprise Zones and Urban Development Corporations as well as a range of grants and subsidies (see Fig. 2.2 for further details). Figure 2.3 shows an example of a residential warehouse conversion undertaken during this period in the area of the London Docklands Development Corporation. However, the approach became discredited by the early 1990s when the property slump and withdrawal of private finance undermined these projects. Critics, particularly those from local communities, also highlighted the limiting preoccupation with high-profile, and often externally orientated projects, the centralised nature of decision-making and lack of consultation, and the tendency for the private sector to bear most of the risk (Edwards 1997).

With these failings in mind, there followed a movement away from the use of physical projects as a solution to employment problems to an approach based on business support and development, and employment training programmes. This approach was supported by the introduction of Training and Enterprise Councils (TECs), Local Enterprise Companies (LECs) and City Challenge projects, as well as by European Union Structural Funds and Community Initiatives. Again, however, the performance of these initiatives did not escape criticism. In this case, the focus on business growth came at the expense of the physical urban environment. In addition, the proliferation of special purpose agencies, some of which have a very local spatial focus, led to a fragmented regeneration programme. In the case of City Challenge, and in the context of limited public resources, the competitive ethos fostered a rivalry, which discourages the exchange of experience and the integration

Fig. 2.3   New Caledonia Wharf: residential conversion in London Docklands.

of activities required in a more holistic approach to tackling the social and economic problems of urban areas (Edwards 1997).

Under the Blair Government regeneration policy has emerged incrementally. There has been no sharp break in policy, even if new initiatives have proliferated. The Government has retained and developed many elements of the Major Government's policies. Central themes of continuity include the emphasis on locally led solutions, competition for regional funds and the promotion of partnerships between public and private sector organisations (Tiesdell & Allmendinger 2001). Despite the broad change in direction, which saw government policy move some way from its reliance on property-led initiatives of the 1980s, there is still a housing element in most of projects undertaken under the policy initiatives introduced by Major and Blair. As Table 2.4 shows, however, the £9.94 billion spend on policies has had only a limited impact on housing development, with only 194 864 new homes being developed through regeneration initiatives (Tyler 2001).

Table 2.4 The impact of area-based urban policy initiatives.

Expenditure	Impacts					
Policy measures 1981–2000	Estimated public sector policy (£bn)	Estimated other public & private sector (£bn)	Land developed and reclaimed (ha)	Floorspace created (million sq. m)	Net additional jobs	Dwellings
London Docklands Development Corporation	2.90	9.69	1756	2.43	44 000	24 000
Other Urban Development Corporations	1.70	9.26	2565	5.66	81 387	18 500
Enterprise Zones	1.00	2.00	2700	6.00	58 000	110 000
City Challenge	1.14	6.25	4000	3.60	32 000	20 000
English Partnerships	1.00	2.30	5650	3.30	90 000	22 364
Single Regeneration Budget	2.20	8.81	1118	1.0	44 728	
Total	**9.94**	**38.31**	**17 789**	**21.99**	**350 115**	**194 864**

Source: Adapted from Tyler (2001); also reported in Adair *et al.* (2001).

The rhetoric of the Blair Government has raised the possibility that future policy may give a greater role to fiscal incentives in regeneration policy (DETR 2000b; see Chapter 8). This is based partly on evidence that two of the most influential incentives introduced through the Enterprise Zones initiative were rates relief and capital allowances (PA Cambridge Economic Consultants 1995). More recent support is provided by Adair *et al.* (1998) who, in their study of mechanisms for attracting private finance into regeneration projects, conclude that more innovative fiscal approaches need to be explored, including the more creative use of the taxation system. This is echoed by the Urban Task Force's (1999) support for tax breaks and by Adams *et al.* (2001b), who propose the designation of Urban Partnership Zones that could include powers to promote capital investment through capital allowances, capital gains tax relief and rate-free periods. The latter are explained in more detail in Chapter 8.

There are arguments both for and against tax-based mechanisms within urban policy. In examining the transferability of the tax break system used in Dublin and Tax Incremental Financing (TIF) districts used in Chicago, Berry *et al.* (2002) highlight several limitations. First, they are critical of the blunt nature of the Irish tax break and the potential for the instrument to be used as a tax shelter rather than for the promotion of regeneration. Second, they acknowledge that the Irish system can exacerbate demand-side pressure on prices. Third, and in both cases, they highlight that while investment flows can be generated they can also cause displacement effects. Fourth, the flow of investment and, by extension, the performance of both schemes is also heavily dependent on general property market performance.

Despite these more negative views, the general support for tax incentives has been brought into focus by recent legislation and by the general direction of policy. On the former, EU competition rules have been interpreted as making the deployment of gap funding grants and subsidies to commercial developers problematic. On the latter, as Berry *et al.* (2002) suggest, taxation measures seem to be broadly in keeping with 'Third Way' thinking in that they provide a basis for the synthesis of traditional forms of market intervention with a more neo-liberal pro-market agenda.

There is also recognition that these supply-side initiatives will need to be accompanied by demand-side changes. The Urban Task Force (1999) highlights the need to create urban environments that will attract households back into the cities. This theme is picked up in the Urban White Paper (DETR 2000b) and suggests a clear role for the public sector in these activities rather than in direct involvement in physical regeneration projects.

In general urban regeneration policy has been subject to marked changes in terms of style and substance. Interestingly, although the reuse of urban land has been given prominence in urban policy discussions, the post-1997 change towards community-based mechanisms for tackling social exclusion has meant less emphasis on brownfield redevelopment within regeneration policy. Of course, this is partly compensated by changes in other policy areas, but it remains a potentially problematic shift in policy content.

Conclusions: housing provision and state–market relations

This chapter has sought to review the way in which housing, planning and urban regeneration policy has influenced the balance of greenfield and brown-field development in Britain. The review suggests that, often, the impact of specific policies has been unintended and the influence of policy change has been subtle. Historically the direction of policy has implicitly supported greenfield development. This has largely been a consequence of changes in the spatial economic structures that shape our cities, and the attempts by policy-makers to tackle the challenges that accompany these structural changes.

In particular, although the trend has slowed since the 1970s, the loss of population from Britain's cities to rural areas has been a continuous source of policy problems. These migration patterns have been inter-connected with social and economic change. Over the past 30 years, the process of economic restructuring has led to the loss of jobs from cities and an increase in the spatial concentration of poverty and deprivation in inner urban areas. The problem of social polarisation has been exacerbated by the selective nature of out-migration. These processes have given rise to the development of polycentric urban regions with new business activity increasingly located outside traditional urban centres.

These changes, accompanied by growth in the rate of household formation, have generated demand for high levels of new housing development. This has caused problems for both urban and rural areas. Parts of urban areas are suf-fering from major social and economic decline, while the increased pressure on rural housing markets is causing shortages and price inflation. These prob-lems cut across a range of public policy areas including urban regeneration, housing and planning. It is apparent from the chapter that public policy has contributed to social and economic change and that the implications of this provide the context for the introduction of current policy issues and debates.

It is also clear from the review that, historically, there has been a tendency for policies to develop in isolation. This tendency has persisted until fairly recently. Although planning policy was to some extent linked to urban policy in the 1980s, the implicit separation of planning and housing policy continued into the 1990s and arguably still continues today. This degree of policy separation has, in part, contributed to the current difficulties surrounding the location of housing development.

Some of the urban social problems, including the shortage of affordable homes and the patterns of urban deprivation, were exacerbated by the housing policies of the 1980s and 1990s. For example, the promotion of home ownership through the RTB has led to the reliance on market price as the means of allocating homes. This has contributed to social polarisation within urban areas, as the poorest groups have been concentrated in poorer-quality unsold stock (Forrest & Murie 1995). The same policy has contributed to problems of social exclusion in rural areas. The sell-off of council homes has created shortages of affordable homes, restricting access and forcing those on lower incomes to seek a private sector solution where the prices are likely to be unreachable. The reliance on home ownership also exposed households to greater risk. This risk now extends across a wider range of social groups (Hamnett 1999). The economic downturn in the 1990s placed large numbers of households in financial difficulty as the risk of job loss increased in tandem with rising mortgage rates and monthly repayments.

In recent policy debates, there has been greater recognition of the extent to which social and economic problems are interwoven. An explicit message emerging from a variety of government policy statements, including the green papers on health and the family as well as the more recent urban and rural white papers, is that there is a clear need for 'joined up thinking' and a holistic approach to policy issues (Brown 1999). This has led to a blurring of the distinction between policy areas, which have been important in the housing development arena.

As Bramley (1997, p. 403) notes, 'people are being housed, moving around, financing their housing, improving or maintaining it and these activities impinge on other areas of life.' Consequently, elements of housing policy are now located within agendas on social security, financial regulation, community care, private finance, health and, in the case of development issues, sustainability, planning and regeneration. Kemp (1999) also highlights the links with the activities of the social exclusion unit and related policies for strengthening communities.

The new role for the planning system in securing affordable housing provides a clear example of the implications of these policy changes for housing development (see Chapter 4). Similarly, the commitment to achieving a social mix in new housing developments represents an attempt to contribute to tackling social inclusion problems (Crook & Whitehead 2002). In addition, as we discuss at length in Chapter 3, planning policies are now much more heavily influenced by the sustainability agenda and environmental policy. What is less clear, however, is whether a more holistic approach to policy has significantly influenced practice (see Chapters 4, 7 and 8).

Another recurring theme in our review of policy has been the changing relationship between state and market. The reorientation of state intervention is clearly evident in the evolution of housing policy. The 1960s saw a gradual switch from public sector to private sector, which dominated development activity. By 1979, various measures were used to encourage private sector involvement, while financial constraints were placed on the public sector. The influence of privatisation was not limited to placing direct restraints on public sector housing development. This was also accompanied by the mass sale of council houses. In addition, the role of the state as housing provider and manager has been increasingly supplanted by housing associations. Although some of the problems highlighted above were, in part, a result of the desire for development of a predominantly market-based housing system, there has been little change in orientation since the change in government.

The changing role of the state in urban policy has also been striking. The evolution of urban policy was underpinned by the assumption that market failure was responsible for urban problems. After 1979, however, the public sector was defined as the cause of urban decline, while the private sector was identified as the solution. This provided the rationale for the central role given to private property development in urban regeneration projects.

Although more recent initiatives emphasise partnership models, the private sector is generally the dominant partner and has continued to play a part in regeneration-related housing development. The market has also become the dominant force in planning policy. Although much of the commentary on this process is dominated by reflections on the urban policy initiatives to which the planning system became subservient, a number of more subtle changes to practice have been observed since 1980. These include the privileged role given to housebuilders in agreeing regional estimates of housing need (Hull 1997). It is also suggested that public expenditure restrictions undermined the ability of the planning system to engage in positive planning through infrastructure investment, or land acquisition and assembly. Although proposals to modernise local government (DETR 2000c) are likely to address this, it had the indirect effect of reducing the incentive for market actors to adhere to plans (Bramley and Lambert 1998).

Overall, the recent ideological dominance of economic liberalisation, and the accompanying decentralisation and devolution of decision-making, have ensured that, often, resource allocation and regulatory decisions are made by the market rather than the state. As we note, one of the features of the RTB is that it transferred responsibility for the allocation of housing from the state to the market. The state now operates in a framework characterised by limited resources, a diminished role for local government, a rise in regional administration, and increased competitive allocation of resources. A potential problem, however, is that economies that are heavily reliant on market mechanisms can be exposed by the fragility of some markets. In particular, there is a tendency for land and property markets to fail or to distribute resources inequitably. Clear examples of these problems are the low levels of private sector investment in urban regeneration property markets, and the tendency for low-income local households to be priced out of rural housing markets (Adair *et al.* 1998; Shucksmith *et al.* 2001, respectively). Additional problems relate to the need to ensure an equitable distribution of externalities from private sector activity.

In this context, the challenge for policy-makers lies in supporting and managing the market. There will inevitably be a range of locality-specific problems to overcome. These might relate, for example, to the need to attract private sector development into declining urban areas or to the accompanying need to redirect housing demand by persuading households of the merits of urban living compared with suburban or rural alternatives. In some areas, there is an ongoing requirement to secure private sector provision of affordable housing in quantities that meet the levels of need experienced in both urban and rural areas. Elsewhere there is, of course, a need to limit the external costs, in terms of environmental damage, that might be associated with meeting the demand for housing generated by household growth and redistribution.

It is clear that the location of new housing development can contribute to social and economic change within particular localities. While planning policy has sought to regulate housing development, it has at times played a positive role in housing and urban regeneration policy. Yet even in the light of potential economic development and social benefits, new development on the scale required to meet household growth cannot be achieved without controversy. From this policy review, it is clear that these problems cannot be addressed by independent sector-specific responses.

3

The Sustainability of New Housing Development

Long before the concept of sustainable development achieved global recognition, the British had sought to limit the outward spread of new housing development through a policy of urban containment (Hall *et al.* 1973). In due course, this was reinforced by an emerging emphasis on urban regeneration, in which it became a priority to accommodate as much housing development as possible on previously used land within urban areas (Llewelyn-Davies 1994; Cullingworth 1999). In one sense, the concept of sustainable development provided a valuable hook on which to fix already-accepted policies for the location of new housing development. In another sense, however, sustainability has proved a potentially troublesome cuckoo in the nest of housing land policy, since the contested nature of sustainable development opens up all sorts of debates that can be deployed to challenge widely held notions of acceptable urban form (Breheny 1996). The purpose of this chapter is to review those debates, specifically in relation to the sustainability of greenfield and brownfield housing development.

In the first part of the chapter, we explore how the concept of sustainable development provides both a common and contested discourse around which controversial debates on the form and location of new housing development now take place. We consider how, at least in terms of public policy, sustainable development has become associated more with the overall quality of life than with mere resource conservation. The second part of the chapter examines how the achievement of sustainable development has increasingly been measured through the use of formal indicators, of which land use is but one. We therefore seek to discern from these indicators the characteristics of a sustainable residential development and to assess the relative importance of residential location within those characteristics.

In the third part of the chapter, we consider why many favour urban compaction as an important means to secure sustainable urban development, while recognising that others doubt whether the compact city is desirable, sustainable or even achievable. Moreover, even if the compact city is accepted as the most appropriate urban form, it does not follow that compaction must necessarily involve intensification of urban areas. The fourth part of the chapter therefore explores how alternative patterns of development requiring greenfield land, such as major urban extensions and new settlements, can be designed to be both compact and sustainable.

The chapter argues that the delivery of sustainable residential development, however defined, is not merely a matter of design and location, but critically requires effective institutional mechanisms and policies to bring about a much higher quality of development than in the recent past. In the final part, we explore how the reuse of brownfield land for housing development has become increasingly paramount within official interpretations of the sustainable development in the UK, and we suggest that this has been attributable, at least in part, to an institutional deficit in ensuring better quality and more sustainable forms of housing, whether developed at brownfield or greenfield locations.

In concluding, we therefore identify three important questions raised by this ever-stronger emphasis on brownfield development, which reach to the heart of our analysis in later chapters of the book:

- How and why has public policy placed so much emphasis on brownfield rather than greenfield residential development?

- To what extent are existing planning and development processes capable of delivering such an emphasis on brownfield development? If they are not capable, what sort of changes may be needed in resource and institutional terms if development is to be successful?

- Which interests are likely to gain and to lose from this policy emphasis, whether or not it is successful?

The contested nature of sustainable development

The Bruntland Commission's (1987, p. 43) original definition of sustainable development as 'development that meets the needs of the present without compromising the ability of future generations to meet their own needs' remains widely quoted in academic and professional literature. Such a broad pronouncement, however, has been open to numerous interpretations, as a result of which over 200 specific definitions of sustainable development were generated in the following seven years alone (Winter 1994).

Attempts were subsequently made to arrive at a better understanding of sustainable development through drawing out its central principles. Those most frequently cited as embodying what is really meant by sustainable development include environmental concern, thought for future generations, equity and social justice, greater participation, transfrontier responsibility, and an enhanced quality of life (see, for example, Environ 1996; Macnaghten & Pinfield 1999; Strange 1999).

What is immediately apparent from attempts to articulate the central principles of sustainable development is how much the concept differs from narrower forms of environmentalism. For sustainability represents 'the merging of economic enterprise, social well-being and environmental integrity' (O'Riordan 1999, p. 11). Hall and Pfeiffer (2000) have taken this holistic view even further, suggesting that sustainable development as a multidimensional concept, should be the central objective of good governance (see Fig. 3.1). They argue that:

> Good governance will act as the motor and political driving force, keeping the different elements of sustainable development in balance, integrating them in policies, and ensuring that all the different agencies in the city share the responsibilities and the benefits. Sustainability as the principle,

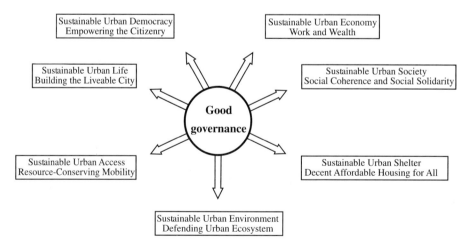

Fig. 3.1   Good governance, an all-embracing concept with sustainable development as its central objective (source: Hall & Pfeiffer 2000).

good governance as the practice, thus become the twin aspects of good urban development.

(Hall & Pfeiffer 2000, p. 164)

In this context, it becomes possible for the UK Government, in its most recent strategy for sustainable development in the United Kingdom, to suggest that 'the simple idea of ensuring a better quality of life for everyone, now and for generations to come' (DETR 1999b, p. 8) lies at the heart of sustainability. From the perspective of land use and development, three profound implications arise from taking a holistic view of sustainable development and linking it so directly with the quality of life.

First, in contrast to the doom-laden debates around environmental limits to growth that took place in the 1960s and 1970, it is now presumed, at least in official circles, that sustainable development can at the same time improve both environmental quality and human welfare (Macnaghten & Pinfield 1999). Secondly, there may be substantial contradictions, at least at the local level, between economic development and environmental protection (Gibbs *et al.* 1998). Thirdly, as we shall argue in this chapter, it is a gross over-simplification to suggest that brownfield development is necessarily always sustainable and greenfield development necessarily always unsustainable.

O'Riordan (1999, p. 7) proclaims that, at least in policy terms, '*environmentalism is dead: long live sustainability*', while Blowers (1997) demonstrates how the planning system is based on ecological modernisation rather than the more pessimistic thesis of the risk society. According to Jacobs (1999), environmentalism carried far too much ideological baggage, being inherently anti-business, anti-modern, anti-poor and anti-aspirational. Environmental modernisation, he suggests, is to be welcomed, since it aligns environmental concerns with people's aspirations and self-interest. Indeed, Jacobs identifies a win–win environmental scenario, in which priority is given towards developing new environmental technologies and industries, promoting better environmental performance and engineering long-term restructuring towards an environmentally efficient, yet profitable, economy, through new forms of environmental taxation. As Rydin (2000a, p. 43) thus comments: 'Environmental modernisation needs to be separated from traditional environmentalism (as typified by the Council for the Protection of Rural England?) which is seeking to protect the countryside at all costs (even if these are costs to the broader environment).'

Such practical distinctions reflect a fundamental conceptual division between what are generally known as strong and weak approaches to sustainability. According to Owens (1994), strong definitions of sustainability believe that environmental capacities must place constraints on economic activities, whereas weak definitions merely accord greater weight to environmental capacities. Applying this theme, Gibbs *et al.* (1998) identify a spectrum of perspectives from technocentric 'very weak sustainability' to ecocentric 'very strong sustainability'. This reflects relative values placed on the importance of natural capital and is shown in Fig. 3.2. While advocates of weak sustainability assume that human and natural capital can be readily substituted, strong definitions of sustainability reject any assumption of infinite substitutability and instead specify minimum levels of environmental quality that take precedence over all other objectives.

Of course, since the concept of sustainability is so much open to interpretation, it can easily degenerate into a bargaining device to be used by sectional interests in pursuit of their own goals (Tate 1994). Counsell (1999), for example, argues that environmental lobbyists such as the Council for the Protection of Rural England are quick to draw on strong interpretations of sustainable development to promote their own beliefs in resource protection. Conversely, those seeking to meet the basic human need for housing are ready to deploy weaker versions of sustainable development in pursuit of their interests. Although, according to Strange (1999), once economic and environmental policy objectives are joined together, weaker versions of urban sustainability are generally preferred over stronger versions; almost to compensate for this, issues such as conservation and preservation are allowed to replace true environmental concern in the discourse of sustainable development. It is therefore essential, when considering the balance between greenfield and brownfield development, to cut through undue reliance on the rhetoric of sustainable development, from whichever quarter, and search instead for hard evidence.

Version	Features
Very weak sustainability	Overall stock of capital assets remains stable over time, complete substitution between human and natural capital. Essential link between willingness to pay and sustainable development
Weak sustainability	Limits set on natural capital usage. Some natural capital is critical, that is, nonsubstitutable. Related to the precautionary principle or safe minimum standards. Trade-offs still possible
Strong sustainability	Not all ecosystem functions and services can be adequately valued economically. Uncertainty means whatever the social benefits foregone, losses of critical natural capital are not possible
Very strong sustainability	Steady-state economic system based on thermodynamic limits and constraints. Matter and energy throughput should be minimised

Fig. 3.2   The spectrum of sustainable development (source: Gibbs *et al.* 1998).

The UK Government's most recent strategy for sustainable development promotes the multidimensional view of sustainability in which economic prosperity, social inclusion and environmental protection are seen as equally important. The Government has thus defined four objectives for its strategy:

- Social progress that recognises the needs of everyone.

- Effective protection of the environment.

- Prudent use of natural resources.

- Maintenance of high and stable levels of economic growth and employment (DETR 1999b, p. 8).

These objectives suggest that official attitudes towards sustainable development in the UK still reflect a technocentrist rather than an ecocentrist perspective (see Fig. 3.3), even though policy is now driven by the 'accommodators' rather than the 'cornucopians' (O'Riordan 1999). In the UK's first sustainable development strategy, continued economic growth was justified on the basis that: 'Sustainable development does not mean having less economic development: on the contrary a healthy economy is better able to generate the resources to meet people's needs and new investment and environmental improvement often go hand in hand' (UK Government 1994, p. 7). We are now told that social and economic advance that improves the quality of life is a justifiable element of sustainable development in its own right and not one that needs to be excused on the basis that it may help fund environmental improvement. The potential contradictions this causes with restrictive land-use controls are explored next by examining how quantitative indicators have been widely developed to measure progress towards sustainable development.

Indicators of sustainable development

It is difficult to know whether human activities are becoming more or less sustainable without formal means of measurement. Numerous attempts have therefore been made to develop sustainability indicators at local, national and international levels. An early list of 150 such indicators was published by the World Bank and UN Centre for Human Settlements (World Bank 1994). Shortly afterwards, the UK produced its own first national list of sustainability indicators (DOE 1996b). After the change of government in 1997, revisions to this list were suggested in order to reflect the social aspects of sustainability more fully (DETR 1998a). Following consultation,

By the early 1970s, two fundamentally different attitudes toward the environment had emerged. The technocentrist view is hierarchical, manipulative and managerial. The ecocentrist view, by contrast, embraces community scale, natural rhythms, and a morality based on ecological principles. As the chart below shows, however, each view has two important variants.

Ecocentrists		Technocentrists	
Deep environmentalists	Soft technologists	Accommodators	Cornucopians
• Lack of faith in modern, large-scale technology and its need for elitist expertise, central authority and inherently undemocratic institutions • Believe that materialism for its own sake is wrong and that economic growth can be geared to provide for the basic needs of those below subsistence levels	• Emphasise small scale (and hence community identity) in settlement, work, and leisure • Attempt to integrate work and leisure through a process of personal and communal improvement • Stress participation in community affairs and the rights of minorities	• Believe that economic growth and resource exploitation can continue indefinitely given (a) a suitable price structure (possibly involving taxes, fees, and so forth); (b) the legal right to a minimum level of environmental quality; and (c) compensation for those who experience adverse environmental or social consequences • Accept new project appraisal techniques and decision review arrangements to allow for wider discussion and a genuine search for consensus among affected parties • Support effective environmental management agencies at the national and local level	• Believe that humans can always find a way out of difficulties, either through politics, science or technology • Believe that scientific and technological expertise is essential on matters of economic growth and public health and safety • Accept growth as the legitimate goal of project appraisal and policy formulation • Are suspicious of attempts to widen participation in project appraisal and policy review • Believe that any impediments will inhibit ingenuity and all obstacles can be overcome given the resources (which arise from wealth)
• Recognise the intrinsic importance of nature to being fully human • Believe that ecological (and other natural) laws determine morality • Accept the right of endangered species of unique landscapes to remain unmolested			

Fig. 3.3   Ecocentrism and technocentrism (source: O'Riordan 1999).

the revised indicators were incorporated in the updated UK Strategy for Sustainable Development (DETR 1999b) and are discussed in detail below.

Separately, the European Commission has developed its own set of common indicators for use by local authorities across the European Union (Rydin 2000b). These European common indicators, shown in Fig. 3.4, are intended both to help local communities across Europe monitor their own progress towards sustainable local development and to facilitate comparison across municipalities within Europe. Rydin (2000b) commends the limited number of indicators chosen, but suggests that the indicators themselves are often both ambitious and ambiguous. This reflects her more general criticism that research interest in sustainability indicators, although extensive, has tended to focus more on definitional and technical issues and less on the process by which they affect policy decisions.

Within the United Kingdom, progress towards sustainable development is now to be measured by a broad set of about 150 indicators and particularly by a subset of 14 headline indicators, shown in Fig. 3.5. Since sustainable development has been officially aligned with improvements in the overall quality of life, these indicators demonstrate concern not only for environmental improvement, but also for economic growth and social advance. Indeed, a further headline indicator is intended to be developed that will measure how satisfied people are with their quality of life as a whole.

An obvious danger of specifying such individual headline indicators is that they encourage single-issue campaigns on particular aspects of sustainability that divert attention from the overall pattern of action on sustainable development. For as Levett (1998) points out, single indicators taken in isolation are open to ambiguity and misinterpretation: they achieve real meaning only in combination. Although the Government has rejected calls for an overall index of progress that would provide a quantitative combination of

Core indicators (compulsory)	1. Citizen satisfaction with the local community
	2. Local contribution to global climate change
	3. Local mobility and passenger transport
	4. Availability of local public green areas and local services
	5. Quality of local outdoor air
Additional indicators (voluntary)	6. Children's journeys to and from school
	7. Sustainable management of the local authority and local business
	8. Noise pollution
	9. Sustainable land use
	10. Products promoting sustainability

Fig. 3.4 First generation of European common indicators (source: Rydin 2000b).

Total output of the economy (GDP)
Investment in public, business and private assets
Proportion of people of working age who are at work
Qualifications at age 19
Expected years of healthy life
Homes judged unfit to live in
Level of crime
Emissions of greenhouse gases
Days when air pollution is moderate or high
Road traffic
Rivers of good or fair quality
Populations of wild birds
New homes on previously developed land
Waste arisings and management

Fig. 3.5   Headline indicators of sustainable development for the United Kingdom (source: DETR 1999b).

the 14 headline indicators, it recognises the importance of links between the various indicators (such as those concerned with transport, health and the environment) and intends to report on the implications of all headline indicators taken together (DETR 1999b).

As O'Riordan (1999) argues, while such indicators may provide a broad basis for assessing progress towards sustainable development, it remains unclear how they will influence strategic policy review. Unless indicators are more clearly justified in cost terms, it is hard to see how they will help resolve the inevitable trade-offs that will need to be made between them. For example, economic growth, as reflected in both total output of the economy and in investment in public, business and private needs, may well be faster, at least in the short term, if new development is concentrated on greenfield rather than brownfield land. Sustainability must involve some assessment of the price that society is prepared to pay (for example, in the costs of derelict land reclamation) to protect the environment in the long term, and of the extent to which that might reduce potential for economic growth in the short term. Thus, in policy and research terms, the relationship between individual indicators of sustainable development is as important as progress on any single indicator.

Nevertheless, by 'headlining' new homes on previously developed land as one of the most important environmental indicators, the Government created 'a new policy dynamic, in which debate about responses to household growth has been dominated and polarised by arguments about the appropriate brownfield percentage and wrangles over exactly what we mean by "brownfield"' (Levett 1998, p. 4). Taking a selection of some of the non-headline indicators identified by DETR (1999b) as shown in Fig. 3.6, it is apparent

Access to local green space
Community spirit
Energy efficiency of new domestic appliances
Energy use per household
Household waste and recycling
Household water use and peak demand
How children get to school
Noise levels
Quality of surroundings
Traffic congestion

Fig. 3.6 Some non-headline indicators of sustainable residential development (source: DETR 1999b).

that consideration of sustainable residential development ranges far wider than matters of mere location.

Of course, it may well be thought easier to measure the proportion of new homes built on previously developed land as an indicator of sustainable development than, for example, the extent of community spirit in a locality or the quality of its surroundings. However, as we subsequently discuss in Chapter 8, while land-use change statistics provide a valuable time series that enable aggregate changes between the most important urban and rural land uses to be tracked, it may be some years before national monitoring of available urban land supplies in England (which commenced with the National Land Use Database in 1998) is able to identify what proportion of vacant and derelict land is well located and capable of early housing development.

As this suggests, reliance on even these apparently simple indicators to measure progress towards sustainable development is likely to require a better-developed framework for collecting and analysing information than currently exists. In the institutional context of housing land release, this will become all the more essential if, as Chapter 4 explains, such decisions are to be made on a continuous basis within the new process approach of 'plan, monitor and manage' now envisaged in PPG 3 (DETR 2000a).

Far more elaborate systems may well be required to gather information on such matters as local community spirit or environmental quality. Indeed, critical information challenges are likely to face those seeking to develop indicators of sustainable development in relation to source (from whom is information collected?), refinement (on what basis it is to be aggregated?) and use (how is it to be interpreted and applied in setting policy?). Unless indicators of sustainable development are to remain merely aspirational, they thus need to be matched by an institutional commitment to create reliable and perhaps costly systems of information.

Yet, if full information were to be collected on all the various indicators included in Fig. 3.6, it would soon become apparent that no simple relationship exists between sustainability and location. New homes can be designed on many greenfield sites, for example, to provide quality surroundings with low noise and excellent access to local green space, to maximise energy efficiency while reducing household waste and to minimise traffic congestion while encouraging children to walk to school. Although such developments may fail the headline test of not being built on previously developed land, Fig. 3.6 suggests that it would be hard to label them as unsustainable simply on the basis of their location. Thus, while the language of sustainability can be used simply to resist pressures for housing development (Lambert & Boddy 1998), it can equally be employed to argue for the creation of sustainable residential communities on greenfield land.

It is thus essential not to allow one headline indicator of sustainability to dominate debate on new housing but instead to take a more measured overview of the factors that most encourage sustainable residential development, wherever it is located. To begin with, much could be done to promote sustainable development in the design and construction of individual new dwellings:

> Simply building a house with a southerly orientation to maximise solar gain, insulating walls, lofts, floors and water tanks to a high standard, and fitting efficient double-glazing and a condensing boiler can reduce energy demand by more than a third compared with a house built to current Building Regulations.
>
> (Burall 2001, p. 82)

Such improvements are significant since housing already accounts for around a third of climate change emissions in the UK which, according to Cambridge Econometrics (2001), is likely to rise by 14% by 2010 in contrast to emissions from electricity generation, which should fall by 23% and those from transport, which are estimated to rise by only 4%. To illustrate what energy-efficient housing can achieve, a super low-energy house, constructed in Oxford in 1995, produced only 10% of the carbon dioxide emissions of an ordinary house as well as reducing the owner's annual gas bill from the average £476 for its type to only £44 (Roaf & Rookwood 2000).

In this context, Bhatti (1996) argues that the main barriers to more efficient energy use in UK housing are not technological but political and institutional.

He suggests that politicians have placed too much reliance on market mechanisms and information campaigns to change prevalent attitudes and behaviour and not enough on direct and effective regulation. For example, although the Building Regulations were apparently tightened in 1990 to promote greater energy efficiency, builders were allowed to offset improvements in one area against another, so making it possible for the thermal efficiency of walls to be decreased if double glazing were introduced. Even though this loophole was closed in 1995, with overall energy ratings introduced for new dwellings, no attempt has been made to highlight, within final housing costs, the total sum of energy consumed in the production of the constituent building materials or to use such information to choose between different building types.

Bhatti (1996) further suggests that, since the amount of new housing built each year is remarkably small in comparison with the existing stock, improvements in the energy efficiency of the stock of existing dwellings are even more important to sustainability than the standards applied in construction of new dwellings. However, reduced expenditure on housing renewal and the switch towards discretionary home improvements grants since the Local Government and Housing Act 1989 have slowed progress towards greater energy efficiency in the existing stock. Moreover, the institutional structure of housing markets serves to deter the emergence of significant numbers of 'green housing consumers', as key actors who structure market behaviour such as mortgage lenders, estate agents and private landlords have little real commitment to energy saving (Bhatti 1996).

An example of recent energy-efficient housing at Greenwich Millennium Village is shown in Fig. 3.7. However, according to Barlow and Bhatti (1997), few speculative housebuilders see marketing advantages in developing energy-efficient homes, since they consider the payback time too long for their additional costs. This view is confirmed by the reaction of many in the industry to the more demanding environmental standards introduced in changes to the Part L of the Building Regulations in 2002, which are intended to reduce the average annual carbon dioxide emissions of a new house from 4.5 to 1.5 tonnes. As Smit (2002, p. 17) commented:

> Most of the housebuilding industry sees the requirements of Part L purely in terms of the £600 to £1,200 it will add to the cost of a house. Few are able to exploit insulation, or other advanced green technology such as photovoltaic panels or water-saving devices, as a marketing opportunity that could attract buyers.

Apart from improved energy efficiency, other important changes that could also be made to house designs to promote sustainable living include water

Fig. 3.7   Energy-efficient housing at Greenwich Millennium Village, London.

conservation features and measures to encourage household waste recycling
(EDAW 1997). In the latter context, Rydin (1992) suggests that recycling
would be encouraged by the provision of space for five separate waste con-
tainers, one each for compostables, metals, glass, paper and plastics. Moreover, the provision of bicycle storage accommodation as part of dwelling
design might encourage greater cycling, while the size and energy consumption of refrigerators could be reduced if ventilated larders were included in
new dwellings. According to the DETR (1999b), greater use of sustainable
materials and prefabrication in construction could also make an important
contribution to reducing the environmental impact of new dwellings.

These limited examples from what is an extensive debate about the design
and form of new housing warn us not to limit consideration of sustainability
issues in residential development simply to matters of location, still less to
those of land use. For as Roaf and Rockwood (2000, p. 182) point out in relation to building standards and design quality, 'the projected construction
of around four million new dwellings over the period 1996–2021 provides a
major opportunity for reducing housing's global warming and other environmental impacts over the next 20 years.' Unfortunately, this opportunity will
be lost if attention is wholly diverted from residential design and construction into residential location. However, with this warning in mind, it is now
time to consider whether, in locational terms, sustainable development is
best served by concentrated or dispersed urban forms.

Sustainable development and urban form: the case for and against the compact city

Urban containment not urban compaction has been the central feature of British planning policy, at least since 1947. Although urban containment has certainly reduced the outward spread of towns and cities on to agricultural and other open land, it has not previously been matched by effective measures to produce a compact urban form within towns and cities. Where suburban housing estates have been developed, for instance, densities have generally been much lower than a compact urban form would require. Since the late 1980s, substantial retail and leisure development too has taken place at the urban periphery, making it more difficult to sustain the vitality and viability of town and city centres.

In this section, we examine the case put forward by those who contend that sustainable development demands a reversal of these processes of urban dispersal and a replacement of the policy of mere urban containment by one of urban compaction. We contrast these views with those who doubt that compact urban forms are achievable in the modern age and believe that, in any event, urban compaction is not necessarily sustainable or desirable. The various arguments revolve around urban design and vitality, transport and energy use, and consumer and market preferences. At this stage, however, it should be noted that urban compaction does not necessarily involve brown-field instead of greenfield development. This is because compact urban forms could be produced either by the intensification of existing settlements (which would be likely to accelerate the rate of brownfield redevelopment) or by the development of new compact towns and cities at greenfield locations.

Policy-makers, however, are quick to link urban compaction directly to urban intensification and to deploy this alleged relationship as a powerful argument against greenfield land release. In this section, we shall therefore seek to demonstrate, in the context of the now accepted multidimensional view of sustainability expressed in the UK Government's current Strategy on Sustainable Development, that excessive reliance on brownfield land to meet housing requirements, while politically popular, could ultimately hinder rather than help the creation of sustainable urban communities.

Urban design and vitality

When in 1990, the Commission of the European Communities published its *Green Paper on the Urban Environment*, in which it championed the case for the compact city, an important stimulus was provided for subsequent debate on sustainable development and the urban form (see for example, Breheny 1992; Blowers 1993; Jenks *et al.* 1996; Hall, P. 1999; Rudlin & Falk 1999; Williams *et al.* 2000). In the Commission's eyes, the compact city meant a high-density mixed-use urban area that mirrored the traditional form and functions of many European cities. It argued that in the European experience such high-density living enhanced the quality of life since it helped produce urban vitality and vibrancy, while encouraging improved cultural facilities and social interaction. Moreover, it was suggested that the very concentration of people within the compact city would better support local services and businesses and thus sustain or renew local economies. Within such urban areas, public facilities and infrastructure could also be provided more efficiently (Williams 1999).

Similar themes are evident in the New Urbanist movement in the USA, which seeks to challenge urban sprawl by diverting growth into well-designed and tightly knit settlements that contain mixed land uses and housing types set within an interconnected street pattern, provide high-quality urban spaces that are universally accessible and physically defined, and aim to facilitate movement as much by foot or public transit as by car (Madanipour 1996; Eppli & Tu 2000; Carmona *et al.* 2002). As we later discuss in Chapter 7, the New Urbanist movement demonstrates how pressures to contain greenfield development, while dominant in their influence in the UK, are also evident within other countries elsewhere in the advanced world.

Whereas in much of Europe the challenge for policy-makers has been seen as one of maintaining traditional urban forms in the name of sustainability, UK debate has centred around how best to re-create denser forms of urban living that began to be abandoned after the First World War. Better urban design has been portrayed as an essential method by which the English could be persuaded to return to urban areas and experience again the benefits of cosmopolitan city life (Rudlin & Falk 1999; Urban Task Force 1999). Yet, much of the literature that calls for a sustainable urban renaissance based on higher-density and mixed-use development looks to continental Europe for its inspiration. The Urban Task Force, for example, speaks glowingly about the success of such continental cities as Amsterdam, Barcelona and Freiburg in pressing its case for denser urban living.

Others, however, criticise the European Commission notion of the compact city for its romantic basis in the architecture of Italian hill-towns that bears no relationship to the way most Europeans actually live (Breheny 1996). As Lock (1991, p. 337) argues: 'the Commission is blind to the merits of the suburbs, to their role as an integral part of the urban system, to the increased

importance of suburban centres as the focus of secondary and tertiary employment, particularly in the fast-growing service and high-technology sectors.' Some commentators are more contemptuous of what they see as the
promotion, within the concept of the compact city, of an imagined pavement
café view of urban life, centred around increased custom for antique shops,
bookshops, restaurants and art galleries (Troy 1996).

More practical concern has been expressed that if the compact city is to be
achieved only by increased intensification of existing urban areas, a poorer
rather than richer quality of urban life will result. This is because without
very careful design and planning, higher densities within cities could merely
aggravate urban congestion and pollution, while damaging the quality of
residential environments by encouraging noise and disturbance (especially
late at night) and reducing privacy. Certainly, if compaction policies cause
people to leave the city, they could not be termed sustainable (Williams *et
al.* 1996). As the Town and Country Planning Association (1997, p. 80) thus
claim 'There is a real danger that poorly conceived and implemented town
cramming policies will prove less sustainable, in every sense, than well-
conceived greenfield development.' Indeed, some critics of the compact city
warn against policies that could return urban areas to the congested squalor
of Victorian Britain or the horrors of high-rise tower blocks constructed from
the late 1950s to the early 1970s (Thomas & Cousins 1996).

The future of brownfield land, of which there is generally considered to be
much within existing British towns and cities, and of urban greenspace in
general, is crucial to this aspect of the compaction debate. To achieve urban
compaction within existing settlements, it will be necessary to accelerate
the reuse of brownfield land, especially for housing, and, where possible, to
replace existing low-density development with higher-density redevelopment. However, as Pratt and Larkham (1996) point out, residential intensification within cities is liable to generate local opposition where it is perceived
to impair residential amenities, encourage overlooking or produce increased
traffic. Certainly, neighbouring residents often resent the intensification of
low-density mature suburbia, especially where the replacement of single
houses by blocks of flats leads to a loss of trees and other vegetation.

More importantly, as far as urban sustainability is concerned, if compaction policies result in an overall diminution of urban greenspace, cities may
become less attractive and less healthy locations in which to live. Troy
(1996), for example, draws attention to the detrimental impact on health,
especially that of children, of excessive urban consolidation. He argues that
public and private garden space is important for health and recreation, both
for young and old. Trees, he points out, make an important contribution

to removing particulates and cleansing the urban environment of carbon dioxide.

Clearly, potential therefore exists for conflict between policies for 'greening the city' and those for urban compaction. This can be most acute where intensification within the city leads to a loss of playing fields or other open space, whether formally designated as such or not. Moreover, while policy-makers may regard brownfield sites as a potential supply of future housing land, there is evidence to suggest that even supposedly derelict sites can be rich in flora and fauna (Woodward 1998; Box & Shirley 1999). Once local residents have become accustomed to the informal use of such land as open space, it is hardly surprising if they resent its subsequent loss for development. As leisure time increases, there is certainly an argument, on sustainability grounds, for retaining open land within cities to meet increased demands for recreation, rather than compacting the city to such an extent that people have to travel further and further for leisure purposes.

According to Rudlin and Falk (1999), such arguments can be resolved only if a clear distinction is made between overcrowding (the number of persons per room) and density (the number of dwellings or people per hectare). The challenge, they argue, is to increase urban densities without making urban areas overcrowded. This calls for a wholesale shift in urban design in which emphasis is placed on the promotion of a rich variety of uses within integrated street patterns that create sociability, community and natural surveillance and which are well linked to surrounding areas.

The main target for elimination in this design-led approach to urban compaction is not urban open space but rather the extensive provision normally made for car parking and car use within towns and cities. Thus Llewelyn-Davies (1994) showed through case studies that if standards of car parking were less demanding, urban housing densities could be increased by up to 25% without significant changes to urban form. Subsequently, urban capacity studies have been increasingly used to determine exactly how much additional development particular urban areas could take, if existing planning policies and residential standards within cities were relaxed. However, as Counsell (1999) points out in the case of West Sussex, such studies can lead to the conclusion that the extent of potential urban intensification assumed at national level cannot be delivered locally without damaging the urban environment and quality of life.

Williams *et al.* (1996, p. 84) therefore suggest that: 'In a number of crucial areas of urban life, achieving the balance between "town cramming" and vibrancy and sustainability will be the key to successful urban development in the future.' In principle, compact cities have clear merits in both reducing the land take of urban development and in creating more interesting and vibrant urban forms but, in practice, intensification is unlikely to work without skilled design and careful management. As far as residential development is concerned, this raises the important institutional issue of whether current planning and development practice is capable of delivering and managing compact urban forms. This is an issue to which we return in more detail in Chapters 4 and 5.

Transport and energy use

The second powerful line of argument deployed in favour of compact cities is that they reduce energy use in general and the need to travel in particular. There is certainly formidable evidence to suggest a strong inverse relationship between urban density and private transport energy use per person (Newman & Kenworthy 1989a, b, 1999). As Fig. 3.8 shows, such energy use is lowest for high-density cities in Asia and highest for low-density cities in North America, with medium-density European cities lying in between. Newman and Kenworthy (2000, p. 113) thus argue that: 'achieving a more sustainable urban form inevitably involves the development of densities that can enable public transport, walking and cycling to be viable options.' In

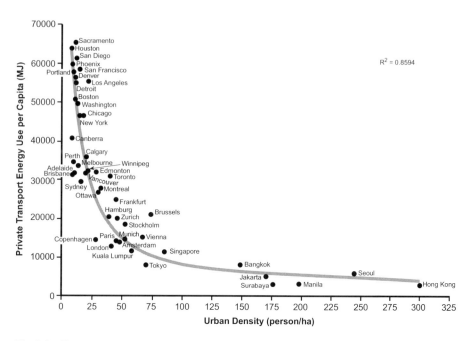

Fig. 3.8   Energy use per capita in private passenger travel versus urban density in global cities, 1990 (source: Newman & Kenworthy 1999).

a British context, research by ECOTEC (1993) has also suggested that higher residential densities are likely to be associated both with reduced travel demand and a shift to more environmentally friendly forms of transport. In particular, it suggested that once density falls below 15 persons per hectare, travel demand rises sharply, but in contrast, falls sharply as densities exceed 50 persons per hectare.

Unfortunately, urban development across many European countries over the past 50 years has made people ever more dependent on the private car. For example, during the 1980s, car ownership in the UK increased by 37% but car use by 52%. By 1995, transport consumed over a third of all energy consumed by final users, itself an increase of a third within a decade (Banister 1997). Since the scale of petrol price increases required to deter car use is likely to be politically unacceptable, Banister argues that it is necessary to promote development patterns and densities that reduce rather than increase car dependence. This was the aim of the revised *Planning Policy Guidance Note 13: Transport* issued by the DOE in 1994, alongside a companion *PPG 13: A Guide to Better Practice: Reducing the Need to Travel through Land Use and Transport Planning* (DOE/DOT 1994a, b). This policy shift was confirmed in a later revision of PPG 13 (DETR 2001) that reinforced the objectives of promoting more sustainable transport choices, including better accessibility by public transport, walking and cycling, while reducing the need to travel, especially by car.

To encourage and enable people to travel less, especially by car, PPG 13 from 1994 onwards urged local authorities to adopt policies that would:

- Locate new development and major generators of traffic where they could be accessed by means other than the private car.

- Restrict parking provision.

- Protect and strengthen existing local centres.

- Maintain and improve choice for people to walk, cycle or catch public transport.

At a strategic level, authorities were urged to concentrate new housing development within existing larger urban areas (giving particular priority to the reuse or conversion of previously used sites and premises) and in locations already or likely to be well served by public transport. Developments to be avoided included significant incremental expansion of villages and small towns that would be dependent on commuting to urban centres, and small new settlements that were unlikely to be self-contained or to reach

10 000 dwellings within 20 years[1]. Additionally, in local plans, authorities were encouraged to place high-density development near public transport or along existing or potential public transport corridors, to maintain, and where appropriate, increase urban densities and seek to juxtapose employment and residential uses within mixed-use developments.

Such policy guidance reflects the collective wisdom that:

> Concentration and diversity of activities result in less travel, less reliance on the car and greater use of 'green' modes. It also maintains the vitality and environmental quality in towns and cities … As the density of development increases, the average trip length, the use of car, and the distance travelled all reduce.
>
> (Banister 1997, pp. 442–3)

Nevertheless, while politically popular, the message that urban densities must be increased to help reduce climate change emissions, remains controversial in the academic world (Breheny 1996).

In the first place, as Breheny (1996) explains, the link between urban densities and private transport energy may not be as simple as Newman and Kenworthy (1989a, b) and others claim, particularly if other factors such as income levels and urban structures are introduced into the analysis to explain differences between cities. Barrett (1996) acknowledges that low-income households with low car ownership typically occupy the highest-density areas but maintains that research controlling for such influences still indicates that density has a significant impact on travel behaviour. However, Gordon and Richardson (1989) argue that polycentric cities with relatively low energy consumption and congestion would probably be created in the advanced world if market mechanisms were allowed to operate.

Stretton (1996) suggests that greater environmental gains could be best obtained by limiting the size and power of vehicles in order to improve fuel efficiency, than by increasing urban densities. Thomas and Cousins (1996) point out that large centralised cities are likely to produce greater traffic congestion, increased travel times, slower traffic speeds and lower fuel efficiency. Conversely, they suggest that Milton Keynes may well be sustainable, despite its extensive reliance on the private car, precisely because its dispersed urban form and limited congestion produce high fuel efficiency and low vehicle emissions. In this respect, as Barrett (1996) recognises, compacting the city may simply produce more congestion and vehicle emissions at precisely the location where they cause most damage and affect most people.

Urban compaction by itself may thus produce harmful environmental side effects, unless matched by significant investment in public transport. As Newman and Kenworthy (1996, p. 22) stress: 'Sustainable and civilised cities are achievable with low automobile dependence but are unlikely to occur without a significant commitment to reconnecting their cities through transit and transit-based planning.' This aspect of the urban compaction debate, widely supported as it is in the literature, is one that politicians least like to hear as it makes substantial demands on public investment, at least in the short to medium term. Yet, since urban decentralisation over past decades has created forms that are no longer centrally based, public transport becomes far more difficult to provide than if organised merely along radial routes into the city centres.

Moreover, even if urban compaction supported by new public transport systems could deliver reduced climate change emissions from vehicles, there are those who suggest that very high densities may be energy-intensive in their construction, while reducing the design potential for solar heating (Goodchild 1994). Although combined heat and power (CHP) systems are most likely to be viable in densely packed urban areas with mixed uses, Owens (1992) confirms that solar heating can be problematic on small urban infill sites and suggests that, in urban areas where land is at a premium, advantage cannot always be taken of microclimatic conditions to reduce energy loss in new developments.

Overall, urban compaction may have potential to deliver energy savings even if, as Breheny (1996) maintains, they would be as low as 2.5% of national energy consumption. According to Breheny, it is questionable whether this is a price worth paying in terms of unpopular restrictions on personal mobility. More significantly, however, taking a holistic view of sustainable development rather than looking at environmental protection alone, it remains unclear how urban compaction intended primarily to reduce energy consumption would help deliver economic growth or social justice, especially if it were not to be matched by large-scale investment in public transport. It is therefore time to consider the case for and against compact cities in relation to consumer and market preferences.

Consumer and market preferences

Breheny and Rockwood (1993) point out that urban compaction will succeed only if it is able to reverse the persistent trend of decentralisation evident over the previous 50 years. Moreover, decentralisation is not merely a feature of housing market but of labour markets as well, as a result of urban–rural shifts in employment. It is likely that this trend will be further encouraged by more leisure time, greater personal control over lifestyle and rejection of work as 'identity' (Thomas & Cousins 1996). As one noted advocate of increased urban densities acknowledges: 'People want to live in low-density urban areas, so increasing density may reduce the attractiveness of towns and cause out-migration' (Banister 1997, p. 443). From an Australian perspective, Stretton (1996) argues that most people prefer public and private open space to dense urbanity while Barrett (1996) suggests that it may be hard to persuade today's population of the benefits of traditional urban lifestyles.

Even studies that emphasise the critical importance of better urban design and management in making cities more attractive places to live recognise that people's needs are many-faceted and that physical improvement alone will not reverse urban decentralisation. As the Urban Task Force acknowledges (1999, pp. 35–6): 'This means looking beyond the design, planning and building of the urban environment at the role played by health, education, security and social services, amongst others.' More pointedly, Rudlin and Falk (1999, p. 145), again strong advocates of the role of better urban design in creating sustainable urban neighbourhoods, comment that 'Children in inner city schools are less likely to succeed and parents cannot be expected to sacrifice their children's education for an ideal of urban living.' This well illustrates why sustainable development has to be taken as a rounded concept and why sustainable compact cities are unlikely to be achieved merely by redeveloping as much brownfield land as possible.

The Urban White Paper (DETR 2000b), which seeks to promote a holistic approach to urban renaissance, thus draws together the Government's proposals to deliver quality urban services in education, health, housing, crime, culture, leisure, sport and community legal services alongside the expected plans for urban environmental, transport and physical improvements. However, even if urban decentralisation can eventually be reversed, it will not happen overnight. Urban renaissance and the compaction of existing cities will inevitably be gradual processes that will need to be actively promoted and carefully nurtured over many years.

It therefore does not follow that urban compaction must involve immediate building on every last urban brownfield site or that it can succeed only through the imposition of very tight controls on greenfield development to deter decentralisation. Moreover, the compaction of existing urban areas must not be allowed to deflect attention from the importance of applying sustainability principles to greenfield developments, whenever they are permitted. It is therefore appropriate to move on from a discussion of urban compaction in principle to an evaluation of alternative patterns of development, wherever located.

Alternative development patterns

If all new housing proposals were to be rigorously evaluated for their contribution to sustainable development, a multidimensional form of analysis would be required in which matters of residential location would be considered not in isolation but in relation to design potential, travel patterns, energy use, consumer preferences and numerous other aspects of social and economic life. Since there is room for considerable debate on how sustainability principles are best applied to the development of new housing, it is important that those who argue for such development to be concentrated at particular locations or on particular types of land should be required to justify their contention by reference to broad economic, social and environmental criteria.

One indicative attempt to evaluate alternative development patterns, undertaken by Breheny *et al.* (1993), provides a helpful illustration of how explicit definition of assessment criteria is essential to any judgement about sustainable residential locations. The research sought to compare and evaluate five different forms of urban growth (namely, urban infill, urban extensions, key village extensions, multiple village extensions and new settlements) against a range of economic, social and environmental criteria shown in Fig. 3.9. Obviously, different weights could be put on these various criteria from different perspectives and indeed other researchers might well wish

Economic criteria	Cost of the end product
	Economy in the provision and use of infrastructure
	Maintenance costs
	Access to employment
Social criteria	Access to social facilities
	Potential sense of community
	Breadth of social mix
	Potential affordable housing contribution
	Local acceptability
Environmental criteria	Loss of land
	Loss of natural habitats
	Energy consumption: transport
	Energy consumption: space heating
	Pollution levels
	Contribution to 'greening' the urban environment
	Town cramming effect

Fig. 3.9 Summary of assessment criteria for evaluation of alternative development patterns (source: Breheny *et al.* 1993).

to add to or subtract from the list in order to reflect the multidimensional nature of sustainability more fully. However, as a starting point for discussion of alternative development patterns, the work of Breheny *et al.* (1993) provides a valuable analytical framework that cautions against any attempt to reduce analysis on the sustainability of new housing development merely to whether it is located on brownfield or greenfield land.

The main conclusions of Breheny *et al.* (1993) are summarised in Fig. 3.10. Here, it is apparent that two forms of development, which have been widely practised in the past, emerged from the analysis with the least favourable performance. Of these, key village extensions, which have been a notable feature of rural settlement planning in many parts of the country, achieved only a modest performance on virtually all the selected criteria. Moreover, multiple village extensions, which almost by default have become a favoured approach to dilute the impact of housing growth in many areas, were considered to deliver the weakest performance of all. It is not intended to discuss either of these in more detail in this chapter since interested readers can turn directly to the original study of Breheny *et al.* (1993).

All the three remaining development alternatives were considered to have the potential to perform well, although in the cases of urban infill and new settlements, Breheny *et al.* (1993) acknowledged that their own conclusions were susceptible to changes in particular weightings since both these options tended to attract extreme judgements on certain criteria. As we indicated in the previous section, brownfield residential development on urban infill sites can certainly make a valuable contribution towards creating sustainable compact cites, provided such developments are well designed, well managed and implemented as part of a co-ordinated urban strategy that seeks to improve the quality of urban life as a whole. In the next section, by concentrating on urban extensions and new settlements, we ask similar questions of greenfield development. In short, in what circumstances could residential development on greenfield land be properly described as sustainable?

Major urban extensions

Over many centuries, existing settlements have gradually spread outwards through expansion onto surrounding agricultural land. Despite the intended policy of urban containment, most new housing still took this form even after the introduction of a comprehensive town and country planning system in 1947. Moreover, apart from two notable exceptions, outward residential expansion has continued to be managed and delivered primarily by the private sector. These exceptions were the construction of major public

Development Type	Good performance	Poor performance	Overall Assessment
Urban infill	On most social criteria; on prevention of loss of land and habitats, on energy conservation; on access to employment and on making use of existing infrastructure	On development costs, public maintenance and potential for planning gain; on 'greening' issues and 'town cramming'	Good overall performance, but susceptible to changes in weighting because of extreme judgements on certain criteria
Peripheral urban extensions	Especially on economic criteria because of low average costs and good potential for planning gain; on most social and environmental criteria as well	On loss of land and possibly on energy consumption from travel	Good performance on virtually all criteria, although important to remember that towns and cities cannot extend indefinitely without social and environmental stress
Key villages	On maintenance costs and social provision	On planning gain and affordable housing prospects; on loss of land and habitats and on energy consumption from travel	Modest performance on virtually all criteria
Multiple village extensions	On existing community base and on limiting loss of habitats	On almost all other economic, social and environmental criteria	Weakest performance of all: extensions to many villages unlikely to be a social success
New settlements	On low development costs, apart from infrastructure, and on potential for planning gain that limits public sector contributions. Social merits modest but can perform well if properly planned. Potential also to create good residential environment	On infrastructure costs; on loss of land and habitats and on energy consumption from travel in smaller settlements	Good performance, but susceptible to changes in weighting because of extreme judgements on certain criteria

Fig. 3.10 Assessment of alternative development patterns (adapted from Breheny *et al.* 1993).

housing estates (such as Kirkby in Merseyside) on the fringes of large cities and the promotion of town extensions under the Town Development Act of 1952, to which we shall return below.

As the main promoters of outward residential expansion, speculative house-builders have been responsible for both the construction of individual housing estates and the development of those major residential areas that, because of their size, have needed to be subdivided between several housebuilders working in a development consortium. As we show in Chapter 5, the main concern of speculative housebuilders is with individual house sales rather than with the creation of sustainable residential communities. While local planning authorities might have been expected to reflect this wider perspective, in practice they have been encouraged to concentrate their attention on the allocation of sufficient land to meet housing requirements rather than on the quality of the residential environment once development had been agreed in principle. An institutional deficit has thus been created by the historic impotence of the planning system to tackle the traditional disinterest of speculative housebuilders in matters other than immediate house sales. This has contributed significantly to the unsustainable nature of much past housing development.

Indeed, the combined result of the speculative residential development process and a planning system that has focused on housing allocations rather than housing quality has too often served to produce monotonous peripheral housing estates built at suburban densities, that are excessively dependent on the private car, provide only limited community facilities and remain deficient in social networks. No wonder then that greenfield land release generates such heated controversy when many of its past products provide ample evidence of unsustainable forms of development. But need this be so?

According to the Prince's Foundation and English Partnerships (2000), sustainable greenfield development is possible if properly planned and developed as a substantial urban extension rather than as a series of separate add-on housing estates. At this scale, greenfield housing development would be designed alongside shopping, employment and other uses in an area large enough to function as a new urban neighbourhood in its own right rather than merely as an outer dormitory suburb of an existing settlement. Indeed, a substantial urban extension, if well located and designed, has the potential to offer a high-quality residential environment in a compact urban form that is both well connected into the public transport system and able to meet a variety of housing needs.

Breheny *et al.* (1993) contend that urban extensions rank alongside urban infill as offering the best access to employment of the five different types of development they investigated, while providing opportunities for 'greening' elsewhere in the city by absorbing substantial development pressure. Moreover, taking a holistic social, economic and environmental view of sustainability, it is arguable that sustainable residential development can be just as easily created from scratch in greenfield locations as pieced together in brownfield locations. To achieve this, however, requires fundamental changes both in the speculative residential development process and in the institutional capacity of the planning system to manage the delivery of major urban extensions.

In this context, although there is now growing recognition that major urban extensions have the potential to deliver sustainable forms of development, this is unlikely to be realised without significant realignment of state–market relations in speculative housebuilding. Specifically, two significant changes will be essential to overcome the institutional deficit that previously allowed extensive housing production to take place in unsustainable ways. First, as is beginning to happen, the quality of new development must become as important to the planning system as the overall quantity of land allocated for the purposes of that development. Secondly, if this is to be fully achieved, it may sometimes be necessary for community interests to be brought to bear throughout the development process and not simply at the point of planning permission.

Unfortunately, the retreat of local planning authorities from participation in the financial and land ownership aspects of major development since the late 1970s has created widespread apprehension that they may lack the institutional commitment and experience necessary to turn what would otherwise be sprawling private housing estates into sustainable urban extensions through concerted intervention in the development process. Yet, as Bell (1998) points out, the Town Development Act of 1952 provides an excellent model of what can be achieved if a supportive institutional framework for major urban expansion is set in place.

The Town Development Act encouraged significant expansion of existing settlements, at a lower cost than building completely new ones, through formal overspill arrangements with London local authorities (Lambert & Boddy 1998). Although many of the towns selected, such as Andover, Basingstoke, Swindon and Wellingborough, were already substantial settlements in their own right, they doubled and, in some cases, tripled in population over a period of 20–30 years. The process was managed not by a specialist development corporation but by the local authority supported by the professional design skills of the London County Council (Bell 1998).

According to Lambert and Boddy (1998), the success of the Town Development Act was primarily attributable to the deployment of additional powers and resources that enabled the local community rather than the private sector to direct the form of new development. Specifically, finance available for land acquisition was accompanied by ministerial support for compulsory purchase. Subsidies were provided for council housebuilding, while per capita grants were offered for social and community facilities. In their case study of Swindon, Lambert and Boddy (1998) argue that since the Town Development Act equipped the local authority with the means of implementation, a clear vision could be articulated for the future of the town. Although responsible for the delivery of particular projects, the private sector operated within a development framework determined by the public sector.

As a result, in Swindon:

> There was strong local support for expansion and the borough council as the major landowner had been able to exert considerable control over the overall development process, ensuring a balance between population and employment, high standards of development, and high-quality, publicly-provided community facilities. It could plough back financial returns from development to finance the ongoing programme of expansion, keeping local taxes down. New housing, new jobs and community facilities benefited the town and its residents.
>
> (Lambert & Boddy 1998, pp. 378–9)

In his detailed history of Swindon's expansion under the Town Development Act, Harloe (1975) highlights the importance of visionary leadership by local politicians and administrators in driving Swindon's development forward and successfully communicating the benefits of planned expansion to the public at large. He argues that although Swindon changed forever as a result of major development, clear benefits resulted in the creation of a wider range of jobs, housing and civic amenities. As well as the rapid growth of owner-occupation and an improved supply of public housing, Swindon witnessed investment in a new town centre, a new road system, new schools, a new college of education and a new hospital. The town also benefited from a significantly increased rateable base that allowed the local authority considerably to improve its services without an unacceptably high rate burden.

Harloe (1975) concludes that such major urban expansion offers two particular advantages over the development of entire new towns. First, since existing settlements are likely to be well connected to existing communication networks and already endowed with some social and recreational facilities, they can provide an immediate and welcome base for new residents from the moment they arrive. Secondly, by placing existing local authorities rather than an imposed development corporation at the centre of political decision-making, town expansion schemes offer a more democratic and satisfactory way to achieve growth, with the likelihood that existing residents will feel some sense of involvement in, and commitment to, the process of major development.

Swindon's experience of major urban expansion demonstrates that the key to making development sustainable is not simply where it is located but how it is managed. Rather than place excessive reliance on the statutory planning system alone for the delivery of sustainable compact cities, the experience of the Town Development Act suggests that the institutional capacity of the state to manage major urban development through active intervention in the development process may need to be restored through emphasis on a broader set of land policies, to which the statutory planning system might well make a significant contribution.

As Harloe and Boddy (1987) show in their analysis of subsequent plans to expand Swindon in the mid-1980s, unless the public sector commands the necessary powers and resources to acquire land for major urban extensions and co-ordinate the activities of various private sector developers, there is a significant danger that strategic planning of such major extensions will be driven primarily by the capacity of individual housebuilders to purchase options on various parcels of land from their original owners. Such reliance on the market alone to bring forward areas for major urban extensions risks the creation of badly designed and poorly co-ordinated urban extensions that are far from sustainable and that, in the end, consume considerably more resources from the public sector over time in order to alleviate inadequate infrastructure provision and other development deficiencies. Of course, the public sector may not always need to control the supply of land to ensure sustainable urban extensions, but its ability and willingness to intervene, if necessary, is likely to ensure a smoother and more effective process of development that is consistent with strategic and detailed planning requirements, even if it is wholly led by the private sector.

In many parts of the country, however, settlement expansion from the mid-1980s has increasingly been driven by private sector priorities alone, as a result of financial cutbacks in the public sector. In Swindon's case, these impaired the local authority's ability to control the supply of land, provide infrastructure and ensure that new development was accompanied by the necessary services and facilities. Moreover, once the benefits of growth, employment and prosperity appeared to pass certain groups by, local opposition to further expansion hardened.

Even though the institutional framework for major residential expansion has changed markedly since the Town Development Act of 1952, it would still be possible to manage the development process as a partnership between the local authority, private sector and existing residents in such a way that it delivers sustainable forms of development rather than a mere proliferation of peripheral housing estates. As 'Planning for Real' exercises have demonstrated (Hall, D. 1999), there can be real value from involving a wide range of stakeholders, including local residents and community groups, in the design and masterplanning of substantial residential extensions. On this principle, the Prince's Foundation and English Partnerships (2000) have promoted the concept of 'Enquiry by Design' in which all relevant stakeholders are encouraged to create masterplans for major greenfield sites through an intensive process of discussion, site visits and design workshops.

To test this, two 'Enquiry by Design' workshops were organised by the Prince's Foundation and English Partnerships in the summer of 1999, for major greenfield extensions to Basildon and Northampton. By bringing together landowners, local authorities, community representatives and local people, it proved possible for conflicts of interest to be addressed and co-operative solutions to emerge with the assistance of an international team of planners, highway engineers, architects and surveyors led by independent designers/facilitators. According to participants, the process proved simultaneous and interactive in contrast to the normally sequential and reactive nature of the statutory planning system. Of course, it would require considerable time and resources to make such an approach common in the design and planning of major new development, but the experience from Basildon and Northampton certainly suggests that it had the potential to improve upon the environmental, economic and social performance of the type of greenfield development produced by more traditional institutional arrangements.

New settlements

According to Breheny *et al.* (1993, p. 9) a new settlement can be defined as 'A free-standing settlement promoted by private or public sector interests, where the completed new development – of whatever size – constitutes 50% or more of the total size of the settlement, measured in terms of population or dwellings.' On this basis, they recorded 184 new settlement schemes proposed in England between 1980 and 1992, of which almost a third were in the South East. Quite separately, Hood (1995) found that a further 65 proposals had been made for new settlements in Scotland since 1980. Most of the schemes identified by Breheny *et al.* (1993) were for less than 1500 dwellings and all were privately sponsored, despite the retention of new town legislation on the statute book. While their designs generally left much to be desired, very few were likely to be built owing to planning restraints and local opposition.

The arguments for and against new settlements are well set out by Stockdale and Lloyd (1998) and their analysis is shown in Fig. 3.11. From this, it is apparent that the principles of sustainable development can be mustered either in support of, or in opposition to, new settlements. This has certainly been the case both at public inquiries and in the academic literature. Goodchild (1997), for example, is particularly scornful of the loss of greenfield land implied even by a relatively modest new settlement, which he estimates will consume 200 to 250 hectares. On the other hand, Breheny *et al.* (1993) argue that new settlements have the potential to incorporate environmentally sustainable features, balance compactness with greenness, include CHP schemes and give priority to non-car forms of transport. However, Rudlin and Falk (1999) comment that even the largest of the private sector new settlements studied by Breheny *et al.* (1993) came nowhere near the threshold for sustainability.

The size of any new settlement is thus crucial to whether it can be considered sustainable, since the larger the settlement, the more self-contained it is likely to be. Stockdale and Lloyd (1998), for example, from their study of two new settlements in the Aberdeen area, each of about 500 houses,

---

Arguments for:
- Deals with pressures from continued decentralisation and counter-urbanisation
- Meets an identified shortfall in housing land and residential dwellings
- Reduces pressure for piecemeal development of existing settlements
- Provides cost-effective investment in infrastructure and other facilities
- Provides a more economic use of land and resources
- Minimum environment impact
- Provides opportunities for balance housing and employment growth
- Competitive house prices
- Channels decentralising populations into planned locations
- Opportunities for new patterns of social mix, by mixing house type, tenure and price

Arguments against:
- Impact on countryside and green belt
- Become commuter settlements lacking employment and social and economic balance
- Some infrastructure and service costs will need to be met by the local authority
- Land unlikely to be sold at less than market values
- Lacking a regional planning context
- Will not reduce pressure for release of additional housing land
- Will attract young and prosperous
- Planned for private profit and unlikely to be best located to meet wider needs

Fig. 3.11   Arguments for and against new settlements (source: Stockdale & Lloyd 1998).

conclude that small free-standing new settlements run the risk of becoming elitist satellite communities that are both dependent on commuting and disadvantaged in service provision. According to Breheny *et al.* (1993), the smallest viable new settlement would need to be between 750 and 1000 houses in order to support a primary school. This would rise to between 3000 and 5000 houses to support a secondary school and a range of other services and facilities.

If, however, sustainability considerations were paramount, then new settlements would need to be of the order of 10 000 dwellings or more (or 25 000 to 30 000 population) to minimise travel to work by car, maximise the viability of public transport and attract a wide range of employment opportunities. Once they reach this size, Breheny *et al.* (1993) argue that new settlements could be the most sustainable form of development after urban infill. To achieve this, they would need to be located either close to existing urban areas so as to reduce commuting and other travel into town, or in relatively remote locations where distance from other major centres would require significant self-containment. Certainly, intermediate locations that necessitate lengthy journeys to existing facilities but that are not large enough to induce self-containment, are best avoided.

Although the DOE/DOT (1994b) subsequently warned against the development of new settlements that were unlikely to reach 10 000 dwellings within 20 years, especially where they would not be self-contained or well-served by public transport, it may be optimistic to expect the private sector to assume the entire development risk of such large projects, even if that risk is shared between several developers and investors within a consortium. Indeed, of the main proposals put forward by Consortium Developments, the company specifically formed by a partnership of volume housebuilders to promote new settlements in the 1980s, Tillingham Hall in Essex was intended to be 5100 dwellings, Foxley Wood in Hampshire 4000, Westmere in Cambridgeshire 1500, and Stone Bassett in Oxfordshire only 1216. This would indicate that, even in buoyant locations, there might well be marketing difficulties in trying to concentrate too much private housing development in a single location unless a lengthy development period is allowed for the local housing market to absorb such a huge increase in local supply. As Great Notley Garden Village in Essex demonstrates (shown in Fig. 3.12), small-scale new settlements are much easier for the industry to market.

This suggests that the potential sustainability benefits of new settlements can be reaped only if there is strong public sector commitment to their development. Indeed, Breheny *et al.* (1993), pointing to historical experience, contend that the development of larger new settlements (from around 8000

Fig. 3.12   Great Notley Garden Village, Essex.

to 10 000 dwellings, or of 20 000 to 25 000 population) should be championed by the public sector, using either new towns legislation or the compulsory purchase powers available under town and country planning legislation. Of course, it is not necessarily easy for even the public sector to find suitably large sites in areas of development pressure that can be justified in sustainability terms. Past controversies would also suggest that substantial local opposition must still be expected to any such proposal.

In Hampshire, for example, the private sector unusually came forward with proposals to develop a new major town of 9000 homes and 12 000 jobs to support an eventual population of 23 000 to 25 000 at Micheldever Station on the main London to Southampton railway line. It was intended that social housing would account for about 20% of the new dwellings, and that land within the new town would be provided for business and industry, shops, schools, health centres and recreation. Despite the site having no particular landscape designation, the proposals generated a wave of protests from conservationists and councillors across Hampshire who argued that its development would undermine a key rural buffer between the north and south of the county (Dewar 1998).

Even though the development was supported in principle by the independent panel report into the Hampshire Structure Plan since it met the sustainability criteria set out in PPG 13, the County Council ignored this recommendation. As we shall discover in subsequent chapters, the case illustrates how, even if professional discourse revolves around the merits or otherwise of development proposals in sustainability terms, political power may well override such conceptual niceties.

In contrast, most of the 16 people sitting on the randomly selected 'Citizen's Jury', established to advise Horsham District Council in West Sussex on how best to accommodate housing growth, voted in favour of a new settlement if the district were to be required to take an additional 5000 new dwellings, and overwhelmingly so if the figure rose to 7000 new dwellings (*Planning* 1998a). Moreover, in East Anglia, the independent panel reporting into the Public Examination of the draft Regional Planning Guidance concluded a new town north of Cambridge with good public transport links into the city, would ensure a more economic provision of infrastructure than could be achieved by scattering the development over a wide area. At 10 000 to 20 000 dwellings, the new town would, it was felt, be likely to justify investment in high-quality, high-volume public transport and so enhance sustainability (Fyson 1999).

Although new settlements remain controversial, especially because they consume significant greenfield land, it should not therefore be presumed that they are unsustainable. Indeed, once of sufficient size to be self-contained and to support good public transport, new settlements offer the opportunity to provide high-quality residential development in a manner that enhances the quality of life to a far greater extent than most peripheral housing estates. However, to achieve sustainable new settlements of this size is likely to require at least tacit approval from the planning system, if not actual promotion and participation.

Alternative development patterns: concluding comments

As Jenks *et al.* (1996) advocate, it may be more constructive to identify a number of sustainable urban forms rather than search for the ultimate sustainable urban form. In this context, it is quite apparent that the sustainability of new housing development is dependent on many other factors as well as location and that, in particular circumstances, alternative patterns of development may each have their own contribution to make to sustainable development.

Although some believe 'that the success, desirability and achievability of the compact city are equivocal' (Thomas & Cousins 1996, p. 61), few would doubt the sustainability of brownfield housing infill, provided it does not produce undue town cramming. However, greenfield development, if well planned and managed, may be equally capable of delivering sustainable urban forms, especially if brownfield sites are incapable of meeting all housing requirements. Since urban compaction needs to be sensitive ecologically, economically and socially (Jenks *et al.* 1996), merit exists in promoting a variety of development patterns on both brownfield and greenfield land.

In this context, the Town and Country Planning Association (1997) has advocated a portfolio approach to new housing development, in which urban infilling, peripheral extensions and selected new settlements can be combined and adapted to suit local circumstances across what is described as the whole of the *social city region*. This flexible approach would enable a range of different solutions to be sought for different circumstances while ensuring that policies were complementary and sustainable across the city region as a whole. The Association has suggested nine practical guidelines for this approach:

- Urban compaction or intensification is desirable to a degree since it may induce less use of the car and protect the open countryside.

- Urban regeneration is essential since the vitality of cities must be restored through investment, design and promotion.

- Opportunities exist for refitting urban areas, and in particular suburban locations.

- Larger cities can be redesigned around new or enhanced suburban centres which would create strong employment and service centres around public transport nodes.

- It is certain that urban decentralisation will continue, driven largely by the geography of jobs.

- Strategic solutions are required to this decentralisation, for example, in channelling growth into transport corridors in fast-growing non-metropolitan areas. This might enable medium-sized and smaller towns along such corridors to be expanded around good-quality public transport nodes typically providing interchanges between longer distance rail and light rail systems and local distributor systems.

- In such zones of pressure, new towns may be an acceptable solution. They are likely to consist of semi-self-contained physically separate towns of

20 000–30 000 people clustered along transport corridors into larger cities of 200 000–250 000 people.

- In more rural areas where decentralisation of jobs and people continues to impose pressures on the local housing market, it may be appropriate to focus growth into key villages.

- In remoter rural areas which are outside the zones of outward pressure from the cities and conurbations, decentralisation should be encouraged (Town and Country Planning Association 1997).

This blending or portfolio approach reflects what Breheny (1996) calls a compromise position between urban centrists and decentrists, which takes account of market forces but is not subservient to them. On the one hand, it involves continued and indeed tougher containment and regeneration strategies, while on the other, it seeks to control the direction of inevitable decentralisation to suburbs and towns with the full range of facilities and public transport and to sites that are likely to cause least environmental damage. Decentralised concentrations of high-density mixed-used development might thus be promoted along fast public transport corridors.

Although the Government has taken up the concept of concentrating large housing development around major nodes along quality public transport corridors (DETR 2000a) there are those who fear that such corridors may result in a twenty-first century equivalent of ribbon development that would damage the landscape and biodiversity or undermine the function of green belts (CPRE/Friends of the Earth 2000). In the end, then, despite the wide-ranging discourse of sustainable development, much of the criticism of the more flexible portfolio approach to accommodating housing growth advocated by the Town and Country Planning Association (1997) comes down to its likely detrimental impact on greenfield land.

In this context, the Town and Country Planning Association (1997, p. 80) contends that

land *per se* has *no privileged place*: it is merely one element in the total ecosystem. It is true that rural land, once urbanised, is unlikely to return to rural uses; but this is not necessarily a key consideration, so long as the remaining land is capable of yielding equivalent amounts of renewable natural resources, and so long as the effect on the total ecosystem is not adversely affected …. What has not been proved is that greenfield development is intrinsically energy-profligate; on the contrary, theoretical work both in the UK and abroad suggests that it is possible to design highly energy-efficient new communities based on local mixed land use and a linear emphasis on strong public transport corridors.

Conclusions

Although it is now widely accepted that the sustainability of a city is related to its shape, size, density and uses, the exact nature of that relationship remains a matter of considerable dispute. 'Certain urban forms appear to be more sustainable in some respects, for example in reducing travel, or enabling fuel efficient technologies, but detrimental in others, perhaps in harming environmental quality or producing social inequalities' (Williams *et al.* 2000, p. 1). While this points to the existence of a variety of urban forms that would be more sustainable than recent development patterns, Williams *et al.* (2000) suggest that their key characteristics are likely to be compactness, mix of uses and interconnected street patterns, supported by strong public transport networks, environmental controls and high standards of urban management. In seeking to apply these characteristics, there remains room for much debate on whether sustainable urban forms are best achieved through centralised or decentralised concentrations of people and especially on the extent to which urban intensification and densification is a prerequisite of sustainable development.

As we have argued in this chapter, if housing development (whether at greenfield or brownfield locations) is to become more sustainable, the institutional deficit in state–market relations in its production will need to be addressed. At one level, issues such as the reluctance of the housebuilding industry to take energy efficiency seriously may demand even tighter building regulations, while at another level, mechanisms to involve local people and communities more closely in the masterplanning of major residential developments may help to break down some of the fears that the industry is concerned solely with the rapid construction and disposal of sprawling peripheral housing estates.

Beyond these, however, real issues arise about the extent to which the state needs to become more closely involved in the residential development process as a whole, perhaps through taking a stake as landowner and financial beneficiary, rather than relying merely on planning control to achieve greater sustainability. This, of course, raises the question of the precise institutional arrangements that may need to be established to ensure that the drive for more sustainable forms of development is not weakened by conflict between various arms of government. A portfolio approach to new housing development across a city region, for example, may well demand particular forms of regional governance that at present do not exist. Again, if the state were to participate more often as landowner to achieve greater sustainability throughout the residential development process, it would need to be determined whether local authorities or specialist development agencies should take on this lead role. It is thus apparent that, even if common ground is ever reached on what sustainable development itself means, plenty of scope will remain for debate on the most appropriate institutional arrangements to deliver it, at least in relation to new housing.

Yet, as a result, at least in part, of the absence of effective institutional mechanisms and policies to deliver sustainable development irrespective of location, public policy in the UK has increasingly concerned itself with a narrow emphasis on brownfield rather than greenfield residential development. As Fig. 3.13 shows, over a 10-year period, policy has gradually evolved under governments of both political persuasions from one that saw its priority as meeting housing demand, even if that involved substantial greenfield development, to one that first adopted a 50% target for new housing on reused land in England, toyed with the idea of increasing this to 75% and eventually settled on a compromise of 60%. This reflects the fact that, despite more varied research findings: 'government and many planners consider that use of brownfield sites and the general maintenance of existing settlement boundaries is the key to sustainable development' (Macnaghten & Pinfield 1999, p. 44).

This powerful policy emphasis on brownfield redevelopment raises three important questions that we seek to address in subsequent chapters. First, it is necessary to explain how and why public policy has placed so much emphasis on brownfield rather than greenfield residential development. For, as this chapter would suggest, it is a gross over-simplification to consider brownfield development always sustainable and greenfield development always unsustainable. Indeed, if sustainability is treated merely as a stalking horse for town cramming, it may eventually fall into disrepute and have to be abandoned (Lock 1991). In later chapters, we therefore explore how the increasing importance of brownfield development in housing land policy is as much attributable to political processes as to the technical merits of the argument.

Secondly, as the Urban Task Force (1999) indicated, even if a 60% brownfield target is to be applauded in policy terms, very real doubts must exist over its implementation unless significant changes are made to the institutional framework for urban development. It is therefore critical to assess whether existing planning and development processes are capable of delivering such an emphasis on brownfield development and, if not, what sorts of changes

Date	Document	Para/Page	Content
1990	This Common Inheritance: Britain's Environmental Strategy (UK Government: Cm 1200)	6.44	There will be a continuing and substantial demand for new housing in most parts of the country well into the next century. Adaptation and subdivision of existing houses can make a major contribution to meeting the need. Even so, substantial new housebuilding will be required.
		6.45	It is one of the most important functions of the land use planning system to assess the need for new housing, and identify enough land in the right places to satisfy it.
		6.46	Communities cannot expect to resist all development.
		6.47	Land in urban areas should be used to meet as much as possible of the demand for sites for new housing.
		6.48	However well urban land is used, there will continue to be a need for building on 'green field' sites.
1991	This Common Inheritance: First Year Report (UK Government: Cm 1655)	4.7	Re-using vacant urban land helps to remove pressure from the countryside and improve the urban environment.
1993	This Common Inheritance: Second Year Report (UK Government: Cm 2068)	7.25	The Government is trying to increase the re-use of previously developed land in preference to encroachment of green field sites.
1994	Sustainable Development: the UK Strategy (Department of the Environment: Cm 2426)	41	The increasing pressures for housing and development require even greater care in optimising the use of finite land resources.
1994	Biodiversity: The UK Action Plan (Department of the Environment: Cm 2428)	4.79	Planning policies preventing unnecessary urbanisation of the countryside also help to protect biodiversity.
1994	PPG 13 Transport (Department of the Environment)	3.2	The overall strategy, to be reflected in structure plan policies to meet housing needs, should be to allocate the maximum amount of housing to existing larger urban areas (market towns and above) . . . with particular priority placed on the re-use or conversion of existing sites and premises.
1995	Our Future Homes: Opportunities, Choice, Responsibility (Department of the Environment: Cm 2901)	11	Aim by 2005 to build half of all new homes on re-used sites.
1996	Household Growth: Where Shall We Live? (Department of the Environment: Cm 3471)	ii	The principle of sustainable development . . . demands that we use every opportunity to protect greenfield sites.
		7.9	The Government is interested in people's views on value of an aspirational target of 60%, or whether we could do even better.
1997	Housing and Urban Capacity (UK Round Table on Sustainable Development)	35/R.1	The Urban White Paper for England should set an aspirational target of 75% of new housing to be built on previously developed land; similarly challenging targets should be set in the Urban White Papers for Wales, Scotland and Northern Ireland.
1998	Planning for the Communities of the Future (Department of the Environment, Transport and the Regions: Cm 3885)	39	With our new policies in place, we expect local planning authorities to be able to raise the national proportion of new homes to be built on previously developed land to 60% over the next 10 years.
1999	A Better Quality of Life: A Strategy for Sustainable Development for the UK (Department of the Environment, Transport and the Regions: Cm 4345)	7.56	In order to create more sustainable patterns of development, we need to concentrate the majority of new development within existing urban areas.
1999	Towards an Urban Renaissance (Urban Task Force)	187	Assuming trends are reasonably stable over 25 years, this implies that the target of 60% of new housing on recycled land, however defined, may not be achieved.
2000	Our Towns and Cities: The Future – Delivering an Urban Renaissance (Department of the Environment, Transport and the Regions : Cm 4911)	4.24	PPG 3 gives priority to the development of brownfield sites before greenfield land. Our national brownfield target is 60% by 2008 and we are asking each region to set targets in Regional Planning Guidance and Development Plans to contribute towards achieving it.

Fig. 3.13   Evolution of brownfield housing land policy 1990–2000.

may be needed in resource and institutional terms to ensure long-term implementation of the intended policy. In later chapters, we therefore look in detail at whether the speculative housebuilding industry has the institutional capacity to switch its emphasis to brownfield development and at the likely effectiveness of current policies that seek to promote this switch. The danger here is that politicians may prove reluctant to provide the necessary powers and resources to make their policies a success and that the long-term costs of policy failure may prove highly damaging in both economic and social terms.

Finally, it is important to consider which interests are likely to gain and to lose from the brownfield policy emphasis, whether it is successful or not. Although it may be too cynical to attribute urban redevelopment potential as a 'codeword for keeping the lower orders off our agreeable rural lawns' (Crookston 1998, p. 9), it can be argued that the costs of urban containment are borne by many in the form of higher house prices and that the benefits in environmental terms are enjoyed by a few, who already happen to be economically better off. In later chapters, we therefore consider the distributional impact of brownfield development in seeking to assess its likely effectiveness as a policy. For, as this chapter has demonstrated, if sustainable development is not merely about environmental protection but extends to social inclusion and economic efficiency, it is essential that the increasing policy emphasis on brownfield land be capable of justification on social and economic grounds and not merely on environmental ones.

Note

(1) Such specific guidance on future development of villages, small towns and new settlements was not included in the revised PPG 13 on Transport, published in 2001 (DETR 2001). Instead, cross-references were inserted to the relevant guidance in the revised PPG 3 on Housing, published in 2000.

4

The Residential Planning Process

The planning system plays a pivotal role in determining the location of new housing development by providing the main arena through which policy-makers can influence development. The operation of the system and the way in which it performs this role has long been surrounded by political controversy as a variety of groups and interests have sought to shape the direction and implementation of planning policy for their own advantage.

This chapter sets out to evaluate how and why the state has used the levers available through the planning system in responding to pressure for new housing development. The analysis begins by reviewing public and political responses to peripheral growth and urban decline. Following from the discussion of the changing policy influences and priorities in Chapters 2 and 3, we highlight the particular problems posed for the planning system by the primacy given to the market over the state.

This provides a context for a discussion of current strategic planning processes, including housing need and demand calculations, land supply estimates and land availability issues. This discussion considers the limitations of the 'predict and provide' and 'plan, monitor and manage' approaches and highlights, in particular, the difficulty in ensuring an adequate supply of housing that offers sufficient choice in terms of type, size and location of homes. It is argued that priority has often been given to increasing the speed of decision-making rather than quality of decisions. The discussion also emphasises the difficulties associated with securing an adequate provision of affordable homes.

The chapter concludes by acknowledging that, while planning guidance and policy appear to have changed little in substance (Cullingworth 1997), it has been over-simplistic to consider the system as simply being based on a technocratic 'predict and provide' approach. Indeed, in order to understand the extent and nature of change in the system, it is necessary to appreciate the processes underlying the rhetoric and to consider recent changes in terms of the role played by bargaining and negotiation. We conclude the review of the system by noting that, notwithstanding the proposals contained in the 2001 Green Paper, it is still focused primarily on land allocation and not visionary futures. Although recent policy changes may herald a rise in planning as place-making, there are still considerable challenges to be faced in facilitating the effective resolution of controversies involving actors in the housing development arena.

Public and political attitudes to urban change

As outlined in Chapter 2, the planning system has sought to cope with urban change that has occurred at a rate and on a scale that were completely unexpected in the immediate postwar period. As Evans (1988) notes, it was thought that the birth rate would remain low and that only a limited amount of land in rural areas would be required to cope with decentralisation of the urban population. However, the levels of growth and accompanying demand for land have been significantly higher than predicted. The predictions also failed to account for the impact of improvements in transport, and the preference for space facilitated by rising real incomes.

The pressure for development brought about by the redistribution of the population from the north to the south and from urban to rural areas has ensured that planning for housing development has retained a prominent place in political debates in the latter part of the twentieth century. This has been exacerbated by the growth in demand for land for uses other than housing, including out-of-town retailing and industrial activity. These debates have taken the form of local disputes over particular development sites as well as more ideologically grounded controversies about state–market relations.

Although, as we will discuss later, it was intended that the planning system should guide rather than restrict development, the dominant policy outcome has been to place a major restriction on the location of development. Since the 1970s, the use of green belt and landscape conservation policies in conjunction with the planning system have served to support the image of contained towns surrounded by open space, and to protect open space from development (Hall 1988). As Chapters 2 and 3 demonstrated, through time, the commitment to urban containment has been buttressed, first by the political prioritisation of urban regeneration in the 1970s and, more recently, by the rise of sustainable development agenda and the accompanying image of a compact city with the presumption in favour of brownfield development sites (Vigar *et al.* 2000).

Although there has been widespread public support for the overall objectives of the planning system, this general policy stance has been the subject of considerable political controversy. In particular, as recent governments have sought to address the negative anti-market view of the planning system by involving housebuilders in the system, environmental interests have campaigned with increasing vigour to prevent urban sprawl. Such political activity has stoked up public concern, for both NIMBYist ('not in my back yard') and environmental reasons, and helped generate increased levels of public participation in local debates about the location of development. This involvement has also become more sophisticated in terms of the political strategy deployed by interest groups. As Vigar *et al.* (2000) note, in this highly politicised context, the discursive solution promoted by the major national stakeholders in housing development has been to turn to technical calculations.

The system of planning for housing that emerged is based on several stages. Demand is estimated on the basis of national level demographic calculations, before being disaggregated to regional and local levels using past trends. The disaggregated figures are then examined in relation to existing supply-side considerations including the estimates of the available stock to arrive at an assessment of the number of dwelling units required in particular localities for specific time periods. The location of these units is then considered in the light of urban capacity or land availability studies and environmental constraints. In the remainder of this chapter we reflect critically on these technical procedures[1]. We note that the system has come under sustained criticism in two main areas. First, its technical basis has been attacked. Second, in operational terms, the system has been criticised for the extent to which it has continued to be influenced heavily by local political considerations.

Such criticism has emanated from a range of stakeholders. While housebuilders contend that the system is overly restrictive, environmentalists suggest it is pro-development and local authorities feel they are constrained by central government involvement. Despite this, Hull (1997) notes that planning for housing is one of only two policy sectors in Britain (the other being mineral extraction) which, as well as incorporating a tiered spatial approach to accommodate local and national policy interests, has given a privileged position to producers in the formulation of policy[2].

Planning for housing

The role and priorities of the planning system

The planning system, together with elements of urban regeneration policy, provides the state with a number of important levers with which to influence the location of housing development. These levers, however, can be deployed only with reference to both the prevailing conditions in the housing market and the over-arching policy concerns of the state. These policy concerns include, *inter alia*, the stated objective of housing policy (which is to ensure that everyone has the opportunity of a decent home) and the Government's commitment to sustainable development (as discussed in Chapters 2 and 3).

In the UK, planning policy operates through the framework provided by the development plan system, where development plan is the generic term covering a number of separate plans such as the structure plan and local plan. The approach adopted, thus, is '… fundamentally a discretionary one in which decisions on particular development proposals are made as they arise against the policy background of a generalised plan' (Cullingworth & Nadin 2001, p. 26). The structure plans provide broad strategic statements of counties' intentions, while the local plans translate the statements into land-use policies within the districts including the allocation of sites for housing development. The two-tiered system applies to much of England with the exception of the larger districts. These are covered by unitary authorities which produce 'unitary development plans' that encompass both strategic and local elements. During the 1990s, the system has broadly been 'plan led' in that development in accordance with the plan should be allowed. Local and regional considerations are set within national planning policy priorities established through planning policy guidance notes (PPGs in England and Wales and NPPGs in Scotland).

In the context of planning for housing, the objective for local planning authorities is to plan to meet the housing requirements of the whole community. This encompasses the requirement to consider those who need affordable or special needs housing and an expectation that authorities will seek to provide wider housing choice, a better mix of size, type and location of housing than is currently available. The objectives for local authorities translate into a requirement to provide sufficient housing land, while giving priority to the reuse of previously developed land within urban areas, using empty homes and converting buildings previously in other uses in preference to using greenfield sites. In England, these and other wider policy considerations are established in *PPG 3: Housing* published, after consultation, in 2000 as a replacement for the previous version that dated from 1992 (DETR 2000a).

In summary, the national priorities continue to show a commitment to the conservation of the countryside and to the assistance of urban regeneration and improved quality of life in towns and cities. This, in turn, influences the requirement to ensure an adequate supply of land for housing. Sufficient sites should be identified in order to accommodate at least the first 5 years or first two phases of housing development (DETR 2000a). The estimate of land allocated for housing is generated by considering demand-side forecasts of population and household formation against supply-side considerations that include the existing stock of housing and land including that with existing planning permission. Local authorities are also required to monitor the uptake of previously developed and greenfield sites and to alter plans in the light of that monitoring. The analysis is translated into a county or regional housing requirement only after entering into a political bargaining process.

Household projections

As Whitehead (1997) points out, until the late 1960s, housing policy was in many respects a relatively simple numbers game. At 1951 there were 6.5% more households than dwellings while around 75% of all households were living in substandard, overcrowded or shared homes. The shortage of decent-quality homes affected households at all levels of the income scale, and consequently all political parties stressed the importance of a public sector building programme. In fact, and perhaps surprisingly given more contemporary views on public spending, the Conservatives achieved the production of 425 000 new units in 1958 under Prime Minister Harold Macmillan.

In the early 1970s, the census showed that there were 700 000 excess dwellings in Britain. Although this figure was subsequently revised downwards, arguments about housing provision became more sophisticated and the nature of housing policy changed markedly (Whitehead 1997). Nevertheless, during the 1960s and 1970s, the level of new construction was generally running much higher than the rate of household growth (King 1993). This can be explained by the strong public sector involvement in slum clearance and rehabilitation.

Since the 1980s, however, as public sector completions have fallen to an all-time low, household growth has outstripped the rate at which new dwellings have been produced. In the 1980s alone, the number of households in England increased at a rate of 1.2% per year or by two million overall (Bramley 1996). However, during the period between 1977 and 1994, perhaps as a consequence of the crude surplus that had existed, no government estimates of housing requirements were published (Jones & Watkins 1999). This almost certainly exacerbated the controversy associated with the new estimates when they were finally made public.

The current demand calculations

The current medium-term estimates of housing need are based on the measurement of any backlog of provision and a projection of new demand and need, which tends to be dominated by new household formation. The figures are produced by the DTLR (and before that by the DETR and its predecessor the DOE) every three years or so. This ensures that the estimates generated are continually revised as new information becomes available and, as such, means that the predicted numbers vary from one estimate to another.

The basic methodology used to produce the household projections begins with the Office of National Statistics' (ONS) population projections, the Government Actuary's Department's estimates of changes in marital status, data on international migration patterns and recent trends on household formation. The approach is trend-based and seeks to illustrate what will happen if historic trends in household formation were to continue into the future.

In recent statements, great care has been taken to stress that the published figures are not forecasts of what the government expects or intends to happen. Rather the figures merely roll forward past experience and are also heavily dependent on the assumptions involved. Of central importance is the fact that people are classified into groups (or household types) based on their potential requirement for a separate dwelling. There are five separate household types: married couples (with or without children), cohabiting couples (with or without children), lone parent households with dependants, one-person households and multiperson households.

Using projected membership rates based on the propensity of people of different age, sex and marital group to form a household, these categories provide the basis by which population figures can be translated into households. Thus the system works from population estimates through household estimates to houses required and housing land allocations (see Fig. 4.1). The method also works down from national to regional and county level. At the regional level, internal migration begins to be accommodated (see Bramley & Watkins 1995; DOE 1996a). The estimates are also converted into a housing requirement using information on vacancies and so on.

The rise in profile of the most recent controversy can be tracked to the first run of 1992-based household formation estimates, published in 1995. These figures suggested that the earlier 1989-based projections had underestimated the level of need and demand by almost one million households (DOE 1995a). The new figures estimated that the number of households in England would grow by 4.4 million (just under 23%) over the 25 years between 1991 and

		Trends	⟶	Policy
	Population	**Households**	**Houses**	**Houses**
National ↓	1. National population projections	4. National household projections		
Regional ↓	2. Regional populations projections	5. Regional household projections	7. Conversion of household total to houses	9. Trend figure used as regional control total in regional guidance
County	3. County population projections	6. County household projections	8. Conversion of household total to houses	10. Policy-based allocation of regional control in regional guidance

Fig. 4.1 Procedure for producing local housing allocations in regional guidance in England (source: Breheny 1999).

2016. This implied that new households would form at the rate of 175 000 per annum and increase from around 19.2 million in 1991 to 23.6 million in 2016. Underpinning this is an increase in the population of 7.6% from 47.5 million in 1991 to 51.1 million in 2016.

Before these projections were published, the debate had tended to focus on the implications of the 'demographic bulldozer' effect (Corner 1991; King 1993). This refers to the projected decrease in households over time and the fact that, should household numbers decrease, then growth in the number of dwellings will also fall. Corner (1991) showed that, up to 1983, there was steady growth averaging around 130 000 new households per year. During the mid-1980s, this increased further to around 200 000 per year but returned to more typical postwar levels after this. The projections at this time suggested that growth would fall to a low of around 100 000 per year by the start of the new millennium. In reality, however, the 'demographic bulldozer' effect has not materialised.

The 1995 projections highlighted changes in household structure (as captured in the mismatch between the population and household growth projections). They suggested that while just under half the new households forming could be attributed to an underlying increase in the population itself, around a third of the estimated growth was attributable to behavioural changes in the rate of households forming because of later marriages, divorces and separations. The changing age structure of the population, and specifically the growth in elderly and young adult groups, accounted for another 21% of the increase. In fact, almost 80% or 3.5 million of the projected increase was attributable to the formation of one-person households. Although less striking in its quantitative impact, this group had also grown enormously, by 2.2 million (or 74%), between 1971 and 1991 (DOE 1996a). The impact of these changes in structure has been to reduce average household size from 2.47 persons per household to 2.17 (Allinson 1999).

In 1996, in response to the 4.4 million debate, the Environment Committee set up an inquiry into the wider question of housing need (DOE 1996c). The inquiry considered evidence on the accuracy of the estimates, the nature of the projections and the technical merits of the approach used. Although, as we outline later, much of the discussion centred on the computation of social housing needs, the debate on methodology led to an acceptance that more information was required on the economic and behavioural factors influencing household formation rates (Whitehead 1997; Bramley *et al.* 1998).

Some of these issues are reflected in the statements surrounding the more recent estimates. For instance, the revisions published in 1999 on the basis of the ONS's 1998 population figures suggested that new household formation would probably be nearer 3.8 million. This was based on a projected increase in household numbers from 20.2 million in 1996 to 24 million in 2016 at a rate of about 150 000 households per year (DETR 1999b).

The most important differences from the 1995 figures related to changes in the marital status projections produced by the Actuary's Department. The newer estimates incorporated recent evidence of an increased rate of cohabitation and a downward revision in the estimated numbers of widows and divorcees. It seems that the earlier estimates had captured some broad trends without incorporating more recent changes in the rate at which single people formed new partnerships. Haskey (1999) notes that while fewer than one in ten couples married in the 1950s were divorced after 15 years of marriage, this had risen to one in five of couples married in the 1970s. As a consequence of this trend, however, new evidence predicts that previously married single people will constitute a fifth of all households in England by 2021 (Shaw & Haskey 1999). This is exacerbated still further by the parallel trends in dissolution and reformation of cohabitation households. The downward revision also reflected a reduction in the contribution of the net inflow of international migrants.

Following the recommendations of the 1998 Environment Select Committee Inquiry on Housing, these new estimates also incorporated an element of sensitivity analysis. This seeks to demonstrate the extent to which the predictions might be influenced by changes in economic conditions (House of Commons Environment, Transport and Regional Affairs Committee 1998). This analysis shows, for example, that a 1% change in real interest rates might cause a fluctuation in the number of projected households by greater than 200 000 in either direction. Similarly, the figures show that a

0.25% decrease in gross domestic product (GDP) would be accompanied by a 150 000 drop in the projected number of households forming (DETR 1999b).

Regional guidance and land availability

As we note above, however, the household projections represent only part of the process of providing land for new housing development. In fact, even before their significance was downgraded with the move away from the 'predict and provide' approach, the Secretary of State for the Environment said that the projections 'represent just one of the factors to be taken into account by local planning authorities ... when arriving at figures for housing provision' (DOE 1996a, p. 48). The next stage requires the preparation of Regional Planning Guidance (RPG) statement which, after consultation with local bodies, is shaped by policy considerations including environmental concerns, the state of the current stock, previous levels of supply and the availability of land.

The primary aim of the RPGs is to provide a framework for development plans, which must be taken into consideration by local authorities in the preparation and review of structure plans, or in metropolitan areas, the unitary development plans. The documents set out future housing land requirements in the region with the figures normally disaggregated down to county or metropolitan district level. As part of this process, many authorities make their own forecasts. Although these do not always accord with the central government projections, strong powers exist that allow the Secretary of State to call in structure plans that do not allocate an adequate supply of land to accommodate the increase in household numbers. In Chapter 7, we discuss the extent to which the Secretary of State has been prepared to use these powers in practice.

The status of regional guidance has grown progressively through the 1990s (Hull 1997) and, in the most recent changes, even greater responsibility has been given to Regional Planning Conferences (RPCs). Through the RPCs, planning authorities are collectively required to discuss how best to accommodate the projected figures with the Government Offices for the Region (GOR) and other stakeholders. The emphasis placed on this local negotiation seeks to improve the local ownership of the numbers (DETR 1998b), although the Secretary of State still has the final say.

At the end of this stage, the local housing requirement is set in terms of an average annual housing provision for each county or unitary planning authority within the region. Although account is taken of the need to use vacant land and to consider transport and local economic development issues, little further detail is provided. The main source of market analysis and information comes from the involvement of producers. The regional officers of the House Builders' Federation (HBF) perform a role in the assessment of demand and in auditing land availability in each of the district local authority areas (DOE 1980b). Although, in many cases, consideration is also given to local migration flows and their implications for the spatial distribution of regional housing requirements, the focus tends to remain on crude numbers (Bramley & Watkins 1995). In fact, the lack of systematic market analysis means that there is no indication of size, density, house type or tenure associated with these estimates. Nevertheless, the crude figures are fed into the structure planning process.

This part of the process encompasses debates about the state of local land markets and, in particular, about the extent to which land is really available for housing development (Cullingworth 1997). In this context, it seems that there are important definitional differences between the key actors. Planners tend to consider availability in terms of the extent of public control over the land, while housebuilders' views are shaped by ownership considerations (Hooper 1980). Successive governments have emphasised the role of land availability studies as a form of economic appraisal of the land market and a means of bringing together planners and housebuilders. Like other aspects of the system, these studies have been subject to criticism for their failure to pay sufficient attention to market forces (Coopers & Lybrand 1985; Roger Tym & Partners 1991). Interestingly, however, the blame is not laid exclusively with the planning authorities. Although they generally fail to consider economic factors, housebuilders' proposals also often lack a sound quantitative basis (Maclennan 1986).

It is thought that the greatest achievement of land availability studies has not been in providing a sound assessment of land availability but, rather, in establishing a better understanding between planners and housebuilders (Barrett & Healey 1985; Cullingworth 1997). More specifically, the process of negotiation and bargaining that underpins the studies provided a basis for learning more about the short- to medium-term flow of land through the development process (Barrett & Healey 1985). Thus, much of the strength of these studies lies in providing a backdrop to the negotiative practice that takes place in local housing markets.

Limitations of the system of planning for new housing

In recent times, the methodology for projecting household formation has been the subject of sustained criticism. Historically, the backward-looking trend-based approach has been questioned. Field and MacGregor (1987) have shown that the estimates produced in the mid-1960s predicted that the population in the UK would now be around 80 million. Allinson (1999) revisits this issue and suggests that there is strong evidence that the current national figures may also represent a serious overestimate. In particular, he is critical of the failure to incorporate any deceleration in the rate of decline of household size.

By way of illustration, Allinson (1999) notes that if some slowing down of this trend is not factored in and the decline in household size continues at past rates then by 2098 every man, woman and child in England will occupy their own dwelling. The CPRE (1998) maintains that analysis of the number of dwellings constructed in the early part of the forecast period also implies that the figures are substantial overestimates. These arguments, however, do not find universal support. In a series of research projects, Holmans presents evidence that is much more supportive of the accuracy of the forecasts (Holmans 1995, 2001b).

A further criticism of the projections is that the system does not take economic considerations into account, even though generally the level of effective demand for housing will be influenced by the employment and income situation of potential households (Bramley & Watkins 1995). The supply and price of homes provided by developers will be affected by current and expected financial and economic conditions. Thus, if economic conditions differ from those that shaped the past trends, the rate of household formation and levels of housing demand may turn out quite different from those forecast. This reliance on economic conditions has, of course, been exacerbated as the role of the state has been reduced (Malpass 1996).

Bramley and Watkins' (1995) criticisms also relate *inter alia* to the 'circularity' inherent in the projections. They suggest that, in effect, the projections are self-fulfilling. The provision of housing to meet expected demand ensures that further demand occurs, and this in turn leads to increased future projections. Importantly, this calls into question the extent to which the housing targets set in plans are in fact based on policy-neutral, technical assessments of housing need. For instance, the pattern of migration is determined on the basis of both past trends and policy objectives relating to issues such as employment or environmental capacity. In cases where land is highly constrained for environmental reasons, then houses will not be available for households to occupy. Thus policy has had a strong influence in determining the housing targets, even though it is not explicitly acknowledged in the rhetoric surrounding the technical calculations.

Elsewhere, it is recognised that the need to account for internal migration flows is the most problematic of all the influences on geographical subdivisions of population projections (Baker & Wong 1997). In particular, although the data used provide a reasonably accurate picture of migration flows in the year immediately preceding the census, they do not reflect the pattern in other years. For non-census years, the information on internal migration is generated from the Family Health Service Association's (FHSA) records of patient moves. The reliability of these records is highly questionable, especially as they are unlikely to capture all movers and those that are not recorded are likely to be of distinct household types or ages.

Similar problems surround the data on international migration flows. Champion *et al.* (1998) provide two estimates of gross international migrants to London for 1990. The first estimate is based on the census and shows an inflow of around 103 000. The second uses the International Passenger Survey (IPS) and puts the inflow at nearer 113 000. The infrequency of the census makes any systematic comparison of the two sources impossible but the divergence is indicative of the measurement problems. The magnitude of the estimate is important as it is broadly in line with the outflow of internal migrants from London during the same period (Breheny 1999).

Hull (1997) makes the more general point that the process of forward planning for housing suffers from lack of reliable market and migration pattern data. She suggests that a prerequisite for more equitable housing outcomes is the systematic collection of data concerning the building stock and housing need within planning authority areas. Others highlight the particular limitations associated with the use of dated census data (Bramley & Watkins 1995; Baker & Wong 1997). It is also clear, owing in part to the Community Charge or 'Poll Tax', that, even after corrections, the census failed to include large number of predominately young male households often referred to as the 'missing millions'.

Confusion also surrounds the use of the terms 'need' and 'demand'. Although the term 'housing need' is commonly used, there is an important distinction between need and demand. By demand, analysts are generally referring to the economic concept, effective demand, which is the requirement for new homes from households willing and able to meet market prices. Housing need refers to the provision of acceptable accommodation for all households regardless of their financial circumstances (see Kleinman *et al.* 1999). By extension while some households in 'need' can secure housing through the market, others cannot and, without support, may be restricted to poor-quality dwellings or become homeless.

Ambiguity surrounds the assumptions that should be made about the need category in projecting household requirements (Bramley & Watkins 1995). It is unclear whether households forced to defer formation and remain living with parents or in other shared accommodation are in need. Suppressed household formation also affects the overall projections. Although, as we discuss in detail below, this has been addressed in recent guidance, problems remain in identifying and meeting housing need arising in addition to housing demand.

As with the national projections, the subregional projections approach has also been the subject of considerable criticism and controversy. Again, much of this has centred on the technical aspects of the procedures employed and the estimates of future land requirements. The figures have typically been the source of conflict between locally based representatives of interest groups such as the HBF and the Council for the Protection of Rural England (CPRE), not least because the procedures from which the figures emerge are considered something of a 'black box'. Baker and Wong (1997) summarise some of the criticisms developed by these groups. They highlight, for instance, that there are a number of sources of potential error. As we note above, the source of error is introduced through the national population projections and, in particular, through the treatment of the 'missing millions', asylum seekers and internal migration flows. The subnational figures are also subject to potential error from the methods used to apply local differentials to the national figures.

Baker and Wong (1997) also suggest that there are specific problems with the 'policy-based' considerations that enter into the calculation of housing requirements in RPG. This is where economic and environmental considerations influence the process, and account is taken of the relationship between metropolitan areas and the adjacent shires in developing a view on urban regeneration requirements and in assessing housing capacities. Baker and Wong felt that generally there has been a tendency for technical considerations to override policy concerns, and for policy and political considerations to be obscured by the technical calculations. Although this has been partly addressed in the revised planning guidance, it remains a concern.

There are also questions about the ability of the system to deliver dwellings of the required type and size or in the appropriate locations. The basis for this criticism is that the system in England does not take account of knowledge of the spatial economic structure of the local housing system and that there is instead an over-reliance on crude numbers. This relates to a more general failure to undertake detailed assessments of local housing markets

(Blackaby 2000). As we discuss in Chapter 5, this allows housebuilders to provide homes of the size, type and quality that best serve their profit motive but are not necessarily those for which there is a shortage within the planning authorities' boundaries. According to Bramley and Watkins (1995), demographic changes are generating a growing diversity of household sizes and types, with the traditional 'couple with children' household a declining minority. It is not clear, however, that the planning system is able to make the link between detailed demographic trends and issues of housing size and type.

Some commentators suggest that aspects of the Scottish system are more sophisticated and potentially instructive in this context (Jones & Watkins 1999). The Scottish system recognises that the Housing Market Area (HMA) is the most appropriate functional area for housing studies and is superior to the ad hoc administrative boundaries of local authorities. Unfortunately, however, the guidance issued does not offer a precise definition of the HMA construct. Rather it states that these 'are ideally areas in which a self contained housing market operates. A pragmatic test is that a substantial majority of people moving house and settling in an area will have sought a house only in that area' (Scottish Office 1996, p. 9).

The advice suggests that HMAs may overlap local authority boundaries around conurbations. Best practice in defining HMA boundaries is presented in research funded by the national housing agency, Scottish Homes (More *et al.* 1993). This research notes that the labour market area and its spatial structure within a region are critical in shaping HMAs and, as such, the self-contained market would capture both the origin and destination of the majority of those moving house without changing job. Thus the housing market area would be defined in a way that the majority of the population would both reside and work within its boundaries. The logic of this construct is that households will move to meet their domestic requirements with changing income or as they pass through the family life cycle without changing employment.

The significance of this guidance is that any assessment of housing demand based on a local authority's administrative boundaries is likely to be inaccurate (Jones & Watkins 1999). However, this framework is also subject to some limitations. In many cases local authority areas are too small to be meaningful in functional terms. The arguments parallel those made by urban geographers in the development of the system of Travel to Work Areas (TTWAs) as an aid to studying labour markets' change and economic development (Peck 1989; Coombes 1995). Within a national system of HMAs, planning authorities will be able to manipulate supply and demand more effectively.

The system of planning for housing, and in particular local plan provisions, also need to be sensitive to the pressures within local markets, and ideally should take account of the neighbourhood-specific nature of housing demand (Maclennan 1992). A useful building block for such analysis is the housing submarket (Hancock & Maclennan 1989). Maclennan and Tu (1996) describe submarkets as the fault lines along which a housing market may fracture or suffer disjunctures.

The conceptual basis for submarket existence is developed in a series of articles (Maclennan 1986, 1992; Maclennan *et al.* 1987; see Watkins 2002 for a review). Within this framework, the supply side of the market is characterised by the existence of a set of product groups comprising dwellings with similar quality characteristics. These dwellings are generally assumed to be relatively close substitutes for each other in terms of their physical and locational features. The demand side of the market consists of a set of consumer groups comprising households with similar housing tastes, preferences and access to finance. The interaction between segmented supply and differentiated demand gives rise to a market that is best conceptualised in terms of a set of inter-related submarkets. House prices within each submarket will be determined by the interaction of segment-specific supply and demand schedules.

For planning purposes, the analysis of prices and migration flows within this framework can aid the identification of local pressure points and provide the basis for understanding the flow of households between neighbourhoods and house types. At present, understanding and analysis of the market is dominated by housebuilders who tend to base their judgement on what seems likely on the basis of their knowledge of past sales and completion rates (Bramley *et al.* 1995), rather than on a systematic assessment of localised patterns of demand pressure.

The submarket framework can potentially facilitate a more sophisticated analysis of the size and type of homes required within housing market areas. In the light of the changes introduced under the 'plan, monitor and manage' system, the submarket framework might also provide a fruitful basis for the strategic collaboration of authorities at regional level and for the involvement of builders in the planning process. Despite this, however, much of the impetus for change in the planning system is driven by a desire to improve the speed of the decision-making process rather than the quality of the decisions taken.

This is not helped by the reliance on private developers to deliver the homes required and the fact that developer behaviour will be governed by current and expected economic and housing market conditions (Bramley *et al.* 1995; Bramley & Watkins 1995, 1996a). Although this makes speed and certainty important issues, there is no clear transmission mechanism between allocating land for housing in structure and local plans and delivery of new homes on to the market. There may be circumstances when development will not be profitable or where, even if the development is profitable, the developer expects to gain a financial advantage by delaying the project. When market conditions are uncertain, developer behaviour may become hard to predict. This makes it particularly difficult to develop a fine-grained system of housing targets at submarket level. This can also cause particular problems with the reliance on the private sector to meet housing need through the provision of affordable homes.

Planning for affordable housing

As part of the fall-out from housing market boom and bust in the late 1980s and early 1990s, housing affordability problems rose up the political agenda (Bramley 1994). During this period, the problem had several dimensions and was transformed from being an issue that simply affected low-income renters. High prices meant that potential buyers were priced out of the market. High mortgage interest rates meant that recent buyers might default and repossessions and arrears rose to record levels (Ford 1994). These households became trapped by negative equity (Gentle *et al.* 1994). In addition, reduced funding in the state sector pushed social rents more towards market levels, and this, coupled with cuts in benefits affecting households in both the private and social rented sector, exacerbated problems for renters. In a clear illustration of the impact of these problems, Bramley (1996) notes that, although there was a reasonable balance between affordable need and supply in the early 1980s, this changed later in the decade as need increased from 90 000 to 140 000 units per year while provision fell from 73 000 to 37 000 units.

There has been a wide range of estimates of the current and future level of affordable housing requirements. Although much controversy surrounds the extent to which there is already a backlog in the system caused by low levels of building in the social housing sector in the 1980s, it seems clear that around 50% of new homes will need to be 'affordable'. Holmans (1995) argues that, without a change in policy, there would be a significant rise in the number of households unable to afford adequate housing without support, and calls for an additional 90 000 to 100 000 social housing units per year. He also argues that the backlog was of the order of 480 000 homes with the major components comprising 110 000 concealed households, 140 000 sharing households and 100 000 single homeless or in hostels (Holmans 1996).

More recently, Holmans *et al.* (1998) estimate that 2.3 million affordable homes, at an equivalent of 115 000 per annum, would be required over the forecast period in order to meet new need and to reduce the backlog by three-quarters. While these figures find support in a recent update (Holmans 2001b), other estimates (still assuming three-quarters of the backlog is met) put the figure at around 1.7 million (Bevis 2001).

Despite these differences, which can be attributed to the fact that there is no widely accepted means of calculating the affordable housing requirement, it is clear that a significant proportion of new housing will need to be targeted at those who will need assistance meeting the costs. In the current market-oriented policy context, it might appear that these low-income households would be priced out of the market or would be limited to homes located in the lowest-quality levels or on the poorest estates.

Against this background, and partly because of the belief that planning con-straints have exacerbated affordability problems by forcing prices upwards, several attempts have been made to use the planning system to address these access problems. The earliest approaches were based on the use of size and density policies or the inclusion of local needs policies in plans in order to meet local requirements in particular areas where tight restraint policies (in-cluding National Parks, for example) and high commuter and second homes demand were pricing out local people (Crook 1996). These approaches were indirect and were not generally endorsed by central government (Crook & Whitehead 2002).

Subsequently, however, announcements made in 1992 heralded a more radical approach based upon seeking planning gain. This approach com-bined use and density policies with legal agreements, and sought to lower land prices and ensure that the dwellings were available at lower prices. One element of this approach was the 'rural exceptions policy', which al-lowed development on sites that would not normally be given planning permission. Legal agreements were also used in principle to persuade de-velopers to build a proportion of affordable homes on larger sites that had not been allocated for housing in development plans. The assumption was that the developer would enter the agreement in return for planning per-mission (Crook 1996). The use of planning gain has become of increasing significance in recent years and has been given a prominent place in policy guidance (DETR 2000a) and in discussions about future policy directions (DTLR 2001b). In this chapter, we concentrate on the role of planning gain in securing affordable housing. Later on, in Chapter 7 we look more generally at its implications for the balance between greenfield and brownfield development, while in Chapter 9 we subject the concept to more detailed economic analysis.

As we note in Chapter 2, one of the significant changes in the land-use planning system has thus been its enhanced role in helping to meet the need for social and affordable housing through planning gain policies. As Crook (1996, p. 61) explains:

> the planning system has been modified in fundamental ways eliminating some of the discretion planning authorities have had over plan preparation and implementation, in order to secure the continued provision of affordable housing while, at the same time, cutting public expenditure on grants to those supplying.

Thus, instead of the traditional approach of direct provision of social rented housing by local authorities, developers are now being asked to provide affordable (including social rented) housing within private schemes and, in effect, to use the market to subsidise the provision of low-cost housing. The planning system has become centrally involved in determining the requirements for affordable housing and in ensuring that these requirements are met.

The current approach to providing affordable housing through the planning system is based on negotiation with developers within the policy framework set out in Circular 6/98 and PPG 3 (DETR 1998c, 2000a). Significantly the recently published PPG 3 stresses the need to plan to meet the housing requirements of the whole community, while Circular 6/98 urges local authorities to create more balanced communities, by requiring the provision of affordable housing (including social rented homes) where existing provision is limited.

This is framed in the context of the Government's stated commitment to securing the economic, social and physical regeneration of urban areas, encompassing socially inclusive developments as part of more environmentally sustainable forms of development (see Chapters 2 and 3). The outcome from this approach has usually been to secure the provision of a supply of social rented housing, owned by RSLs rather than local authorities, or to a lesser extent low-cost homes for owner-occupation or shared ownership.

Circular 6/98 sets out that there should be a presumption that affordable housing should be provided and that failure to do so could justify the refusal of planning permission. PPG 3 emphasises that the provision of affordable housing should be a material concern when agreeing planning permission. This requires local authorities to define what is affordable, conduct housing needs surveys, determine how many affordable homes need to be provided, and identify the amount to be sought from developers (given that some will still be secured through the provision of the Social Housing Grant, SHG).

It is only since the early 1990s, however, that local planning authorities have tried to identify separate affordable housing requirements in statutory development plans. Although in exercising their development control function, they do not have the power to allocate land separately for market or affordable homes, this is nevertheless indicative of the rising profile of the issue. In fact, the development of housing affordability policies is now almost universal. By 1993, 90% of planning authorities had policies adopted or in draft (Crook 1996). More recently, from their postal survey of 180 planning authorities, Bishop Associates (2001) note that 95% of respondents had developed affordable housing policies within their plans and that almost a quarter of these had developed supplementary planning guidance on the topic.

In practice, developers have several options in honouring planning obligations (Crook & Whitehead 2002). These include directly providing a mix of affordable and market homes on the same site; providing affordable homes on other sites owned by the developer and thus avoiding a mix of market and affordable homes; and providing financial contributions to the local planning authority in the form of commuted sums that may be earmarked for subsequent provision of affordable housing by other parties. The first option appears to be preferred because it is consistent with the wider aim of creating socially inclusive developments, while the others will achieve this only if the site is linked with market provision (DETR 2000a).

However, it seems clear that, even at this relatively early stage, the system is not securing sufficient levels of affordable housing provision. There is clear gap between policy and implementation. Over the five years from 1997 to 2002, only about half of the requirement for affordable housing has been delivered (Crook & Whitehead 2002). Barlow *et al.* (1994) suggest that between 10 000 and 12 000 affordable homes were produced between 1991 and 1994. Monk (2001) suggests that, in recent years, the annual figure is around 12 000. Elsewhere, Holmans *et al.* (1998) maintain that 15 000 affordable homes per annum are likely to be the maximum achievable. Significantly there is no evidence whether these homes were additional to those that might have been produced. Monk (2001) suggests that the intervention of the planning system may simply have helped spread the impact of the SHG.

There are a number of possible explanations for the low levels of affordable homes secured. Several commentators suggest that successful co-ordination of land use with housing policy at local level has tended to prove difficult (Poxon 1994, cited in Crook 1996; House of Commons Environment, Transport and Regional Affairs Committee 1998). Crook and Whitehead (2002) indicate that output is further diminished by the desire simultaneously to pursue affordable housing, social balance and urban regeneration goals through the same planning mechanisms. Crook (1996) also notes that the policy tends to work better in certain land-value contexts, namely on large greenfield sites at the edge of cities. In these cases, the higher land values allow owners to retain some development value even after a proportion of the site has been allocated for affordable housing. We pick up the policy implications of this in Chapter 7.

The extent to which planning gain can be extracted is also limited by the varying negotiation skills of planners, as well as procedural costs and informational problems (Crook & Whitehead 2002). In addition, Crook and Jackson (2001) present some preliminary findings from a postal survey of 117 local planning authorities in England to show that local authorities find the current policy framework difficult to interpret. There appears to be considerable variation in terms of the form and extent of subsidy obtained by planning authorities for affordable housing. These differences seem to relate directly to ambiguity surrounding the application of the policy framework in practice. Bishop Associates (2001) confirm this and suggest that the lack of clear guidance may often lead to protracted negotiations about planning gain.

In a similar vein, Bishop Associates (2001) highlight *inter alia* the need to increase the clarity of affordable definitions used in local policies and in the types of households targeted. After much delay the Government defined affordable housing as encompassing 'a range of both subsidised and market housing designed for those whose incomes generally deny them the opportunity to purchase on the open market as a result of the local relationship between income and the market price' (DOE 1995c, p. 4). The imprecision of this official definition of affordable housing, however, leaves local policymakers with a difficult task in setting guidelines on the local relationship between incomes and costs. Indeed, there is considerable debate among housing economists about the basis for defining households with affordability problems (see Hancock 1993; Whitehead 1993; Hulchanski 1995).

The two most common approaches to affordability in the housing economics literature are based on housing cost to income ratios and residual income measures (Chaplin & Freeman 1999; Wilcox 1999). Both types of definition are tied to normative assessments about acceptable levels of housing quality and quality of life (Bramley 1994). The former suggests that there is an accepted maximum proportion of a household's income that should not be exceeded in paying for a home of adequate size and quality. The latter is based on an assessment of the ability of the household to meet other basic living expenses after it has paid for the cost of a decent home. Although both of these conventions have formed the basis of attempts to measure the numbers of households in different tenures facing affordability problems at local and national level (see respectively Bramley & Smart 1995; Bramley 1991; Hancock *et al.* 1991), there is no generally acceptable 'best practice' approach available to local policy-makers. In fact, the term 'affordable housing' is generally used as shorthand for low cost rather than in any consistent, technical sense.

Despite these problems and the limited success in securing the provision of affordable housing through the planning system and in the form of new development, this is not the only option available to government. Kleinman *et al.* (1999) note that there are four additional ways in which housing demand and need might be addressed. The first of these would be to reduce the number of homes that are vacant. Crook *et al.* (1996) have shown that recently constructed housing association stock on local authority areas has proved difficult to let. This evidence is supported by the work of Pawson and Kearns (1998) who have also identified high levels of difficult-to-let stock, particularly in the North of England. Kleinman *et al.* (1999) suggest that vacant stock might account for an additional flow, admittedly of only the low tens of thousands, to the social sector. The second option is to use the existing stock more intensively. This is largely discounted as a potential source of additional affordable homes as shared accommodation is generally unpopular (Holmans *et al.* 1998).

Potentially more useful is the third option, which is the provision of flats by subdividing larger homes. Although Kleinman *et al.* (1999) note that the number of flats provided in this way is unlikely to be above 15 000 per year, this of a similar scale to the volume of new homes secured through planning gain. The fourth option is to convert non-residential buildings into housing. There are several highly visible examples of this in the urban regeneration literature but this source of new homes is often constrained by financial considerations (see, for example, Rosenburg & Watkins 1999). In particular, the grant regime for housing associations discourages conversion work as the costs are much less predictable than those associated with the building of new houses or flats (Kleinman *et al.* 1999).

Thus, with the planning system failing to secure a sufficient supply of affordable homes and despite the evidence that the majority of affordable homes will have to come from new investment, there is scope to augment this with regeneration policy initiatives.

Conclusions: planning as process and vision

Although the planning system has remained largely unchanged for 50 years, its remit has contracted over time, reflecting the shift from a position of central importance in postwar restructuring to the current narrow regulatory function it performs. The system was designed to perform a positive proactive role underpinned by the nationalisation of development rights and to facilitate the strategic development of the right land in the right place and time. The nationalisation of development rights was accepted on the basis that the developers would have the right to a fair hearing and that local strategies would represent the views of the community. This implicit contract brings with it considerable procedural implications for the planning system (Hull 1998).

Against this background, policy-making on the allocation and development of housing land is based on a cascading system of accumulated decisions flowing from ministerial statements and national Planning Policy Guidance through Regional Planning Guidance, Structure Plans and Local Plans (and in some cases Unitary Development Plans). Typically the role of the planning system in influencing housing development has been twofold. First it has been the responsibility of housing planners to calculate the requirement for new housing units and to set these out in statutory plans. Secondly, the planning system has had responsibility for the provision of an adequate supply of land to meet the overall requirements, either by identifying specific sites or by setting out policies to be used in response to applications to develop other sites. These policies have then been implemented through the development control system.

This overall approach has been the subject of sustained criticism for a variety of reasons. The technical and procedural basis of the housing need estimates have been subject to such scrutiny that their role has now been de-emphasised since the abandonment of the 'predict and provide' system. In addition, the ability of the system to deliver homes of the appropriate size, type and quality and in the best locations has been the subject of critical comment from both the housebuilding industry and academic analysts. Notwithstanding these problems, however, a further challenge has been presented in that the planning system has now been given a central role in securing the provision of affordable housing. To date, the system has had only limited success in securing affordable homes. While local planning authorities have tended to complain about the ambiguity of the system, this has emphasised the operational difficulties of a system that, despite rhetoric to the contrary, really operates on the basis of bargaining and negotiation.

Vigar *et al.* (2000) consider the discourse involved in the housing numbers game. They note that the technical discourse was elaborated through the 1980s in the light of the growing intensity of local political conflicts. During this period, developers, for whom large sites are generally most attractive, appeared to recognise that the most commercially appealing sites were often the most politically contentious. The ideological climate at the time, however, appears to have provided an opportunity to exercise greater influence and, ultimately, national policy allowed housebuilders the opportunity to become involved in decisions about the location of housing.

Specifically, since 1980, the regional officers of the HBF have had a direct role in assessing housing demand and in auditing housing land availability in each planning authority district. This has introduced 'market criteria' such as site marketability into the decision-making toolkit. As we note above, however, the environmental lobby also became more vigorous in its involvement in the planning system and operated successfully as a counter-balance against the housebuilders. Although involvement has been limited to groups who have sufficient resources to participate, such as the CPRE, this lobby has been prominent in the planning inquiry process and in determining consensus on future supply and demand estimates. This theme is taken up further in Chapter 6.

Against this background, the system of planning for housing became characterised by negotiative practice and the language used was punctuated with metaphors such as 'windfall sites' and 'land qualities' (Vigar *et al.* 2000). In this politically contested context, the technical basis of the system provided a stable frame of reference for the stakeholders involved. Usefully planners were able to negotiate agreement on a range of matters by the process of bargaining and negotiating planning permission. Although the agreements and planning gain secured were not without controversy (Healey *et al.* 1993), the strength of the system lay in its ability to blur the reality of this negotiative process while resolving conflicts about the location of land for development.

The relative success and underlying justificatory logic of the system, however, were undermined in the 1990s by two main forces (Vigar *et al.* 2000). First, the nature of housing demand had become far more differentiated and the actors operating in the housing market had become much more sensitive to its segmented structure. As we note above, the system was unable to locate housing on the basis of a sound conceptualisation of the economic workings of local housing systems. Secondly, the increasing pressure to resist greenfield development and to concentrate brownfield development within cities or near existing transport corridors, brought into focus concerns about environmental capacity and the quality of urban areas. The failure to reconcile the environmental concerns with the need to achieve sustainable development patterns and market demand for more homes, brought the curtain down on this period.

These tensions helped question the narrow, technocratic focus of the system and demonstrate the need for a broader vision based on considerations of the quality of life, the sustainable spatial organisation of development and the wider role of housing in individual and community activities. The limits of the system, and reliance on the market, are most clearly seen in the failure to deliver affordable housing. Indeed, this failure is indicative of the need for a system that has a clearly defined sense of social justice. At present, without a clear articulation of the links to social and other policy areas, the planning system lacks the tools required to secure the provision of an adequate supply of land to meet housing needs, to contribute to the quality of places or, in particular, to secure an adequate provision of affordable housing at the levels required.

Encouragingly, however, recent policy statements appear to be reasserting plan-led planning and have begun to search for a new vision for planning (DETR 1999a; Urban Task Force 1999). In this context, Healey (2001) notes that there are two different directions in which the system might be led. She states it:

> could go down the narrow path of regulation of particular sorts of externality, and jostle for power with the Environment Agency over who has the duty to regulate which bit of the externality effect. Or it could evolve into an active role in place-making in an interactive and facilitative way, involving many stakeholders, in processes of collaborative planning.
>
> (Healey 2001, p. 268)

Despite the emphasis given to place-making by the Urban Task Force report, however, Healey points out that it is not clear that this tension has been resolved with respect to the planning system. She goes on to note that a new system, with a positive role in place-making, will require a considerable transformation in the parameters of the current system and of current practice. At the centre of this challenge lies the need to provide a basis on which controversies and conflicts surrounding strategic decisions about new housing development might be resolved. Within this, the tension between the use of greenfield and brownfield sites and the growing influence of the sustainability agenda must be addressed. As we will begin to show in Chapter 5, under any new system policy can only succeed if some subtle pressure is exerted over the behaviour of private interests in the housebuilding industry. This challenge is made more difficult by the highly contested political framework within which the planning decisions are taken, which we explore in detail in Chapter 6.

Notes

(1) Land availability studies have been superseded in England (but not Wales or Scotland) by urban capacity studies (see Chapter 8).
(2) Although we discuss specific aspects of the policy guidance in Scotland and Wales, the system in England is the primary focus of this chapter.

Part II

Market, Economic and Political Context

5

The Speculative Housebuilding Industry

Speculative housebuilders are now responsible for about 80% of all new homes built in the UK. Over the years, speculative housebuilding has grown and prospered primarily through the conversion of greenfield land into new housing estates. In the first part of this chapter, we examine how the current structure of the speculative housebuilding industry reflects this conventional form of production. We show how capital in the industry has become increasingly concentrated and how strategies such as internal regional competition are adopted by the larger housebuilders to enhance corporate profitability.

The Government's desire to switch the balance of residential development to brownfield sites represents a significant challenge to prevalent behaviour and attitudes in much of the housebuilding industry. Brownfield redevelopment has generally been perceived as more problematic and risky than new development on greenfield land and has tended to be promoted by either specialist companies or subsidiaries. The second part of the chapter therefore investigates the speculative housing development process, with a view to pinpointing how any redirection of emphasis towards brownfield land may call for different skills and strategies.

This analysis of the producers and process of residential development is followed up in the third part of the chapter by consideration of the industry's product range. Here, the policy switch to brownfield redevelopment is more likely to require individually tailored products for specific locations rather than the standardised products for standardised locations traditionally produced by speculative housebuilders. Although the industry has not been well known for its capacity to innovate, government policy towards housebuilding is likely to place increasing constraints on its ability to continue to earn its living in the same way as in past decades.

In the fourth part of the chapter, we summarise the main distinctions for the industry between brownfield and greenfield development and seek to evaluate whether speculative housebuilders are capable of making significant changes in their product range and locations over the next few years. To illustrate the argument, we look in particular at some of the more innovative housebuilding companies and try to decipher whether their recent success in brownfield development offers any pointers to the industry as a whole. In conclusion, the chapter contends that, unless most currently dominant producers are able to demonstrate a greater capacity for innovation in terms of both process and product, a new structure of provision in speculative housebuilding will be necessary to ensure the successful implementation of the Government's preference for brownfield redevelopment.

Speculative housing producers[1]

Although there are about 18 000 housebuilders registered with the National House Building Council (NHBC), speculative production of new homes is dominated by a small number of major companies, each with an annual output of 500 units or more. In 2000, there were 43 such companies in the UK, which together accounted for almost 71% of all the homes built by the industry (Wellings 2001). Earlier figures from the NHBC's *Private Housebuilding Statistics*, reported by Nicol and Hooper (1999), indicate that in 1990 there were 32 companies starting 500 or more units who together claimed a 41% market share, while the returns for 1980 revealed only 24 such companies with a 39% market share. Nicol and Hooper (1999) therefore contend that there has been a long-term trend towards increased concentration of housebuilding capital, at least in terms of unit output.

Those companies completing an average of 2000 or more dwellings each year are often termed volume or mass housebuilders. In 2000, there were 14 such companies in comparison with 8 in 1990 and only 4 in 1980. The market share of the top ten builders by unit output, which in 1990 had stood at 26%, rose inexorably throughout the decade and was estimated to have reached 44% by 2001 (Wellings 2001). Although other measures of market share such as turnover or number of employees may also be valid (Monk 1991), unit output has been widely used to assess the growing concentration of capital in the industry. Indeed, as Fig. 5.1 shows, eight of the top ten housebuilders by unit output in 2000 reappear in the top ten rankings by both turnover and profitability for that year (Wellings 2001). Although there may well be important regional or local variations in the extent to which housebuilding is dominated by relatively few companies (Gibb 1999), it is apparent that, at a UK level, the industry is becoming more rather than less concentrated.

	Unit Completions		Turnover		Profits	
	Rank	No	Rank	£ million	Rank	£ million
Wimpey	1	11437	1	1254	2	142.5
Barratt	2	10636	2	1165	1	150.0
Beazer	3	8223	3	841	5	104.0
Persimmon	4	7035	5	742	4	116.0
Bellway	5	5714	6	634	8	95.6
Westbury	6	4435	10	476	13	60.8
Wilcon	7	4215	9	571	9	78.6
Alfred McAlpine	8	4007	11	463	14	53.7
Bryant	9	3961	7	594	7	98.1
David Wilson	10	3604	8	569	6	103.5
Totals		63267		7309		1002.8

Fig. 5.1   Top 10 housebuilders in 2000 (source: Wellings 2001).

The increasing importance of large housebuilding capital was originally noticed by Ball (1983) who showed that builders with an output of over 250 units a year doubled their share of the market from 25% to 50% during the 1970s. He explained the relative growth of larger producers by their ready access to finance capital, often supplied by parent companies. In contrast, small and medium-sized producers were dependent for finance on the banks, which restricted the availability of capital especially during cyclical downturns.

According to Ball (1983) such financial constraints prevented small and medium-sized builders from taking advantage of booms and slumps in the same way as the larger companies which had the ability to acquire land cheaply during periods of slump and, as a result, were well placed to sell houses early in a boom. Indeed, the growth and structure of the British housebuilding industry, from the 1920s period onwards, have been predicated on the ready availability of greenfield land that is both ripe for development and free from costly site constraints. Later in the chapter, we therefore return to the critical importance of land in the residential development process and suggest that brownfield redevelopment demands different acquisition skills from those conventionally learnt in the housebuilding industry.

Of the 20 top housebuilders in 1980 identified by Ball (1983), only 11 remained in the business as separately identifiable companies in 2001. Most have been subsumed as a result of takeovers by or mergers with other housebuilding companies. Figure 5.2 summarises how all but 3 of the top 15 companies of 2000 had expanded their operations through takeovers, or mergers since 1990. One explanation for this process is put forward by Wellings (2000, p. 19):

> The driving force towards consolidation, to the extent that there are sufficient companies prepared to be on the receiving end, remains the desire

Company	Completions in 2000	Main Corporate Events 1990-2001	
Wimpey	11437	1996	Asset swap whereby Wimpey acquired McLean from Tarmac in exchange for Wimpey's construction and mineral division
		2001	Acquisition of Alfred McAlpine for £461m
Barratt	10636		
Beazer	8223	1991	Takeover by Hanson plc
		1994	De-merger from Hanson plc
		1994	Acquisition of John Mowlem Homes for £31m
		1996	Acquisition of Charles Church for £36m
		2001	Takeover by Persimmon for £610m
Persimmon	7035	1996	Acquisition of Ideal Homes for £178m
		1997	Acquisition of Mightover for £6m
		1998	Acquisition of Laing Homes (Scotland) for £18m
		2000	Acquisition of Douglas Tilbury Homes (Scotland) for £19m
		2001	Acquisition of Beazer for £610m
Bellway	5714		
Westbury	4435	1995	Acquisition of Clarke Homes for £61m
		1998	Acquisition of John Maunders for £55m
Wilcon	4215	1995	Acquisition of London and Clydeside for £12.5m
		2001	Acquisition of Wain Homes for £62m
Alfred McAlpine	4007	1997	Acquisition of Raine for £38m
		2001	Takeover by Wimpey for £461m
Bryant	3961	1996	Acquisition of Admiral Homes for £4.2m plus assumption of £58m debt
		2001	Takeover by Taylor Woodrow for £613 m
David Wilson	3604	1996	Acquisition of Trencherwood for £10m
Redrow	3330	1993	Acquisition of Costain Homes for initial £17m
Berkeley	3210	1991	Acquisition of Crosby Homes for £11m
		1991	Purchase of remaining 50% of St George
		1998	Acquisition of Thirlstone Group for £15m
Bovis	2173	1997	De-merger from P&O
Countryside	1919	2000	Sale of Northern Region to Miller Group for £30m
Taylor Woodrow	1844	2001	Acquisition of Bryant for £613m

Fig. 5.2   Recent corporate history of top 15 housebuilders of 2000 (source: Wellings 2001).

of most quoted company managements to produce profits growth and the only way that this can be done in a static market is by increasing market share.

Most of the corporate acquisitions shown in Fig. 5.2 involved the takeover of smaller companies by volume builders. Such purchases offered a simple way to break into new market areas or to expand land holdings by capturing prime sites carefully nurtured by smaller competitors. However, major acquisitions took place in 1996 and 1997 and again in 2001 that involved volume housebuilders alone.

In 1996, Persimmon bought Ideal Homes, previously part of the Trafalgar House Group and one of the longest-established names in British house-building, for £177 million. In the same year, the two largest UK housebuilders, Wimpey and Tarmac/McLean struck a historic asset swap in which Wimpey acquired McLean Homes from Tarmac in exchange for its own construction and minerals division.

Subsequently in 1997, Alfred McAlpine bought Raine Industries, a company that had originally been based in the steel industry but that had expanded significantly into housebuilding, shopfitting and general construction from the mid-1980s, largely as a result of takeovers. In 1995, Raine built almost 1900 private dwellings (under the Hassall Homes brand) and, unusually for a volume builder, a further 1600 units of social housing. However, an overall reduction in housing production of about 900 units in 1996 coupled with difficulties in other parts of the business made Raine Industries ripe for takeover by McAlpine.

An even more significant process of consolidation occurred in 2001. This was sparked by an intended merger between Beazer and Bryant that was overtaken by separate bids for each company. As a result of these, Beazer was acquired by its rival Persimmon for £610 million, while Bryant was taken over by Taylor Woodrow for £613 million. Later than year, Wimpey bought Alfred McAlpine Homes from Alfred McAlpine PLC for £461 million. According to one commentator, this rise of 'super builders' with an annual output of at least 10 000 units was driven by the City's demand for better capitalised and funded housebuilding companies that are not dominated by a single entrepreneur but are able to produce consistent and stable earnings (Simpkins 2001). Indeed, as Peter Johnson, Chief Executive of Wimpey, made clear: 'The City would rather have a small number of strong companies which are more liquid, which they can better understand and which they can more easily compare' (quoted in Simpkins 2001).

Whereas Ball (1983) categorised volume housebuilders as either independent companies, divisions of major building contractors and subsidiaries of large industrial conglomerates, by 2000, all but 2 of the top 15 companies were specialist housebuilders with their own stockmarket quotation. The withdrawal of the conglomerates from housebuilding was demonstrated not only by Persimmon's purchase of Ideal Homes in 1996 but also by the de-merger of Bovis Homes from P&O a year later.

While the impact of the Wimpey/Tarmac deal was to split housebuilding from general contracting in two companies, another major contractor, John

Laing, saw its housebuilding output fall from around 3400 dwellings in 1988 to just under 1200 a decade later. Moreover, during the 1990s, other contractors such as Amec, Costain and Mowlem pulled out of housebuilding completely. More recently, however, Wellings (2000) reported some re-emergence of interest in housebuilding among general contractors. While Taylor Woodrow bought Bryant as a first step in its ambitious plans to expand residential development both at home and abroad, some medium-sized regionally based contractors, such as Kier, Henry Boot and Morrison, significantly expanded their residential output between 1996 and 1999, although to a level still below that of the top 20 UK housebuilders.

Although profitability in the housebuilding industry is highly dependent on the state of both the housing market and development cycle, Gibb *et al.* (1995) have shown that, even in the depth of the early 1990s recession, profit as a proportion of turnover among 20 Scottish housebuilders varied from 0.3% to 26%. During that period, average margins in UK housebuilding fell below 5%, in stark contrast to the record 17.5% reached at the height of the housing boom in 1989 (Wellings 2000). Noticeably, while even Barratt recorded its first ever pre-tax loss in 1991 (of £106 million), at least one specialist inner city builder went into receivership while other larger companies closed down their inner city operations (Adams 1994). This experience made many housebuilders fearful that, in contrast to greenfield development, brownfield redevelopment could be made profitable only in specific locations at the height of the boom. Although it has taken time for this perception to break down, more recent experience suggests there is considerable potential to make profits out of well-chosen brownfield sites. For example, two of three companies with the highest return on capital in British housebuilding in 1999, Fairview and Linden, concentrated almost exclusively on brownfield development.

Overall, while the mid-1990s saw a slow recovery in the fortunes of many housebuilders, the end of the decade witnessed a sharp improvement in both margins and return on capital. In the five-year period from 1996 to 2001, Wellings (2000) estimated a doubling of turnover among 18 quoted housebuilders but a trebling of profits, as a result of the increased turnover combined with house price inflation and a rise in average margins to around 14.5%. Housebuilders had also become adept at turning their capital over more rapidly, so that by 1998, capital turn was above 1.5% compared with a figure of less than 1% in the depths of the recession. However, even in 2000, considerable variation was seen in the recorded margins of the 18 quoted housebuilders, from a high of over 31% for McCarthy & Stone to a low of 10% for Wimpey. Moreover, while Wimpey has seen its UK housing profits rise by 125% to £104 million between 1994 and 1999, during the same period

Berkeley, which had switched its attention almost entirely to urban development, saw a 315% rise in profits to £105 million.

Although the late 1990s were generally prosperous years for the housebuilding industry, significant variation in profitability among companies both
reflects and instils a strong sense of corporate competition, especially as the
fear of losing market share or indeed, of a wider cyclical downturn in the
housing market is omnipresent. Paradoxically, however, such competition
takes place as much within volume housebuilders as between them. Many of
these builders increasingly operate not as single unified companies but rather
as collections of regional offices or subsidiaries (Freeman 2000). Some companies such as Bellway, which has 14 regional offices throughout England and
Scotland, operate these arrangements informally, but others such as Linden,
which has five regional subsidiary companies each with its own corporate
status, treat regionalisation of the company's business as a formal strategy.

Regionalisation in housebuilding helps address the fact that:

> Unlike manufacturing, there are no operational economies of scale: there is
> no housebuilding equivalent of doubling the size of the chemical plant again
> and again and again to drive down costs. In contrast, there are diseconomies
> of scale. Reach 400–500 units and the consensus is that you need to form
> another subsidiary; keep going and you need an additional layer of manage-
> ment to control that which you used to be able to oversee directly.
>
> (Wellings 2000, p. 18)

Nevertheless, in terms of corporate strategy, regionalisation in the housebuilding industry has the distinct advantage of enabling national management separately to identify the financial performance of each region (unit
sales, turnover, margin, return on capital, etc.) and to encourage a strong
sense of internal regional competition within the company. Not only does
underperformance by any one region in comparison with the corporate average become easier to identify, if that underperformance persists, the separate
organisational structure at regional level allows national management to
close down that particular regional office or merge it with another one, in a
reasonably painless manner as far as the company as a whole is concerned.
In the meantime, the threat of such closure or, more positively, the internal
publication of league tables comparing the financial results of each region
and distributing annual bonuses accordingly, keeps everyone on their toes.
Barratt, for example, shut down several regions as a result of its financial
setbacks in the early 1990s. However, in contrast, in early 2000, the company
announced the launch of four new divisions with a strategic emphasis on the

south of England, in order to produce 2000 to 3000 more homes a year over the next few years (Minton 2000).

Corporate regionalisation thus provides housebuilders with the institutional flexibility to respond to the varying pace of change in housing and employment markets at the regional level. More than that, however, it enables companies to connect with greater effectiveness to the devolved political decision-making process that increasingly determines the release of housebuilding land at the regional and local levels. Such important institutional factors mean that successful housebuilders are likely to grow ever more sophisticated in the way they create and deploy regionalisation as an explicit corporate strategy.

In the end, even though the corporate structure of the housebuilding industry has changed markedly over the past 20 years, there are those who argue that, at heart, housebuilding as a production activity has changed little in the past century. Gibb (1999), for instance, suggests that the sector is relatively inefficient in comparison both with other forms of productive enterprise and with its counterparts elsewhere in Europe. This he attributes to the labour-intensive nature of production, the difficulties of site management, the endemic low skills level of the workforce, the fragmentation of design from production, the sequential nature of the production process and the cyclical nature of housing demand and land prices.

Indeed, as a result of the high cost of land relative to the selling prices of completed dwellings coupled with the high historic volatility of real land prices, much greater attention has been accorded in the UK than elsewhere in Europe to the financial gains and losses that potentially arise while land is banked. At certain times, UK housebuilders have thus been able to make substantial inflationary gains on land held freehold in their land banks, although after the housing market slump of the early 1990s, they also had to cope with substantial write-downs in land value. In other European countries, where land has been supplied more cheaply, the housebuilding industry has been obliged to concentrate on productivity gains and cost savings as the basis for enhanced corporate profitability.

In the next section, we therefore turn our attention from this initial overview of the strategies and organisation of the housebuilding industry to the detailed operations of the housing development process. By looking particularly at how that process differs between brownfield and greenfield locations, we aim to provide a more informed basis for subsequent discussion of whether the Government's intention to switch the balance of residential development increasingly to brownfield locations is likely to induce a fundamental restructuring in the nature of British housebuilding.

The speculative housing development process

Most models of the residential development process, at least those that contribute to or draw on the US literature (see, for example, Weiss *et al.* 1966; Kaiser & Weiss 1970), are constructed around the conversion of greenfield land to new housing estates. In such models, housing demand is primarily driven by economic growth and demographic change to the extent that the outward expansion of urban residential areas is seen as both a source and a reflection of a prosperous society. In contrast, models that seek to capture the essentials of brownfield redevelopment are more likely to be policy-led than market-led, even if such policies operate primarily by seeking to influence market decisions, for example, through taxes or subsidies.

Whether residential development takes place on brownfield or greenfield land, a key component of the development process remains that of testing development feasibility. In their classic event-based model of the development process, Barrett *et al.* (1978) identified five tests of development feasibility, namely physical conditions, ownership, public procedures, market conditions and project viability. British housebuilders have traditionally made their money from greenfield sites with relatively easy physical conditions. They often argue that the problematic condition of brownfield sites makes public subsidy necessary to encourage their participation in its redevelopment.

As a result, the three basic skills required to establish development feasibility in housebuilding have traditionally been those firstly of controlling ownership through land acquisition, secondly, of securing planning permission and other public consents, and thirdly, of creating attractive marketing images to pull in customers. Thus, apart from those locations or times of poor housing demand, the viability of speculative residential development and indeed the profitability of British housebuilding as a whole has depended on finding land at the right price, gaining planning permission and marketing the completed product. Over the years, these three basic skills have been honed and sharpened primarily through greenfield experience. In one sense, exactly the same skills are needed for brownfield redevelopment but in another, the very different way in which they need to be applied presents a severe test to those housebuilders whose staff have grown up and built their careers primarily on greenfield projects.

In this section, we therefore look in turn at these three key aspects of the residential development process, explaining why they are so vital to the profitability of the speculative housebuilding industry and identifying the challenges that a policy switch to brownfield land presents to the traditional skill base in speculative housebuilding. Although, for analytical purposes, we separate out land acquisition, planning permission and marketing strategies, we aim to present a linked and integrated discussion since, to the industry at least, these three skills are but three dimensions of the same activity.

Land acquisition

For speculative housebuilders, land is an essential raw material that needs to be controlled well before construction is due to start. At the minimum, sites are normally held in a land bank for a period of 2–3 years prior to the planned commencement of on-site production (Smyth 1984). Land banking can be viewed as a strategic response to uncertainty in housebuilding (Bramley *et al.* 1995) since it not only allows time for pre-development preparations to be completed but, crucially, enables flexibility of response to any planning, demand or other external changes.

According to Ball (1983, p. 148):

> A useful way of conceptualising the nature of a housebuilder's land bank is to treat it as a portfolio of land just as a commercial bank or other financial institution has a portfolio of assets. In both cases, the portfolios consist of a spread of high-yielding but potentially risky assets (in the builder's case these will usually be sites of white land) and safer but less profitable assets that can ensure a steady cash flow and corporate stability. Portfolios also have a temporal profile consisting of assets with different dates of maturity and profit realization. In general, a land bank portfolio spreads risks and takes the pain out of speculation.

Within such a land bank portfolio, most housebuilders normally seek to control land by option or conditional contract until planning permission is certain and only then to complete acquisition of the freehold. As a result, the amount of land held under option or conditional contract within housebuilders' portfolios is generally many times that owned freehold (Adams 1994). Options and conditional contracts enable housebuilders to commit only limited resources to land acquisition before planning permission is secure. However, substantial professional fees may well be incurred in the meantime on hiring lawyers and consultants to negotiate the passage of such land through the protracted process of planning applications, planning appeals and development plan inquiries.

According to Barlow (1999), housebuilders reduced their holdings of land with planning permission during the 1990s, with the mean stocks falling from 4.4 years' supply in 1991 to 3.0 years' supply in 1997[2]. This latter figure was supported by Jones and Leishman (1998) who found that the average land bank maintained by 20 housebuilders in the Glasgow area was 2.8 years. However, as Bramley *et al.* (1995) point out, land banking strategies can vary over the development cycle since well-resourced firms may well seek to make strategic land purchases counter-cyclically in order to benefit most from relatively low prices in a development downturn. Barratt, for example, was reported as having undertaken a spending spree towards the end of 1995, acquiring 15 residential development sites in the South of England with potential for almost 1000 new homes. 'With dipping land values these recent weeks have proved a particularly good time to buy', commented David Pretty, chairman of Barratt Southern (Hazell 1996).

Such advance purchases of potential development sites offer larger housebuilders another significant advantage by allowing them to benefit from any inflationary gains in land value between freehold purchase of the site and the eventual sale of the completed dwellings. Indeed, Barlow (1999, p. 23) claims that: 'From the 1960s to the late 1980s their main business strategy focused on capturing inflationary gains from housing and land markets.' Over the years, such a strategy has been encouraged by the release of substantial greenfield land, especially during periods of high price inflation. However, even at a time of lower general inflation, there are still profits to be made from the practice of land banking in an active housing market. According to Wellings (2000), housebuilders were able to make excess stock profits in the late 1990s mainly because house price inflation had been greater than anticipated. 'Take away the inflation and the stock profit goes. This may take time to materialise as old land still generates healthy profits, but as the more recent land works its way through it is inevitable that trading margins will come under pressure' (Wellings 2000, p. 8).

The practice of land banking has thus helped structure the British housebuilding industry, not only because it has generated an undue reliance on inflationary increases in land value as a source of profitability but also because it advantaged larger housebuilders with the financial muscle to buy counter-cyclically and almost close down the market to potential later entrants. Indeed, as Gibb *et al.* (1995, p. ix) argue in a Scottish context, 'the difficulty of buying land limits competition by restricting entry of new firms to the market.'

The importance of a ready flow of potential development sites into their land banks thus ensures intense competition between housebuilders to acquire suitable land. Most maintain specialist teams of land buyers, precisely for this purpose. They tend to operate in several ways. Local knowledge and informal contacts remain an important first source of information on potential development sites. Some housebuilders also make use of the specialist property press, mostly to respond to notices offering land for sale but some-times to place their own advertisements seeking land with development po-tential. Many will also retain estate agents, especially in pressured areas, to bring sites to their attention. Such agents are expected to know when poten-tial development sites are likely to be marketed, who owns them, when any lease will expire and whether planning permission can be easily obtained. They would normally be rewarded with a fee of approximately 1% of pur-chase price when a site is eventually acquired by the housebuilder. Finally, of course, it is now common practice within the housebuilding industry to monitor new development plans as they emerge and, as we shall soon see, to seek to influence their content during preparation.

Options on potential development land can normally be secured at a fraction of the cost of freehold purchase, and are usually expressed either as a small percentage of estimated development value or as a small absolute sum. Ob-viously, if the option to purchase is never taken up, the landowner retains the original option payment. Bramley *et al.* (1995) suggest that conditional contracts can be more costly to housebuilders, since they typically pay the landowner 10% of market value when the conditional contract is signed, but thereafter benefit from a 10% discount on market value once planning permission is secured. Of course, such a division of gains will differ both in time and location, depending on the state of the housing market and the likelihood of securing planning permission.

Housebuilders' bidding prices for land are formulated as the residual sum in a development appraisal which attempts to forecast likely selling prices at the time when the proposed dwellings are eventually marketed. Here there are two schools of thought. On the one hand, Leishman *et al.* (2000) have constructed a model of residential land prices derived from forecasting fu-ture house prices and construction costs. By testing the model empirically with detailed data from 16 Scottish housing developments, they conclude that in bidding for land, housebuilders tend to make excessive allowance for uncertainty in the development process. They argue that this conservatism means that prices paid for land are approximately 20% lower than if the housebuilders had had perfect foresight.

On the other hand, these findings offer little comfort to hard-pressed house purchasers and ignore the historical experience noted by Ball (1999a) that over-building and optimistic land purchases are prime causes of housebuilding fail-ures. Since the financial appraisal of development projects is in practice such an inexact science whose results can be readily manipulated by minor changes in component assumptions, it is important to recall that, even in a recession, nearly 75% of the housebuilders investigated by Gibb *et al.* (1997) perceived land supply to be a severe problem for the industry. Thus, while it is theoretically conceivable that housebuilders could pay more for land than they do, strong competitive pressures exist within the industry for each developer to maximise their own particular bid for available development sites.

There are four reasons why brownfield land purchase presents the industry with a new challenge to its tried and tested methods of acquisition. First, the very nature of brownfield sites with their history of previous uses often results in abnormal site preparation costs, and makes the task of development appraisal an even more uncertain exercise than usual. Secondly, brownfield landowners are unlikely to be as willing as their greenfield counterparts to grant options or conditional contracts allowing housebuilders lengthy periods of time to bargain with planning authorities. On brownfield sites, housebuilders may thus have to be more willing to take the risk of freehold purchase prior to planning permission or alternatively be more prepared to work within the adopted planning context. Thirdly, if brownfield sites need to be pieced together from a multiple of ownerships, the acquisition process itself can be highly protracted. Finally, for many housebuilders, brownfield land markets remain a relatively unknown arena in which, as Gibb *et al.* (1997) point out, it will be necessary to build up contacts, networks and practices before large-scale entry. It should not therefore be assumed that the housebuilding industry can continue extracting inflationary gains between site purchase and the sale of completed dwellings under a different policy regime.

Fig. 5.3   Delta Building, award-winning brownfield development in East London.

According to Freeman (2000), the price of brownfield sites is already being driven up by their becoming a highly prized counterbalance to greenfield land banks. At a corporate level, Wellings (2000, p. 19) argues that since brownfield sites are often more expensive to purchase and develop, and cannot, unlike major greenfield locations, be readily parcelled out between different builders, 'the capital requirements of urban regeneration will drive the industry further towards larger units and hence consolidation.' Moreover, it may well be that housebuilding companies most likely to take advantage of this policy switch are not the current top ten housebuilders with their different skills in land acquisition and development, but rather the contractor/housebuilder/property hybrids and smaller specialist companies. This suggestion connects with a later theme in the chapter where we consider current housebuilding products and assess how a brownfield emphasis may necessitate significant changes in what much of the industry now offers its consumers.

Planning permission

The importance of the planning policy in structuring residential development has already been discussed in detail in Chapter 4. Here, we wish merely to acknowledge the ways in which the housebuilding industry uses the planning system to its own advantage and to reflect on whether the current structure of the industry is itself a product of the planning system.

Leishman *et al.* (2000) argue that planning policies aggravate market uncertainty over the permissibility and intensity of uses to which land can be put. Certainly, there has been no shortage of critics of the planning system among residential developers. Over 20 years ago, Tom Baron, at the time both one of the UK's leading housebuilders and a special adviser to Michael Heseltine, the Secretary of State for the Environment, described the housebuilding industry as the biggest and least satisfied customer of the planning system. More recently, Steve Morgan, then chairman of the housebuilders Redrow, berated the planning system for its constant delays, lack of effectiveness and failure to provide enough building land (*Planning* 1998b). Yet, according to a more independent source: 'Developers complain about planners like farmers complain about the weather, despite the fact that it is the planning complexities that give many of the companies in this review their competitive edge' (Wellings 2000, p. 10).

Two particular aspects of the relationship between housebuilders and planning authority are worthy of note in relation to the residential development process. First, there is now strong evidence that housebuilders no longer make indiscriminate use of options and conditional contracts, relentlessly pursuing the release of such land by submitting planning applications and appeals. Most housebuilders have long since replaced such an unsophisti-cated approach by one that attempts to use the planning process to their own advantage through influencing policy formulation (Adams *et al.* 1992). This involves targeting options and conditional contracts on land likely to be re-leased in the next round of development plans and using the best professional representation to ensure that it is allocated for housing development sooner rather than later. Moreover, it is not unknown for such companies to argue at local plan inquiries for the early release of their own land in preference to that of their competitors on the basis of good planning reasons.

Farthing (1995) goes further, suggesting that while housebuilders are quite prepared to adopt a coercive strategy towards the local planning authority by seeking to challenge allocations publicly though the local plan arena, it is as likely that earlier negotiations and contacts over a long period of time prove productive to housebuilders' interests by ensuring that their sites are already allocated for development before the first draft of a new development plan reaches the public arena. Whatever the process, and this will vary from area to area, if the unwitting outcome of the planning system is to favour land already owned or controlled by one or two housebuilders in a locality, it may well create a degree of monopoly power in favour of those developers (Adams *et al.* 1992).

This possibility is reinforced by the second aspect of the recent relationship between the housebuilders and the planning system, namely the tendency for planners to concentrate the release of greenfield land into a small number of very large allocations. From the planning authority's point of view, this has the advantage of maximising the potential for infrastructural costs to be borne by the private rather than the public sector, normally on the basis of planning obligations offered, or entered into, by a consortium of builders. However, as Lambert (1990) pointed out, in the Bristol area such a strategy tends to exclude small, local builders from the development market not simply because they may not have the financial resources to contribute to large-scale, off-site infrastructure provision but also because the larger housebuilders are better placed to secure control of major development sites through early and extensive purchase of options from landowners.

As Chapter 3 explained, such concentration of greenfield land release in a small number of large sites rather than a large number of small sites is likely to be increasingly favoured on sustainability grounds. Although major urban extensions, for example, can have significant sustainability advantages over a scattering of disparate housing estates, the scale of capital investment needed for their development is likely to be well beyond the resources of other than the larger housebuilders and may even require a consortium of large housebuilders. As this suggests, urban forms preferred by policy-makers can be an important influence on the institutional structure of the housebuilding industry.

During the 1990s, housebuilders found it increasingly hard to secure the re-lease of major greenfield sites to the extent that by 2000, it became necessary for any proposed development on greenfield land in England of more than 5 hectares or 150 dwellings to be notified by the local planning authority to the Secretary of State before any planning approval was granted. Neverthe-less, despite the policy imperative in favour of residential development on brownfield sites, housebuilders cannot presume that planning permission will be easily obtained for the reuse of urban land for speculative housing. There are two main reasons for this.

In the first place, local planning authorities often desire to maintain a bal-ance of uses within urban areas and can be particularly reluctant to accede to the redevelopment of former industrial land for non-employment uses. On this basis, the Managing Director of Strategic Land Management at Brit-ain's largest housebuilder, Wimpey, was quoted as lambasting the planning system for not enabling the company to build more than 40% of its output on brownfield land. He argued that 'We could do a lot more if the planning system would just get out of the way' (Dewar 2000).

Secondly, as discussed in Chapter 3, very real concern exists in urban com-munities that increased urban housing development reflects a policy of town cramming rather than town planning. As a result, housebuilders can equally well face opposition to their development proposals from local residents and communities on brownfield as on greenfield sites. Moreover, since the task of fitting new development into existing urban areas is more challenging than building on greenfield land, housebuilders may well need to develop fresh skills and approaches to convince planning authorities and local com-munities that their proposed brownfield developments, even if welcome in principle, represent a worthwhile contribution to the quality of urban life rather than a mere translation of the greenfield development model to a brownfield location.

Marketing strategies

Ball (1983) divided the owner-occupied housing market into three sectors – lower, middle and upper – while Nicol and Hooper (1999) suggest that housebuilders wishing to compete across the whole of the new housing markets must maintain at least one standardised type of starter home, middle home and executive home. Housebuilders will give careful thought to the target market sector(s) and proposed product mix, prior to site acquisition. Thereafter, especially for large estates constructed in phases, exact product mix may well be revised during production in response to marketing and sales information on units already completed.

In recent years, housebuilders have tended to move upmarket in pursuit of wider margins. This has been achieved by the increased emphasis of individual housebuilders on more expensive, high-quality products and through corporate acquisitions. As an example of the latter, Alfred McAlpine's higher selling prices and margins was one of the main reasons why it proved an attractive acquisition target for Wimpey in 2001. As the formal statement issued by Wimpey at the time explained:

> McAlpine Homes owns high quality sites in other regions which will enable Wimpey to move more rapidly into higher price and higher margin business. This is demonstrated by the higher achieved average selling price of McAlpine Homes, which, at £145,000 in the first half of 2001 (excluding Cumbria), was more than 20 per cent higher than that achieved by Wimpey.
>
> (George Wimpey PLC 2001)

Marketing strategies are designed to produce a regular flow of sales since 'failure to achieve required rate of sales can lead to a significant erosion of profit' (Leishman *et al.* 2000, p. 163). Obviously, the number of sales required on a weekly basis will vary according to the size of the development, but for other than small housing schemes, housebuilders will generally become concerned about cash flow if average sales fall below at least one unit per week. Unlike commercial and industrial developers, the speculative nature of residential development in the UK means that housebuilders do not normally rely on any level of pre-sales before commencing construction. Instead, they set out their pitch in the form of a show house or show flat at the very start of a development project and combine this with extensive advertising and promotion in order to lure potential customers.

To achieve this, marketing images have always played a very important role in British housebuilding (see Fig. 5.4). What is marketed to the purchaser is not so much bricks and mortar but rather a whole new lifestyle that implies upward mobility in both family prospects and social interaction. A journalist, who in the late 1990s visited a major housing development in

Fig. 5.4   Marketing brochure for North Country Homes.

Hertfordshire and collected the company's brochures, neatly captured such images. The brochures:

> stuck to the dream of the gleaming family living in perfect harmony in their 'unique' and 'traditional' home, set among green fields and birdsong … The hunky blond husband in New Labour weekend gear tosses his blonde pony-tailed daughter, who sports pastel-coloured leisurewear into the squeaky-clean air as a sparkling blonde wife lays a manicured hand lightly on his manly shoulder and grins with confidence. Here's dad again, this time walking along a spotless path, carrying one golden child on one arm, one on another and a third on his broad shoulders. Not a splash of mud on the children's dungarees, much less a tear or pout on their angelic faces.
>
> (Glancey 1997)

While such images can be readily caricatured in an almost comical way, the reason they have such powerful resonance within the British psyche is that they readily connect with a long-standing desire to escape the city and live in the countryside. According to a Countryside Commission survey undertaken in England in 1997, 51% of inner-city residents and 43% of those living in city suburbs would prefer to live in a village or in the countryside. The main appeal of such rural locations was seen as the greenery of the countryside, the traditional nature of the buildings and the pattern of social relationships (Champion 2000).

In this sense, then, housebuilders are highly skilled in the marketing images they portray for their greenfield development sites since they connect very effectively with much of the detailed research on urban decentralisation. The extent to which images of the 'mythical golden family' located on the 'estate fit for a fantasy of traditional living' (Glancey 1997) merely reflect or actually promote such decentralisation is, of course, a matter for some debate. Nevertheless, it is quite apparent that the marketing strategies of British housebuilders have evolved and matured over the years in order primarily to sell greenfield housing estates.

Quite different approaches and quite different images will be needed for brownfield locations set in the midst of urban complexity. The challenge that some housebuilders, such as Berkeley and Bellway, have begun to take up is not simply to transfer greenfield images to brownfield locations, but rather to realise that entirely new marketing skills and concepts will be required, which fully appreciate that the nature of both the clientele and the purchase have changed significantly. On this point, we move on to the form of speculative housing products since, while they may encapsulate greenfield marketing images, they are again not readily transferred to brownfield locations.

Speculative housing products

Standardisation of product is an essential feature of speculative housebuilding in the UK in the sense that most builders have devised and use standard house types. Such products contrast with customised one-off designs for specific sites, since they are reproduced in a repetitive unmodified way in a range of different locations (Nicol & Hooper 1999). In this section, we first investigate how and why the industry relies on standard house types, secondly consider the implications of standardisation for residential design more generally and finally evaluate the capacity of the industry to innovate and radically alter its product range in future.

Standard house types

Within the industry, standard house types are defined by their 'footprint', which enables different facades to be bolted on to a standard structural design (Nicol & Hooper 1999). Although standardisation of house types is widely employed throughout the British housebuilding industry, their use becomes more prevalent the greater the number of dwellings produced by a particular company. Hooper and Nicol (1999), for example, reported that 100% of those firms questioned producing more than 2000 units per annum employed standard house types, in contrast to 69% of those producing 501 to 2000 units per annum. Although the largest firms offered the widest range of house types, Hooper and Nicol (1999, p. 796) found that 'Irrespective of firm size, however, the utilisation of standard house types is a central characteristic of private-sector housing production.'

Hooper and Nicol's detailed interviews with 14 large housebuilders each producing at least 1000 units per annum revealed that three companies employed 20–30 standard house types, five companies 30–40 types, another five 50–70 types, while one company used over 100 types. Companies were thus able to vary the standard product mix offered at each site according to the particular target audience. Some house types such as bungalows may be retained within the production portfolio, even if they are used only occasionally. Indeed, according to Hooper and Nicol (1999), several companies identified a core of standard types they used most frequently. For example, one of the companies that had over 50 different products relied on only 12 of them for most of its turnover.

Most housebuilders allow purchasers a choice of internal fittings even within a standard type and a significant minority, according to Hooper and Nicol (1999), are prepared to make some alteration to room layouts in response to a purchaser's wishes. However, less than a quarter of the builders questioned were prepared to make any alteration to the façade or structure of a standard house to meet individual requests. In another study, Barlow (1999) found that some firms, which regarded themselves as mass builders, remained resolutely antagonistic towards greater customer input into production decisions. Others, however, had been forced to take a more flexible line as a result of the recession in the early 1990s. Most firms, according to Barlow (1999), had attempted to overcome lack of direct customer input by maintaining a wide range of standard house types, by rationalising their portfolios of standard design and particularly, by seeking to increase the frequency of redesign. By this process, standard house types gradually evolve over time, with the emphasis upon incremental changes rather than radical overhaul (Leopold & Bishop 1983).

The widespread use of standard house types in speculative residential development reflects the intense pressures within the industry to maintain profitability by cost minimisation and price competition (Hooper & Nicol 1999). Standard house types facilitate construction by a low-skilled workforce, enable central purchasing of components and limit design costs both directly and through blanket building control approval. Moreover, by using tried and tested products, housebuilders are able to reduce risks by more accurate cost forecasting when they bid for land and by reliance on designs known to have sold well in the past. Indeed, Ball (1999a) argues that house purchasers are notoriously conservative in their tastes in house styles since they worry over the future resale value of their property. He suggests that this conformity is reinforcing to the extent that it deters builders from more innovative or exciting house designs.

Residential design

Most house purchasers are primarily concerned that their investment will at least maintain its value until they wish to sell (which may well be sooner rather than later) and are driven by cost, value for money, functionality and size of the property, and only then by intrinsic design (Carmona 1999a). This helps explain why housebuilders are interested in better design only if it produces higher sales, wins planning approval more speedily or contributes to marketing strategies. In design terms, the main incentive of housebuilders is therefore to improve the 'kerb appeal' of their products (Goodchild & Karn 1997) by attaching mock features to façades in order to give the pretence of individuality, improving internal amenities and facilities, and developing detached and semi-detached houses rather than terraces and flats.

Nevertheless, a recent attitude survey revealed widely held negative perceptions of the products of speculative housebuilding among potential customers and non-customers alike (Popular Housing Forum 1998). New homes were generally considered cramped, boxy and lacking in individuality, and were generally associated with the bottom end of the housing market. Even those most likely to purchase new houses from builders had generally unfavourable impressions of their appearance and layout. Detached houses, for example, were felt to be too close together and were not always designed to allow people to walk comfortably between them. According to the survey, most people wanted to live in a safe, green and village-like environment that was quiet and peaceful. Suburban development was preferred, provided it was designed to fit into an already-established location and was not built at too high a density. New homes should be suitable for family and parking, while communal facilities such as parks and shops needed to be planned and provided alongside the housing.

Such surveys suggest that, while housebuilders' marketing images may connect very well with the broader desires of the house-buying public, a serious implementation gap exists between the image with which the consumer is presented at the sales house and the reality of life on a new greenfield housing estate. In this context, Bartlett (1997) argues that most consumers have more confidence in the second-hand market than in new housing and remain unenthusiastic about the actual products of the housebuilding industry. The challenge for the industry, he suggests, is to devise an imaginative product range that attracts consumers as much as new cars.

Over the years, the industry's reliance on 'a factory style box-building approach' (Fulford 1996, p. 128) and its disdain for 'any dedicated architectural input … because of the product-orientated nature of the volume house-building sector' (Carmona 1999b, p. 408) have arguably produced too many developments that 'do not bear any relationship to their regional context (and) could have been built anywhere, having no sense of place' (Scottish Office Environment Department 1994, p. 9). As Nick Raynsford, then Minister for Housing and Planning, contended: 'Good design is the key to creating places where people can live, work and relax. We need to avoid the predictable soulless estates that have been built in the recent past' (*Planning* 2000a, p. 3). Traditionally, however, the builder's product has been the individual house and only to a much less extent, the context it defines (Carmona 1999a).

According to the DOE (1996a), public disenchantment with the products of the speculative housebuilding industry and in particular with ugly development that make places seem just like everywhere else, is an important component behind the growing public resistance to greenfield encroachment. As a result, recent planning guidance for England emphasises the importance of urban design, local distinctiveness and public sector intervention in the cause of better design (Carmona 1999b). Indeed, the Minister subsequently threatened housebuilders with greater difficulty in securing planning permission unless they were willing to invest in higher-quality design (DETR 2000d). Such controversies over product design in speculative housebuilding raise important questions for the industry about its wider capacity for product innovation.

Innovation in speculative housebuilding

In a classic cartoon, Hellman (1995) portrays the products of the speculative housebuilding industry as having stood still for a hundred years, while all around, remarkable innovation has taken place in other consumer products. According to Ball (1999a, p. 9) 'British housebuilding has an exceptionally poor record of innovation in designs and production methods', while Barlow (1999, p. 23) too chides the industry as 'notoriously slow to innovate'. Empirical evidence of housebuilding in practice tends to support such claims. For example, Gibb *et al.* (1995), in their study of Scottish housebuilders, found that the majority questioned could not identify a single technical innovation in the previous five years. Another survey of over 100 firms involved in the UK industry found that less than 10% were developing new designs or trying out new technologies (Barlow & Bhatti 1997).

Ball (1999a) argues that housebuilders face particular market constraints on innovation in both their output and input markets. Planning policies towards new housebuilding, for example, have evolved incrementally and without concern for best practice. The conservatism of consumers on design is reflected in the reluctance of lenders to lend on non-traditional forms of construction, while the uncertainty induced by cycles in the housing market persuades builders to organise in ways that maximise flexibility. These include widespread subcontracting, traditional building techniques and low amounts of fixed capital on building sites. Such structural constraints encourage firms to adopt low-cost strategies (apart from land acquisition) that require minimum sophistication and forecasting ability, while discouraging innovation.

Barlow (1999) suggests that the external environmental for housebuilding is now changing as a result of tighter controls over energy efficiency and land release, as well as probable increased shortages in skilled labour. The short-term challenge for housebuilding, he maintains, will be to lower its construction costs while improving the quality and functionality of its products. In the longer term, the industry will need to broaden its appeal to consumers by creating attractive new products rather than merely redesigning existing house types. In this context, the Construction Task Force (1998) highlighted the role of well-informed, demanding clients at the design stage as an essential prerequisite to the creation of a modern, efficient and world-class housebuilding industry in the UK. On this basis, it is contended that the social housing sector offered much greater potential for improvement and innovation since only a few major clients were responsible for the majority of development commissioned.

Unfortunately, memories of construction failures such as those associated with systems building in the 1960s and 1970s and with certain types of timber-framed housing in the early 1980s reinforce the reluctance of housebuilders to innovate (Barlow & Bhatti 1997). Indeed, most firms are unwilling to take on the role of technical pioneers for the industry, preferring instead to free-ride as someone else bears the cost of ironing out any snags. Overall, then, the housebuilding industry 'seems to have particular difficulties in improving building design and quality; in responding to consumer needs; in reducing the long-term rise in real construction costs; and in moving beyond the traditional two-storey, pitched roof structure to new forms that appeal to particular market segments' (Ball 1999a, p. 9).

Although the British housebuilding industry has developed its reputation around the delivery of standardised products for standardised greenfield locations, it is clear that brownfield development is more likely to require individually tailored products for specific locations. This is both because brownfield sites themselves are likely to be more problematic, requiring layouts that take account of particular site conditions, and because successful brownfield development needs to be carefully woven into the existing urban fabric. It is therefore pertinent now to examine the likely capacity of the speculative housebuilding industry to adapt to the new policy agenda.

Brownfield development – the challenge for housebuilders

According to Black (1997), the housebuilding industry has been characterised by its commitment to a manufacturing rather than a design process, its minimal interest in the public realm, its disdain for urban design and local consultation and its build and walk away trading ethos. In one sense, this is indeed a harsh judgement on an industry that has made a significant contribution to the growth of home ownership and economic prosperity over several decades. In another sense, however, it summarises all the worst features of the greenfield housing on which the industry has built both its fortunes and its reputation.

Now that the concept of sustainable development has become so well enshrined in political philosophy, it is implicit that time has been called on the manner in which the speculative housebuilding industry has traditionally earned its living. In this section, we look first at what this means for brownfield redevelopment. We then examine how the industry is already beginning to restructure and reorientate its strategies and practices to match this policy switch, while questioning whether all housebuilders are equally capable of making such an adjustment.

If speculative developers are to make a significant contribution to brownfield redevelopment, it is apparent that new skills and strategies will be required. The problematic nature of many brownfield locations means that developers will need to deliver value added directly from housing products rather than rely on gaining profits from inflation in land prices. Moreover,

Fig. 5.5 Crossland House, Virginia Park, Surrey: new apartments built in Gothic style to complement adjacent restored Grade 1 listed building.

standardised solutions are unlikely to suffice, not only because brownfield sites will require careful individual design, but also because the milieu of potential urban purchasers, with their social and economic diversity, is unlikely to be satisfied with a narrow and inflexible product range.

Housebuilders will therefore need to develop greater skills in integrating with and supporting local communities rather than in merely constructing housing estates. Much higher standards of urban design are likely to be required, not simply to secure planning approval but also to cope with the tricky task of resolving potential conflicts within mixed-use schemes. To achieve all of this, partnership with planning authorities and with local communities is likely to become the norm rather than the exception. Indeed, as Gibb *et al.* (1995) note, the public sector is likely to play an increasingly important co-ordinating role at both greenfield and brownfield locations.

In many ways, such requirements appear a tall order for an industry whose mode of operations has been so distinctively different until relatively recently. However, if either housebuilders or planning authorities consider that the Government's brownfield aspirations can be achieved merely by taking existing greenfield housing estates and planting them, lock, stock and barrel, in brownfield locations, then, in due course, the intended policy switch will break down in a failure of implementation. It is therefore pertinent to consider how far the speculative housebuilding industry has yet moved in the direction of a brownfield emphasis.

In an early survey Fulford (1998) found that the 39 housebuilders he questioned were divided into three main categories: 18 mainly greenfield, 9 mainly urban and 9 mixed. In output terms, 60% of the units constructed by the housebuilders questioned were described as greenfield and 40% as urban. Although the companies as a whole were generally positive about the need for sustainable patterns of urban development, they expressed concern about constraints upon their ability to deliver brownfield schemes, such as land contamination, restrictive planning policies and difficulties in creating successful mixed-use development. In the end, however, they contended that the prospect of further brownfield projects would depend on the relationship between the costs of development and the strength of demand.

According to Wellings (2000), the contractor/housebuilder/property hybrids such as Taylor Woodrow and Miller are arguably better suited to brownfield sites than some greenfield volume builders. Indeed, only 3 of the 14 volume builders in business in 2000 (Barratt, Bellway and Berkeley) could be considered to be at the forefront of urban residential development. Of these, perhaps the most interesting is Berkeley, which has transformed itself from a greenfield developer to one whose production is 90% on brownfield sites. Its previous approach reflected the land-dealing tactics of most volume builders for, as Stewart (1995, p. 33) reported, it originally became 'a favourite of analysts for having bought land cheaply before the last boom, sold at the top of the market and then bought again in the early 1990s – just before the values started shooting up again.' However, by the late 1990s, it had established itself 'at the forefront of post recession urban regeneration' (Wellings 2000, p. 53), having become a leading player in both London and provincial city centre schemes. To those who consider urban redevelopment unprofitable, it should be noted that, in 2000, Berkeley achieved a 23% return on capital employed, while seeing its pre-tax profits rise by 20%. Over the period 1994 to 2000, its asset value per share was the second best among all 18 leading quoted housebuilders.

Several other housebuilders that have begun to take brownfield development seriously, such as Crest Nicholson and Fairview, appear in the top 25 builders by unit output in 2000. Crest Nicholson builds across Southern England and the Midlands, but its activities are concentrated in the Home Counties and around Bristol. It acquired five flagship urban regeneration sites in late 1998, during a lull in the land market, and expects to see these developments come to fruition between 2000 and 2002 and to have an end sales value of more than £500 million. Fairview, which expanded its output from 620 units in 1989 to over 2000 in the mid-1990s, concentrates on low-to medium-cost housing within the Greater London area. It has consistently achieved above average margins (above 30% in 1999) through selective brownfield acquisitions in an active housing market. According to Stewart (1995, p. 33) its strategy involves 'Buying cheap land in derelict inner-city areas and targeting almost cash-strapped first-time buyers'.

Further down the list of housebuilders by unit output in 2000, Linden Homes, at number 32, was specially founded by Philip Davies, its Chief Executive in 1991 as 'he had grown sick of standard house types' and instead wished to concentrate on individually designed units within mixed-use schemes (Forrester 1999). The company now produces over 750 units per annum and returned pre-tax profits of over £15 million in 2000. At its flagship Caterham Barracks site in Surrey, Linden has converted 61 dwellings left vacant by the Army and built a further 287 new homes, both private and social, alongside business and retail space and a 60-bed nursing home. Facilities will include a school, community centre, doctor's surgery, temporary church, gymnasium and cricket pitch, while the developer has also promoted a new bus service to the local train station. Interestingly, the development proposals for this 22-hectare brownfield site emerged out of a community-planning weekend organised by a well-known architectural practice with particular expertise in 'Planning for Real' exercises.

As Wellings (2000) points out, some quite small companies such as Try Homes and County & Metropolitan have also played an important role in pioneering brownfield schemes. It may well be that most volume builders are waiting for such smaller fish to gain experience from their own mistakes, before seeking to swallow them up and benefit from their experience. Alternatively, however, unless most volume builders seriously begin to adapt themselves to the new policy environment, they run the risk of finding themselves sidelined in an emerging business and increasingly marginalised as market leaders.

In the late 1990s, for example, Bryant had to make provision for a £4 million write-down in its accounts against carrying greenfield land options, knowing that sites that may have previously been thought likely to obtain residential permission will not now be released for development. Wellings (2000) suggests that this reflects general uncertainty among leading housebuilders over the implications of revised planning policy for the value of their land banks. However, there are already positive indications elsewhere that the industry is beginning to respond to the new policy agenda. For instance, in April 2000, Wilcon announced that it would undertake a sustainability test on all its potential developments to assess whether, for example, they were well served by public transport and amenities and would provide for a broader social mix. Developments failing the test would be either amended or scrapped (Baker 2000).

As this section has indicated, there are already hopeful but small signs that the housebuilding industry is beginning to adapt to the demands for more sustainable forms of development, including the reuse of brownfield sites. Examples have shown that housebuilders who concentrate on brownfield development can succeed within a highly competitive industry, if sites are carefully chosen and development takes place in an active housing market. However, since most of the examples are drawn from London or the centre of major provincial cities, they are not necessarily representative of the fortunes of brownfield development through the UK as a whole. In this context, doubt must still remain as to whether and how quickly the industry as a whole, and in particular most of the volume housebuilders, can alter their attitudes and behaviour to accord with the new policy agenda.

Indeed, it may be that not all today's leading housebuilders have the institutional capacity to replace their traditional emphasis on greenfield land dealing, planning battles and marketing strategies with the new strategies and skills required for successful brownfield development. However, since the new discourse on sustainable development is not confined to brownfield locations, but will increasingly impinge on the form and design of any remaining greenfield development, the challenge for the industry as a whole is whether and how fast it can adapt to changed political priorities to prevent subsequent major restructuring.

Conclusions

This chapter has demonstrated how the provision of speculative housing for sale in the UK has become increasingly dominated by a small number of very large companies that have built their experience and reputation on a particular mode of production that is now threatened by an emerging policy agenda. The Government's determination to switch the balance of new residential development from greenfield to brownfield locations is, however, but one component of the changing institutional context for speculative housebuilding. In an increasingly affluent age, for example, consumers are likely to require better-quality designs and environments from housebuilders and seek higher standards of customer service. Again, demographic changes coupled with competition and diversification within the financial services sector mean that housebuilders now operate in a very different institutional context for housing demand from that of 20 years ago.

From a historical perspective, the significant changes reported in this chapter in the composition of the industry over those 20 years would indicate that the structure of housebuilding is unlikely to stand still, even in the immediate future. In this context, it is pertinent to ask whether many of the leading housebuilders at the beginning of the twenty-first century will be able to survive and adapt to the new policy agenda or if, with some notable exceptions, they will fall victim to takeover by an emerging generation of more innovative companies. For, whether by stimulating innovation among currently dominant producers or by encouraging corporate reorganisation, it is likely that the successful implementation of the intended policy switch in favour of brownfield sites will both demand and encourage the emergence of a new structure of provision in speculative housebuilding.

Notes

(1) Much of the factual information in this section is drawn from the Private Housebuilding Annual, written each year by Fred Wellings and published by Credit Lyonnais Securities Europe. The authors are grateful to be able to draw on this source of information and appreciate the further assistance of Mr Wellings in commenting on the draft chapter. He is, of course, entirely absolved from any responsibility for the views and comments expressed in the chapter.

(2) It should be noted that there can be wide variation in size between the land banks of different companies and that no consistent method exists for the definition or measurement of land banks within company reports. Industry-wide averages therefore need to be treated with some caution.

6

The Politics of Planning and Housing Development

Controversy so often surrounds new housing development, especially where it involves encroachment on to greenfield land. As a result, debate is often highly politicised and conducted using emotive language. The CPRE, for instance, has invoked images of 'concreting over' the countryside, while critics of intervention have deployed the term 'planning rape' in retaliation (McFarquhar 1999). The complex issues associated with the location of, and need for, new housing development are presented by the media in terms of stark choices – which is more important (a) new homes or (b) 1000 hectares of green belt? (Harrison & Wintour 1998).

As Grayson (2000, p. 56) notes

> the building industry is often cast as the villain of the piece in the public debate about urban sprawl, deliberately choosing to plough up greenfield sites for up-market 'executive' homes because these generate the highest profits. It is accused of environmental sins by those who favour a much higher use of recycled brownfield land in urban areas, and of social sins by those who believe it is indifferent to issues of affordability and social housing need.

This strongly negative perception of the market is countered elsewhere, when commentators turn on the insidious effects of the state or, more precisely, of local planning authorities. Abbott (1999), for instance, expresses deep despair at the extent to which green belt controls, low housing output targets in plans, development taxes and other policy constraints prevent the housebuilding industry from pursuing its business and economic goals.

In this politicised context, this chapter seeks to address the following research questions:

- What are the ideological and party political influences on planning?

- What is the basis for political power struggles surrounding housing development and housing land allocations?

- Who are the main stakeholders with an interest in political decisions?

- How are political decisions on housing development and land allocations made in practice? Who appears to win and lose in the process?

- How does this compare with theoretical explanations of the distribution of power and the decision-making process?

The first part of the chapter seeks to explore the intellectual and theoretical bases for conflict over new housing development and planning intervention. It begins by considering ideological views on the role of the state versus the market. The chapter explores the private property rights arguments for the creation of a market-based mechanism for allocating development rights. The analysis shows that, despite the rhetoric about the strong market orientation of public policy, these arguments fail to capture significant support within any of the major political parties. Instead, there has been a relatively high degree of policy continuity between successive Conservative and Labour governments and changes to the system have been far less radical than those proposed. Indeed, conflict surrounding planning and housing development, rather being party political, is best understood by examining stakeholder interests and the nature of their involvement at local and national level.

The second part of the chapter focuses on these stakeholders. It considers the key groups involved in influencing planning decisions and summarises the basis for their involvement, their policy preferences and degree of influence. We argue that the interaction among stakeholders ensures that planning decisions are essentially political in nature and that outcomes are determined by negotiative practices, rather than purely by technical analysis.

A number of theoretical explanations of planning decisions and influence are examined in the third part of the chapter. This review first considers public choice explanations of interest group involvement in the policy process. This explanation is then contrasted with other views, including Marxist and corporatist theories, to identify who asserts most influence on political decisions. In the fourth section, we examine evidence of how decisions have been made in practice, which, in turn, provides some insight into the winners and losers from the process. The concluding part of the chapter highlights some of the unresolved debates within which the greenfield and brownfield debate is played out.

Ideological perspectives and party politics

By the 1950s it was possible to talk of the postwar consensus in British politics (Kavanagh 1997). The two major parties alternated in power with a large measure of policy continuity from one administration to the next. Up to the mid-1960s, Labour and Conservative shadowed each other as they moved to the right and left of the political spectrum. As far as the provision of new housing is concerned, there was general agreement that high levels of construction were required to eliminate housing shortages, replace slums and keep pace with household growth (Malpass & Murie 1999). As Whitehead (1997) explains, until the late 1960s, successive administrations were simply engaged in the 'numbers game' of who could deliver the highest annual level of housebuilding.

In the 1970s, however, the postwar political consensus broke down. Kavanagh (1997) highlights the loss of support for key political actors including those prominent in Labour's right wing and the progressive Conservative 'One Nation' group. This coincided with a period during which arguments about housing provision became more sophisticated at the political level. The debate moved on from a crude numbers game, and began to consider what type of housing should be produced, and where it ought to be located (Whitehead 1997).

Towards the end of this period, with Michael Foot and Margaret Thatcher heading Labour and the Conservatives respectively, both parties had their most left-wing and right-wing leaders since the war. This had important ramifications for debates about the role and nature of state involvement in the provision of new housing. While in keeping with tradition, the Left continued to support state provision of public services, the New Right embarked on a programme of 'rolling back' the frontiers of the state through privatisation.

When the Conservatives returned to power in 1979, there was a significant crude surplus of homes over households and a growing belief that what really mattered was the ability of the private sector to respond to demand (Whitehead 1997). This had implications for the institutional structures involved in housing provision. In the early 1980s, a number of specific criticisms were levelled at the planning system. These focused, *inter alia*, on the financial costs of delays imposed on developers, the standardisation of development type and design, and the high administrative costs of the system. With this in mind, the Thatcher Government brought about a number of important changes to the system. These changes were driven by a general desire to extend the political and economic ideas of the New Right to a range of public policy arenas (Jordan & Ashcroft 1993).

The economic strand of New Right thinking, which was influenced by the public choice (or 'economics of politics') school and the Austrian economist, Hayek, provided the basis for a critical analysis of participatory democracy. This critique asserted that democratic decision-making was not necessarily the same as efficient decision-making. This argument provided the rationale for reducing the scope for collective decision-making by limiting local government and/or by replacing or 'commodifying' state activities. A related critique from the 'economics of bureaucracy' literature argues that bureaucrats act in their own self-interest, in pursuit of empire building or budget maximisation (Niskanen 1971). Since they use the control of information in their relationship with elected politicians to emphasise their own role and significance, this leads to excessive bureaucratisation. Such analysis lends further support to the perceived need to privatise state functions as a means of providing more efficient management and delivery of public services.

Together, these separate strands of economic analysis provide the intellectual basis for the Conservatives' sustained attack on the state, or more precisely, on 'state failure' (Bramley & Lambert 1998). This analysis was buttressed by the deployment of Hayekian ideas. These provided an alternative to arguments based in welfare economics that planning was an essential response to 'market failure'. Hayek's ideas, in essence, suggest that successful planning intervention is ultimately inoperable because of the inability to collate or process the information required to make fully informed, effective planning decisions.

The political basis for New Right ideology is centred on a neo-liberal emphasis on individual freedom within the free market and a neo-conservative (or social authoritarian) desire for discipline and social order (Allmendinger & Thomas 1998). The aggregate effect of these economic and political ideas meant that, from a New Right perspective, the planning system was ripe for reform. Although originally designed to guide development to acceptable locations, planning was now characterised as imposing a restriction on development across the board (Evans 1988). Critics highlighted the significant costs imposed on the economy, through higher house prices, crowded urban areas and reduced quality of urban life, which resulted from unintended and unrecognised impacts of the system.

In these economic and political terms, the Thatcher Government made a strong case for a less bureaucratic and more market-orientated system. As such, the primacy of the market over the planning system began to be asserted in the 1980s through 'project-based' approaches to planning and development, including Urban Development Corporations (UDCs), Enterprise Zones (EZs) and Simplified Planning Zones (SPZs) (Thornley 1996; see also Chapter 2). Other features of the reforms included a reduction of unnecessary planning regulation, and the removal or reduction of the role of local government decision-making and implementation in the planning system (Bramley & Lambert 1998). In parallel with these changes, housing policy became dominated by a range of initiatives designed to promote private housing provision over state provision, increased home ownership and deregulation of the rented sector (Whitehead 1993).

These ideas appear to have helped shape a new consensus in British politics. There seems to have been some policy continuity between the Major and Blair Administrations and the New Right appears to have left its imprint on New Labour. In this respect, some commentators claim that the success of Thatcherism as an economic and political project is most clearly demonstrated by the transformation of the Labour Party into New Labour. Specifically they highlight Labour's ideological realignment towards a neo-liberal socio-economic programme and away from its social-democratic tradition (Heferman 2001). At a general level, Ellison and Pierson (1998) outline changes in New Labour's values and note that the normative position held by the Labour Party displays a more individualistic interpretation of social justice than would normally be associated with centre left parties.

Nevertheless, there are distinctive features of the New Labour project. Notions of 'social cohesion' and 'social inclusion' form part of a conception of 'citizenship', which is perceived as a mix of individual rights and duties. Yet, this approach to social justice sits more comfortably with the acceptance of a central role for the market as a means of allocating resources. This is also consistent with the use of notions of economic efficiency and social equity as a framework for the evaluation of public service provision in the influential quasi-markets literature (Le Grand & Bartlett 1993).

This new consensus might have important implications for the direction of British planning. Allmendinger (Allmendinger *et al.* 2002), for example, argues that planning could have an important role in meeting the Government's wider objectives and, in particular, dealing with the spatial dimensions of urban regeneration and social justice issues. To date, however, devolution aside, such radical change has not emerged. Rather, in the context of planning for the housing market, Jones and Watkins (1999) highlight the extent to which the market orientation and commodification of the system has continued largely unchecked. It seems that, over the past three governments, despite differences in emphasis and approach, the changes to the planning system have all sought to achieve the same broad goals. These have been, *inter alia*, the removal of supply-side constraints from the development process and the promotion of economic development. Although the impact of these changes has been mixed, one clear manifestation of the concerted effort to alter planning is that planners and planning are now much more market-sensitive while the market-supportive role of planning is now hegemonic.

Housing development and party politics

Arguably, there is currently little difference in ideological terms between the successive New Right and New Left administrations. While election manifestos and ministerial statements do not always reflect the substance of policies implemented by parties in power, they provide some insights into the general stance adopted by each party, their social and political beliefs and, by extension, the policy options that they are likely to favour. In this sense, the normative position of parties, the values and principles that shape their attitudes to housing policy and the housing land debate can shed some light on the sort of specific policy measures and instruments that may be favoured by each party.

In their manifestos for the 2001 General Election the two major parties express strong support for setting targets of 60% of new housebuilding on derelict and under-used urban land, in order to ease pressure on greenfield sites. Other than this, Labour's only mention of the planning system can be found in reference to a commitment to the establishment of regional chambers with responsibility for, *inter alia*, co-ordinating planning. This, of course, continues to be supported in the Government's recent Green Paper (DTLR 2001b).

The Conservative Party made rather more of issues surrounding new housing development. In the course of William Hague's 'common-sense revolution', the party attempted to extract political capital from Labour's difficulties over the scale and location of new housing provision, and in particular, the local, community-based opposition to planning proposals in former Tory seats. Although Conservative politicians regarded their proposed regulation of new housing development as a vote-winner in their former heartlands, such potential electoral advantage conflicts with the party's ideological suspicion of state intervention in commercial and business activities. In the summer of 2000, Archie Norman, then shadow Environment Secretary, dubbed Labour 'the enemies of the countryside' and announced his party's intention to strengthen the role of local communities in the planning system (Dewar 2000). However, this statement brought dissent from within the party, with former Environment Secretary, John Gummer, highlighting the difficulties that this 'right to be NIMBYist' might cause to the necessary development of housing and commerce.

The Liberal Democrats' position has been less ambiguous, with their 2001 manifesto making a strong commitment to reforming the planning system. Their 'Strategy for Sustainability' set out a desire to give more prominence to protection of the natural environment (Liberal Democrats 2000). In this area, they went further than the Conservative and Labour parties and set an interim overall target of 75% of all development on brownfield sites, to be applied as nationally but with some local flexibility.

The broad ideological and party political consensus in favour of brownfield development at national level, however, masks the extent to which the development control and new housing development have become a highly contested and highly politicised battleground at local level. At that level at least, it seems that self-interest has replaced ideological principle as the central basis for debates about development. These disputes, however, are often legitimised by drawing on wider social or environmental concerns and by mobilising national support for local action.

As Bramley (1998a) notes, local concerns cut across party political interests. This is not a new phenomenon. In the 1980s, resistance to Michael Heseltine's attempts to facilitate large-scale development in green belt areas through the reduction of planning constraints came under fire from Conservative councils and MPs in the suburbs and shires. The precedent this set has been followed more recently in 'labour versus labour versus labour' battles over the countryside. In debating plans to allow 10 000 new homes on green belt land west of Stevenage, David Kearns, Leader of the Labour-controlled West Hertfordshire District Council, is quoted as saying 'the Government claims to be committed to protecting the environment and regenerating urban areas and we have them supporting plans to rape 2,000 acres of green belt' (Harrison & Wintour 1998, p. 21).

As Bramley (1998a) points out, the pronounced geographical skew of the issue, which has clear association with 'middle England', is rather more important politically than the old ideological debates. This is echoed in the press where, for example, Hetherington and May (1998, p. 15) use the banner headline 'middle England's mad, bad dream in bricks and mortar' to launch a story about the housing numbers debate. The story highlights the passionate debate surrounding this issue in the middle England constituencies, which were critical to Tony Blair's victory in the 1997 General Election and remained with Labour in 2001.

Property rights arguments

Although the preceding analysis suggests that there has been little substantive difference in the policies of successive governments, there has been an ongoing debate about the means by which development rights are allocated. Under the Town and Country Planning Act of 1947, land development rights were in effect nationalised. Since planning permission creates the opportunity for an owner to capture value created by the potential for development, ideological debate has focused on whether that value should be shared with, or indeed wholly diverted to, the wider community (Corkindale 1998). It is argued that the more valuable planning permission becomes to the owner, the greater is the incentive to engage in 'rent seeking' behaviour to obtain it (Evans 1982). As we discuss in Chapters 7 and 9, the state now seeks to extract what it can from the potential value of planning permission through the growing practice of planning gain.

More generally, property developers, land-owning lobby groups and New Right 'think tanks' have argued for a private property rights alternative to development control based on the expansion and easier exchange of development rights. The justification for changing to this approach has its intellectual antecedents in the rise of 'property rights economics' in the USA and is based on the seminal work of Ronald H. Coase (1960). The main thrust of Coase's Theorem suggests that if property rights are clearly delineated, and if all transaction costs are zero, then resource use will be the same regardless of who owns property rights. This can be taken to imply that intervention is unnecessary because the market can address the problem of externalities. In effect, planning authorities seek to assign, reassign or attenuate the rights of landowners (Chung 1994). What is open to debate is whether the cost associated with this intervention is greater or less than allowing an unregulated market to resolve these matters.

Corkindale (1998) believes strongly that the cost is indeed too great and proposes the privatisation of development rights in Britain. He argues that the efficiency of planning decisions would be improved if planning permission could be bought and sold. On this basis, he suggests that what is required is an application of the User Pays Principle (UPP) under which landowners would be permitted to develop their land provided there was some conformity with certain preset legal standards. This principle would be augmented by arrangements for compensatory payments designed to meet external costs. The analysis is extended to suggest that there may be advantages to designating 'conservation zones' and 'development zones' and introducing a system of tradable development rights. Within conservation zones, landowners would be allocated certain development rights and future development would be permitted only through exercising these rights. Should landowners, however, choose not to exercise their development rights, they could sell them to others.

While these ideas are interesting, there would be many practical difficulties with their implementation. In addition, as Grant (1998a) notes, there are many possible models for a privatised system of development rights which would each require systematic analysis. At this stage, however, even Corkindale (1998) is uncertain about which model might be best. Elsewhere McFarquhar (1999) is generally supportive of the proposals but thinks that the presence of quality controls means that even market-led solutions can fail to allow the private sector sufficient creativity in the development process. This appears to be a minority position.

Despite the success of New Right 'think tanks' in influencing the climate of opinion, and in particular the views of Keith Joseph and Margaret Thatcher during the developmental stages of the New Right project (Denham & Garnett 1998), there has been no political commitment to recent pro-property rights contributions to the debate about the nature and form of the development control system. The essence of the problem is captured by Barker (2000, p. 26) when he suggests that, although nationalised development rights are almost the only remnant of postwar nationalisation yet to be repealed, any attempt to repeal this aspect of the 1947 Act 'would have the middle classes marching on Whitehall and Westminster … in even greater numbers than the defenders of fox hunting'.

Stakeholder involvement

What is the role of stakeholders?

The planning system provides the framework within which complicated interactions between a range of public and private, political and professional interest groups (and their policy preferences) take place. These interactions ensure that planning decisions are essentially political in nature, occurring as a result of a process of bargaining and negotiation, rather than as outputs from a purely technical process.

For this reason, planning academics have a long tradition of analysing power relations within local politics (Simmie 1974; Blowers 1980). Typically, these studies examined the formal and informal processes underpinning the structures of government and sought to explore the ways influence has been exerted over policy decisions. They show that conflict occurs in both overt and covert ways and that it is an oversimplification to characterise planning decisions on the basis of planner–developer disputes (Rydin 1985). Such work highlights the pervasiveness of bargaining and negotiation in the decision-making process (Healey *et al.* 1988).

For example, in a relatively early investigation of the public participation programme introduced by Warwick District Council, Bruton (1980) suggests that, as a result of conflicts of interest, some form of distributional bargaining takes place. Groups of stakeholders involved in the decision-making process operate by establishing (or using) bargaining agents to advance their cause and to achieve 'group' goals. This study shows only limited evidence of the general public's involvement; the main form of public participation is through the formation of community interest groups with specific concerns about development.

Healey *et al.* (1988) also show that the outcomes from land-use decisions are biased in favour of particular groups and interests. In particular, they identify landowners, developers and investors, for whom the land provides an exchange value, as 'privileged groups'. They also note that the most significant gains were accrued by some affluent and articulate groups who were able to combine concerns over conservation with an interest in the exchange value of their property (see below). In the planning for housing context, Murdoch *et al.* (2000) show that the only actors able to exercise influence are policymakers, developers and, to a lesser extent, those groups seeking to protect the rural environment.

What is the basis for stakeholder involvement?

Interest in public participation in planning was reawakened in the 1980s. During this period, government attempts to 'roll back the frontiers of the state' coincided with growth in anti-development protest and NIMBY behaviour by local resident groups. As the social composition of rural and urban fringe areas altered in response to the changing distribution of employment and the changing locational patterns of housing provision, pressure on greenfield development grew and so did activity by interest and protest groups.

This period also saw a blurring of localised 'single issue' protest with environmental and conservation issues that increased the ability of protest groups to court support from the general public and the media. Barlow (1995) notes that this most concerned the Conservative Party in the 1980s because anti-development protest groups represented their natural electoral base. More recently, Bramley (1998a) suggests that the effect of dressing what were previously considered to be NIMBYist views in environmental sustainability clothing, has helped win support among a new tranche of Labour Party members representing southern shire councils. As such, the motives for seeking to influence decisions about housing development can be varied and overlapping.

In a detailed study of planning practice, Healey *et al.* (1988) sought to unravel the motives for the involvement of particular groups by focusing on their 'interests'. In this sense, the term interest might describe the relationship between stakeholders and planning decisions. Healey *et al.* established that interests in land, and its development, are a reflection of complex inter-relationships of economic structure and civic society, as brought together through the political system.

As we note above, they identify use-value interests and exchange-value interests. Use-value interests take different forms, and encompass both consumer and producer interests. This implies that groups may be interested in preventing the development of land to keep it in its current use or they may be interested in securing the right to develop for economic reasons. Groups with divergent interests in the use value of land may clash through the planning process. Exchange-value interests would include landowners, who can profit from the sale of land. However, there is a close relationship between use and exchange values. A landowner might consider the returns available to alternative uses. This would also require consideration of the use of other plots of land, including those adjacent to that under ownership. Thus Healey *et al.* (1988) argue that use and exchange values are inter-linked and also have influence on the way others are concerned with land parcels. These 'interests' provide the rationale for the involvement of a wide range of consumer and producer groups in debates about the location of new housing development.

Who are the main stakeholders with an interest in housing development decisions?

Several researchers have sought to classify the interest groups involved in planning decisions (Rydin 1986; Smith *et al.* 1986; Pennington 2000).

Smith *et al.* (1986), for example, identify two main forms of interest groups operating within the planning system. First there are interest or sectional groups that tend to be well established. These groups are described as being socially homogeneous, often defenders of the status quo and communicate with the local public administrators. Secondly, there are 'promotional' or 'cause' groups who are socially heterogeneous and advocate policy change. This type of group usually attempts to influence the political arm of local government rather than the administrators.

Alternatively, Rydin (1986) categorises groups according to their interests in the land market and discusses, in particular, the housebuilders' (or development) lobby, the professional lobby, the rural lobby and reformist organisations. Pennington (2000) adopts a similar approach but links the policy focus of the planning system, and in particular the emphasis on urban containment, to the incentives for interest group formation and activities. The result is a slightly different classification, which highlights five important types of group rather than four. These are the building lobby, the agricultural lobby, the local amenity/NIMBY lobby, the (other) environmental lobby and the professional lobby, and also describes the 'forgotten groups' or those 'who suffer in silence'.

It is, of course, possible to debate the detail of these classifications. It seems clear that both are influenced by the political conditions and state of the policy debate at the time of writing. Thus Rydin, like Evans (1991), emphasises the influence of the rural lobby. However, the research pre-dates the increase in prominence of environmental groups in the 1990s and, as such, would seem to understate the influence of this lobby. In addition, under Rydin's classification, the TCPA is labelled as a reformist rather than a professional group, while under Pennington's classification the CPRE, which might be classified as an environmental group, is categorised as NIMBYist[1]. The important point, however, is that both classifications recognise that interest groups play an important role within the structure of political institutions and emphasise that particular types of groups have shared interests and goals. Analysis of the inequalities and differences between these groups, including the way in which groups are able to influence public and political opinion and the manner of information flows between groups and the state, are important in developing an understanding of planning policy formulation and change.

Of all the major groups involved in housing development policy debates, the CPRE has probably had most success in recent years. It has successfully emphasised the broader environmental issues in shaping debates about new household development. The Council has dominated media exchanges, has become a prolific publisher in a range of popular media and more specialist professional outlets, and has a strong track record of submitting evidence to government consultation exercises and Select Committee proceedings (see *inter alia* CPRE 1997a, 1998, 1999; Green Balance 1994; Bramley 1996; Wenban-Smith 1999). Pennington (2000) presents an analysis of the *Financial Times* media database between 1992 and 1995, which shows that the CPRE has achieved prominence in almost five times more articles on the urban containment debate than any other interest group, with the HBF the next most successful. This represents a reversal of the picture of media coverage in the 1980s, which Rydin (1986) shows was dominated by 'pro' land release articles, and HBF-based articles.

The CPRE's strategy has been effective for two reasons. First, as shown in Chapter 1, it has been able to attract media attention by presenting an environmental protectionist message in terms of stark choices. Secondly, underpinning its high-profile and attention-grabbing efforts to alter the climate of opinion, the CPRE has also changed the way in which it seeks to provide opposition to local housing needs estimates.

Murdoch *et al.* (2000) describe the tendency, in the recent past, for housebuilders to employ professional planning consultants who used their expertise to challenge housing estimates by exposing the underlying political assumptions. This strategy was based on recognition that the figures could be disputed only on technical grounds. This contrasted with the approach of local groups, voluntary agencies and the CPRE. These groups were less well placed to provide opposition that was anything other than 'political' and, although they expressed reservations about housing calculations, the local participants were not able to make any impact. Now, of course, the CPRE recognises that the technical calculations are of critical importance in the entire process of planning for new housing and has sought to weaken the power of the household projections by lobbying for their downgrading in the structure plan process (see DOE 1996c). It argues instead for placing greater weight on environmental capacity considerations.

Earlier notable successes achieved by the CPRE include the reversal of the Thatcher Government's 1983 proposals to redraw the boundaries of green belts and, in tandem with the National Farmers' Union (NFU), the successful opposition to the 1987 Alternative Land Use and Rural Economy (ALURE) proposals which suggested that farming should cease to have first claim on rural land. Perhaps the CPRE's greatest success, however, was with the amendment, during the final parliamentary stages, of the Planning and Compensation Bill (1991), which resulted in the new plan-led development control system requiring planning applications to be judged in accordance with the local development plan. Significantly, this reduced the ability of the development lobby to use the DETR appeals procedure to alter local planning decisions (Marsden *et al.* 1993; Pennington 2000). The CPRE is strongly supported in developing its agenda by other prominent environmental groups. Friends of the Earth, for example, also contend that urban living should be boosted in order to reduce pressure on the countryside (see Friends of the Earth 1998). The majority of CPRE's members are derived from local amenity interests (Shucksmith 1990; Pennington 2000).

The housebuilding lobby has responded by seeking to exploit the tainted image of town planners. Although this lobby has included the Volume Builders Study Group (VBSG), the Federation of Master Builders (FMB) and the Building Employers Confederation (BEC), the most prominent member is the HBF. Its response to several government policy initiatives provides a useful insight into the different dimensions of its strategy.

For instance, in response to an announcement in March 2000 that sought to dampen the approval of plans for 215 000 new homes in the South East, the HBF claimed that this would stifle development and lead to a shortage of homes for key workers (such as teachers, nurses and police officers) who are currently priced out of the market (Hetherington 2000). Another example of the strategy has seen the HBF focus on the preference among families for dwellings located in 'leafy' areas rather than in towns and cities, which are depicted as unpleasant physical and hostile social environments (House Builders' Federation 1999). In arguing in favour of edge of town developments and against the reuse of urban land, the Federation suggests that 'Britain deserves better' (House Builders' Federation 1997). These comments were illustrative of the way the HBF typically sought to present planning intervention as anti-growth or as a means of circumscribing the individual's ability to make lifestyle choices. More recently, the HBF has begun to emphasise its desire to work with communities, in delivering the sort of homes consumers want. They also highlight the contribution new homes can make in tackling the social ills caused by affordability problems (House Builders' Federation 2001).

The housebuilding lobby has also had its share of political success. Rydin (1986) describes the role played by the HBF and VBSG in the formulation of DOE Circulars 9/80, 16/84 and 14/85, which increased developers' involvement in the identification of housing sites. In the Scottish context, Shucksmith *et al.* (1993) note the parallel influence of the housebuilding lobby on PAN38 'Structure plans – housing land requirements' (Scottish Office 1996).

The agricultural lobby includes the NFU and the Country Landowners' Association (CLA). This represents a second set of producer interests, who broadly set out to protect the traditional rural activities. Both groups are supportive of a relatively strict system of planning control and promote urban containment (Marsden *et al.* 1993). In Scotland, the Scottish Landowners' Federation (SLF) began to work closely with the national housing agency, Scottish Homes, and approves of 'sensitive and sensible development' (Shucksmith *et al.* 1993). This lobby has also had some success in influencing policy both in conjunction with other groups, as mentioned above in the context of defending the green belts and opposing ALURE, and in acting independently. Newby (1985), for instance, documents the role of the NFU in redistributing development rights away from landowners and towards tenants.

Professional groups, including the Town and Country Planning Association, provide policy prescriptions that are (arguably) somewhere in between the building and environmental view. As Chapter 3 explained, the TCPA's preferred 'portfolio approach' suggests a role for new settlements, urban extensions and infill with, for example, taxation incentives for promoting urban development (see *inter alia* Town and Country Planning Association 1997; Evans & Bate 2000). Media attention, however, has tended to be driven by the CPRE/environmentalist agenda and this has seen the TCPA attacked for its advocacy of new settlements and urban extensions that include proposals for three conurbations: 'City of Mercia' from Milton Keynes to Northampton, 'City of Kent' around Ashford and Kent, and 'City of Anglia' from Stevenage to Peterborough. Part of the TCPA's problem is that this particular initiative has been endorsed by the development industry. Seidl (1997), for example, quotes CNT's John Walker as a supporter of new settlements; David Birchall (of Beazer Strategic Land) as a supporter of urban extensions; and David Coates of the HBF as a supporter of building along transport corridors.

Despite strenuous attempts by the TCPA to change media perception, it tends to be cast as the developer's friend. The media describes Sir Peter Hall, former chairman of the TCPA, as the urban planning expert who wants to concrete over the countryside (Hugill 1999). This simplification, of course, does not accept Hall's argument that development is needed and that his (and the TCPA's) policy prescription is a pragmatic attempt to protect much of the countryside. Equally, it does no justice to the more subtle argument that, by predominantly accommodating new development on urban brownfield sites, there will be a systematic removal of small parks, playing fields and green sites. For, as we explained in Chapter 3, there are strong and valid arguments put forward by a range of expert commentators both for and against the notion of the compact city.

Irrespective of the validity (or otherwise) of their arguments, these groups face a difficult task in winning ground back from the combined arguments of the environmental and NIMBYist lobbies. In summarising the TCPA's position, Grayson (2000, p. 7) states that such

> initiatives (including the use of green wedges) may help change percep-
> tions in the long term, but, in the meantime, the political instincts of
> ministers tell them that any overt threat to the protective shield around
> England's green and pleasant land – even when the case for development
> is strong – will rebound on them with a vengeance.

The evident success of particular interest groups operating within the planning system seems to demonstrate that some groups are able to exercise
greater powers than others. Ball (1999b) explains, in part, the basis on which
interest groups can exert pressure. He suggests that because gains from restricting land release are concentrated, policy-makers can attract votes by
supporting the winners, while the fact that the costs are dispersed makes
it unlikely that the policy-maker will lose many votes. Specific cases provide evidence of the incidence of local, community-based NIMBY groups
successfully achieving their goals. More generally, however, the politics of
planning and housing development is dominated by the success of the environmental lobby. This lobby has managed to shape the climate of opinion
by providing a grander motive for relatively narrow interests. This grander
motive has proved capable of winning popular support.

Theoretical perspectives

A number of different theoretical explanations of power relations have
emerged over time. Some explanations have been essentially 'corporatist' and suggest that a relatively small number of key political actors and
members of the business community act together to determine the direction of policy. Under the corporatist model, it is possible that planning
decisions could be used to support the agenda of a local elite and to pursue
the goals of those with particular interests in the land market or development industry. Others might suggest that the power and interests of elite
groups dominate local planning. This power might be expressed in terms
of the way policy is both designed and implemented. Such an approach
locates individuals within wider networks, and looks at the relationships
between networks.

Pluralists would suggest that these views are overly limiting. Pluralists
study actual decisions and analyse the multiple influences on decision-
makers. In the pluralist model, the state is independent of any one sectional
or group interest. Power is dispersed rather than concentrated and policy

agendas are determined by interaction and negotiation between groups. Under this model, planning serves to mediate conflicts between different interests (Healey *et al.* 1988; Brindley *et al.* 1996).

As an alternative, Marxists locate their analysis of local political decisions within the structures of the capitalist state. The Marxist view is based on an understanding of social order as a struggle between the capitalist and working classes over control of the means of production. This suggests that the planning system, and local government more generally, is an instrument of the capitalist class (Castells 1977). This approach is rather closer to the corporatist model in that it places less emphasis on the extent to which a range of different interests might influence decisions. A key contribution of the Marxist studies derives from their focus on economic interests and their political strategies, at the expense of the relations between politicians, officials and voters (Hill 2000). As Rydin (1985) argues, this perspective underemphasises the role of many actors in favour of structural influences. In essence, a difference in emphasis on structural influences as against human agency lies at the heart of the divergence between these competing explanations. Within elitist, corporatist and pluralist frameworks it is human agency that matters most, while to Marxist and neo-Marxists the structures of capitalism dominate. In contrast, institutional theory indicates the need to weave together structure and agency influences in explaining policy directions and development outcomes.

Interest in the role of groups has also been given impetus by relatively recent developments in communicative (or collaborative) planning theory. This emphasises consensus building and this requires the participation of interest groups and stakeholders in the political decision-making process (Healey 1997, 2001). Other recent contributions from public choice theorists are fundamentally concerned about the motives of groups (Pennington 2000).

Public choice theory (or economic theory of politics) ascribes economic modes of reasoning to the analysis of collective action. Academic discussions of public interest group formation derive primarily from Mancur Olson's seminal book *The Logic of Collective Action* (Olson 1965). Olson stresses that, from a rational choice perspective, the involvement of a single individual will not influence the outcome of the democratic decision-making process. As the product of interest group activity is not indivisible, some individuals will free-ride on the membership and collective action of others. In short, rational individuals will operate within a collective setting (such as an interest group or political institution) if this is the best way to accomplish their purpose (or to maximise their benefits).

As a result, this means that only certain interests are likely to form into groups. These include 'privileged groups', which exist where the gains to at least one member from acting alone to achieve the collective good exceed the costs of this action. For larger groups to achieve mobilisation there must be private benefits. These may take the form of material or non-material selective incentives, solidarity benefits including the opportunity to socialise with like-minded people, or expressive benefits that may come from the entertainment value of group events. Without these, public choice theorists believe groups would not form.

However, empirical evidence shows a proliferation of public interest groups and thus points to a 'mobilisation paradox' (Jordan & Maloney 1997). This paradox is explained with reference to the fact that individuals accept a broad range of benefits, not just material or selective. Jordan and Maloney suggest, in particular, that many environmental groups are operating a protest business and can influence potential memberships from the supply side. This recognises that individuals will join groups in order conspicuously to consume membership via, for instance, the display of stickers and badges that provide evidence of lifestyle orientation.

In the planning context, Pennington (2000) applies public choice theory to interest groups and collective action in the political marketplace. He associates different forms of incentive with different types of group. Development industry groups, for instance, are driven by material incentives, while farming groups offer members the chance for networking and social interaction.

Ball (1999b) also offers a public choice explanation of the role of (suburbanite) Territorial Interest Groups (TIGs) engaged in a strategy that constrains urban development. He highlights two types of benefit. First, a policy of constraint enables suburbanites to enjoy the benefits of relatively easy access to urban agglomeration economies while maintaining an environment that suits their preferences for space, layout and design. Secondly, by restricting new housing supply, the value of members' housing is raised.

Ball (1999b) argues that the wider costs of this strategy arise through greater travelling costs caused by more dispersed urban development, generally higher house prices (and their impact on business costs through inflationary pressure on wages) and diminished urban economic growth because of lost agglomeration economies. These costs, however, are more widely diffused than the gains and, from a public choice perspective, do not impact on the rational individual's 'maximisation' strategy. Although this explanation has some merit, it is worth noting that not everyone accepts the underlying assumption that individuals act rationally (Munro 1995).

Irrespective of the merits of these theoretical explanations, it seems clear that the commodified nature of planning for housing has had a marked effect on the mobilisation of homeowners. Conflicts over the location of new development are often motivated by defensive urges. Towards the end of periods of sustained economic growth, for example, protest activity may result from perceived threats to house prices within a locality. Planning decisions, and particularly those on the location of new housing developments, are now played out in a relatively sophisticated political environment within which a number of stakeholders have proved able to influence decisions.

Political decision-making in practice

Naturally, there are tensions between the use of technical planning procedures and the requirement to allow public participation in the decision-making process. Research by Murdoch *et al.* (2000) into the contest between technical expertise and public participation in Buckinghamshire, a shire county north of London, is illustrative of the way in which planning for housing decisions are made in practice. The case study depicts a county that experienced a flow of middle-class migrants into its rural areas over a long period. The residents of these villages, in turn, proved to be strongly opposed to economic development and the provision of additional new homes. By focusing on the Structure Plan Review process, Murdoch *et al.* (2000) identify two significant dimensions to the analysis. These are, first, spatially defined interests and, secondly, lobby groups and professional interests.

Significantly an uneven spatial distribution of development pressure emerged across the five districts within the county, with considerable pressure in the southern districts of High Wycombe, South Buckinghamshire and the Chilterns that are closer to London, compared with Milton Keynes and Aylesbury Vale to the north. In the 1970s, a coalition of environmental and NIMBYist interests, including the local branch of the CPRE and the Chilterns and High Wycombe amenity societies, forced the adoption of restrictive growth policy in the south of the county. At the centre of this policy were Green Belt and Area of Outstanding Natural Beauty (AONB) designations. As a consequence, further growth was pushed to the north. During the 1980s, the local political coalition continued to support growth in the north and sought to ensure that the protectionist principles applied to the south were adhered to in development plans.

When local planning officers were interviewed by Murdoch *et al.* (2000), they acknowledged that as a result of the strength of local opposition to development, they had never sought to overturn the long-standing Green

Belt and AONB restrictions. This suggests that, from the earliest stages in the process, the coalition of anti-development interest groups was successful in ensuring that these policy preferences were entrenched in the review and were accepted by all participants. The muted response from urban areas was interpreted as implicit support for the plan. There had been no history of collective action in response to planning issues and, as such, no alternative view was put forward to challenge the protectionist interests.

The study also shows that, within Buckinghamshire, there was also dissatisfaction with the high level of development expected within the county as a whole. On this issue, however, the anti-development interests had less success than they might have hoped for. At the resultant examination-in-public, housebuilding interests presented a sustained justification for growth, which was underpinned by detailed technical assessments of housing demand. Despite expressing deep reservations about the validity of statistical estimates and their assumptions, local participants did not provide alternative analyses and, as such, were unable to present any challenge to the predictions. In this case, the national to local structure of the land-use regulation that was imposed by technical and legal procedures proved more powerful than local actors. From this, it does appear that planning for housing may have resisted the influence of institutional change evident in the apparent demise of the 'predict and provide' approach (Murdoch *et al.* 2000).

At a national level, however, the CPRE and other environmentalist groups helped secure the end of the 'predict and provide' approach. Despite representations from housebuilders and professional planning interests, the projections method previously at the core of planning for housing appears to have lost its pre-eminence. The new approach indicates that the figures should be used only for guidance rather than being seen as prescriptive (DETR 1998b). This policy shift acknowledges that the projections have to be understood in the context of sustainable development and environmental capacity.

Nevertheless, evidence from local case studies suggests that this victory may have been less than emphatic. As Murdoch (2000) shows, even under these new terms, the findings of SERPLAN's regional capacity study for the South East were unable to make an impression on projection-led policy. After considering local land resources and environmental factors, SERPLAN's draft regional strategy sought to demonstrate that the regional projection of 1.1 million new homes could not be accommodated. Rather, a figure of 780 000 was considered viable within the plan period. The findings of the capacity study were bolstered with reference to sustainability and social inclusion objectives. In response, the Government appointed a panel of stakeholders, including representatives of the housebuilding industry, to discuss the regional strategy. The panel was critical of SERPLAN's attempt to shift the policy debate towards the sustainability agenda. The panel also argued that regional considerations did not undermine the national projections and, as such, the figures retained their place at the core of policy. Perhaps this is not entirely surprising. It may be unrealistic to expect that the influence of technical aspects of the system would vanish instantly. This seems particularly unlikely given that the relatively protracted debates in most regions will have begun before the end of 'predict and provide'.

Conclusions

In the context of household growth and concerns over sustainable futures, debates over planning for housing and about the location and form of new housing development are highly politicised. The nature of the political debate, however, is not ideological or party political. The most recent Labour and Conservative administrations have adopted broadly the same policy stance. The changes that have taken place have been described as 'institutional tinkering' (Pennington 1998). It seems that both major parties accept a greater role for the market than in the past but there is no commitment to radical changes such as the development of a wholly market-based approach to allocating development rights.

Although there has been some national-level debate about the use of household projections, most of the conflict surrounding development decisions takes place at the local level, especially in the shires. In this context, it is common for local politicians to oppose national policy. The positions adopted tend to relate to the sensitivity of particular proposals within the local arena, with the approach adopted by local politicians best described as voter-centric.

In much of the coverage of debates about greenfield and brownfield development and about the scale of new development, commentators tend to present the positions of the protagonists as polar opposites and firmly entrenched. On the one hand, state intervention is welcomed as acting in the wider social interests while, on the other, it is represented as a force working against the market that potentially harms local business and industry goals. In reality, however, characterisation of planning decisions as a conflict between state and market or between planner and developer significantly over-simplifies the political context. The politics of planning and development are based on complex interactions between a number of stakeholders including local NIMBYist, environmental and rural interests and coalitions as well as professional and development industry interests. The interests of these groups embrace consumer and producer motives, use and exchange interests, and groups' interests are often inter-linked or blurred. In this sense, the politics of planning provides a classic case study of interest group politics.

The state is faced with mediating and balancing the conflicting interests. In this context, an analysis of policy implementation at local level reveals more about the political pressures on the planning system than any study of central government's policy pronouncements. Evidence from a number of studies shows that interest groups have been acting with increasing sophistication as they seek to influence decisions about the location of housing development. These studies clearly show that planning and development decisions emerge from a process of bargaining and negotiation at local level. They also demonstrate that the extent to which particular lobbies achieve their goals varies from case to case. Although the CPRE has been successful in influencing both the direction of policy and specific planning decisions, they have also suffered many reversals. Although, in general, politicised decisions tend to have primacy over technical decisions, the rhetoric surrounding the decisions may often be used to obscure this (Vigar *et al.* 2000; see also Chapter 4).

In recent years, decision-making in planning practice has been the subject of renewed research interest. Researchers have examined the extent to which interest groups have been able to influence decisions and have examined the capacity of groups to represent a broad range of public views. Despite this, there remains considerable scope for further research in this area. Questions remain unanswered about who becomes involved in planning decisions and, in particular, about interest group membership and representation. In addition, in the context of new forms of local governance, further investigation of the influence of groups on the formulation of policy and in determining local planning decisions is required. These questions lie at the heart of any understanding of the institutional context within which housing land policy is formulated and implemented.

Note

(1) This categorisation can be justified if, for example, we considered overlaps in personnel with other NIMBYist groups. The vice-chairman of CPRE's South-East Regional Advice is also vice-president of Sane Planning in the South East (SPISE).

Part III

Policy Evaluation

7

Greenfield Housing Development

Although most politicians would wish to concentrate new housing development increasingly within existing towns and cities, there remains substantial pressure in many areas of the country for greenfield land release. As a result, policies to facilitate brownfield development are usually matched by those that seek to limit greenfield development. Such policies, however, are not limited to the UK but are found in many parts of the developed world. We therefore start this chapter by reflecting on the international nature of efforts to protect greenfield land from urban encroachment. We then explain the supply and demand factors that create market preferences for greenfield development before comparing three different policy responses: management, resistance or accommodation.

While there has been some variation in policy response from one region to another, recent years have generally seen attitudes towards greenfield development pressure in the UK harden from management to resistance, with very few authorities now pursuing a policy of open accommodation. Yet, as the Urban Task Force (1999) pointed out, over the period 1996–2021, at least 850 000 new dwellings in England had been built or were expected to be built on greenfield sites as a consequence of planning permissions already granted or of allocations already made or expected to be made in development plans. Furthermore, even if six in every ten homes in England were actually to be built on previously developed land over this 25-year period, additional land would still need to be released for a further 670 000 dwellings on greenfield sites to meet projected household growth.

The chapter therefore examines whether current policy mechanisms will be able to contain future greenfield development or whether more radical proposals, such as the introduction of a greenfield development tax, would be beneficial in reinforcing planning restrictions. More fundamentally, we ask whether, as a result of the prevalent determination of politicians to protect greenfield land, the British planning system has focused too much on limiting the quantity and impact of greenfield development, and not enough on raising the quality and sustainability of such development, when it actually takes place.

Greenfield protection: some international experiences

The themes of this chapter, while discussed primarily in a British context, are international in nature. In Japan, for example, areas within and around most cities are delineated as either *toshika kuiki* (urbanising districts) or *chosei kuiki* (urbanisation-curbing districts) (Mori 1998). Land within the former is expected to be developed within 10 years, while new development in the latter is strictly regulated. However, since these delineations are reviewed about once a decade, landowners even in remote areas remain hopeful that their land may one day be made available for development, especially when the economy is booming. According to Mori (1998), land delineated for urban development in Japan is valued at between 50 and 150 times the value of land delineated for agriculture. He suggests that this multiplier is lower than in the UK since it is easier for farmers and landowners in Japan eventually to secure permission to develop agricultural land for urban use.

Razin (1998) reports that the control of urban sprawl became a high-priority issue in Israel, as a result of rapid economic growth and mass immigration from the former Soviet Union, which created intense pressure for urban expansion in the 1990s. Urban sprawl in Israel, Razin (1998) argues, has been associated with two particular problems: over-investment in too many industrial and employment centres and the rapid loss of scarce open space. In the latter context, policies to preserve agricultural land are gradually being replaced by those to preserve open space and land resources as a whole.

Whereas severe restrictions have been placed in Israel on the transfer of land into housing use, policies in the Netherlands have long sought to provide a plentiful supply of cheap development land (Needham & Verhage 1998). To achieve this, Dutch municipalities have operated as both planning authorities and land market intermediaries to meet the demand for housing land in the region where it arises. However, in the mid-1990s, political concern that the urbanised part of the Netherlands had increased from 6% to 14% of the country's land area over the previous 40 years led to a significant policy change. As a result, it is now intended that housing development should be concentrated within or adjacent to existing large towns in seven city regions, but restricted in more peripheral locations. Needham and Verhage (1998) claim that this shift in policy will cause house and land prices to rise and, as a result, encourage the emergence of land speculation as its unforeseen side effect.

Even in the USA, what originated as localised concern over urban sprawl has now achieved more national prominence (Teitz 1999). While three decades have passed since growth management and growth controls were first introduced in the state of Oregon (Nelson & Moore 1993), the success of its most famous example, Portland's urban growth boundary, still remains a matter of dispute (Peiser 2001). Nevertheless, it is apparent that American debates on urban containment differ from those in Europe only in respect of contrasting cultural attitudes towards government intervention (Hall 2001).

Many of those who press for the containment of urban sprawl in the USA from a New Urbanist perspective emphasise the same benefits of higher urban densities and better access to public transport espoused by European advocates of the compact city. Duany *et al.* (2000), for example, identifying bored teenagers, stranded elderly, weary commuters, bankrupt municipalities and the immobile poor as among the victims of urban sprawl, argue passionately for the New Urbanist approach to settlement design based on clear town centres, short walking distances to everyday facilities, grid patterns of block layouts, narrow versatile streets, mixed-use development and special sites for special buildings.

Moreover, the New Urbanist concept of 'transit-oriented development' proposed by Calthorpe (1994) demands a rich mixture of housing, offices and shops creating a dense, tightly woven and compact community, all within walking distance of the transit station. The New Urbanist movement has been implemented primarily through private initiatives, with, for example, Andres Duany and Elizabeth Plater-Zyberk, the leading New Urbanist architects behind the much-acclaimed community of Seaside in Florida (see Fig. 7.1), having received over 40 subsequent commissions for town design (Ellin 1996). However, Madanipour (1996) suggests that its design principles derive primarily from a revival of early town planning concepts adjusted for the demands of modern life.

Eppli and Tu (2000) regard the reform of sprawling North American suburban development as one of the primary goals of the New Urbanist movement, claiming that such extensive conversion of greenfield land to new residential development in the USA is directly responsible for increased vehicle mileage, rising infrastructure and public service costs, loss of agricultural and other resource land, declining environmental quality and loss of community values. Once urban sprawl became a visible media issue in the USA, the

Fig. 7.1   New Urbanism at Seaside, Florida.

Clinton Government showed greater interest in promoting what has come to be known as 'smart growth' (Teitz 1999).

According to the Urban Land Institute (1999, p. 3) 'smart growth' commonly has the following characteristics:

- Development is economically viable and preserves open space and natural resources.

- Land-use planning is comprehensive, integrated and regional.

- Public, private and non-profit sectors collaborate on growth and development issues to achieve mutually beneficial outcomes.

- Certainty and predictability are inherent to the development process.

- Infrastructure is maintained and enhanced to serve existing and new residents.

- Redevelopment of infill housing, brownfield sites and obsolete buildings is actively pursued.

- Urban centres and neighbourhoods are integral components of a healthy regional economy.

- Compact suburban development is integrated into existing commercial areas, new town centres, and/or near existing or planned transportation facilities.

- Development on the urban fringe integrates a mix of land use, preserves open space, is fiscally responsible and provides transportation options.

Although many of these themes appear remarkably familiar in a British context, the Urban Land Institute provides example of 'smart' approaches to growth under consideration or implementation across the USA in locations such as Arlington in Virginia, Envision in Utah, Lincoln in Nebraska and Orange County in California. Nevertheless, as Teitz (1999) points out, the growing opposition to urban sprawl in the USA has generated a reaction of its own from conservative and libertarian organisations who have actively campaigned against any further restriction of development.

Against this background, Peiser (2001) attempts to classify the outcomes of US urban sprawl, according to whether they should be considered positive, negative or neutral. He argues that the concept of urban sprawl embraces a complex set of urban issues that are often ignored in the intensity of public and political debate generated about growth and development in the USA. Thus, as this short review of international experience demonstrates, controversies about the management of urban growth in the UK, to which we now turn, find a resonance elsewhere in the developed world.

Greenfield development pressure

Demand factors

On the demand side, greenfield development pressure is primarily attributable to the continued decentralisation from large urban areas explored in detail in Chapter 2. This occurs for social, economic and demographic reasons. Socially, Newman and Kenworthy (1999) argue that the idyllic view of rural life known as 'pastoralism', which asserts that the countryside provides solitude, innocence and happiness, lies deep in Anglo-Saxon traditions and culture. They suggest that 'Many English, American and Australian artists and writers have idealized rural places, and their literary heroes are from the countryside,

Fig. 7.2   'Rustic-style' greenfield development at Stoke sub Hamdon, Somerset.

the prairie, and the bush. Cities, in this view, serve only to corrupt the purifying aspects of country life' (Newman & Kenworthy 1999, p. 135).

Of course, as Newman and Kenworthy (1999) point out, the pastoral tradition has not served to re-create village life (even though it may affect individual design, as Fig. 7.2 shows): instead it has provided a rationale for the suburban lifestyle. Ironically, as each spacious new 'rural' suburb is soon engulfed by the next, the appeal of rural life is never quite what the real estate brochures promised. Yet, the mythical world created by such writers as George Eliot and Thomas Hardy in England, Banjo Patterson and Henry Lawson in Australia and Ralph Waldo Emerson and Henry James in the USA, which is continued in the ecology literature of today, remains powerful but wholly elusive to most of the population.

In practical terms, research has identified more tangible reasons why people move to large new estates built on greenfield land. In a study of 600 households who had purchased new homes on two such estates in Bristol and Luton constructed for owner-occupation in the late 1980s, Forrest *et al.* (1997) found that most new entrants were young couples and families who had moved only a short distance and thus remained well connected to their existing networks of close family relatives and friends. Although many were drawn by the environmental attractions of living near to open countryside, particularly if moving from a distance, other factors also accounted for the pull of the estates. For instance, new homes were felt not to have the physical problems associated with older inner city dwellings. More importantly, during the booming market of the late 1980s, newly built properties offered the chance to climb on to the ladder of owner-occupation at affordable prices. Some years later, in the depressed market of the 1990s, the variety of attractive incentives offered by builders desperate to sell made estate properties among the cheapest in the local market.

This indicates that consumer demand for greenfield housing is not merely a matter of social taste and cultural tradition but is the outcome of a complex interweaving of social and economic factors. Indeed, urban decentralisation reflects not simply demographic change but the outward shift of economic activity from the centre of conurbations and large cities to their peripheries and to towns and rural areas. This is why the UK Round Table on Sustainable Development (1997) criticised excessive reliance on the proportion of new housing constructed on previously developed land as the best indicator of sustainable land use. Since in many growth areas, pressure for greenfield housing development is a direct consequence of decisions to allow employment growth, the Round Table concluded that it would be better to measure greenfield land-take for new building of any kind rather than restrict consideration to that for housing.

Indeed, if this more holistic view is taken of urban growth, it can be argued that planning authorities should be required to provide whatever level of new housing land is commensurate with their proposed allocations of land for employment provision. Otherwise, the continued expansion of employment development at greenfield locations, combined with the concentration of new housing within towns and cities (and in many cases on abandoned industrial land), will lead at best, to extensive patterns of reverse commuting and at worst, to an increasingly dysfunctional relationship between housing and labour markets. However, whereas strong public and political opposition is often evident to greenfield housing development, it is usually less vocal in the case of greenfield employment development where it is accompanied by the promise of new jobs and increased local prosperity.

For example, in the late 1990s, the West Midlands Regional Forum identified two greenfield locations, each of about 50 hectares, as suitable for major investment by single very large companies. According to Johnston (1999, p. 16):

> The idea was to ensure that the region does not miss out on potential
> jobs and investment because of a lack of suitable sites for footloose major

investors. The project group behind the study predicted that the two sites pinpointed could create 8,000 jobs directly and twice as many among suppliers and service industries.

Subsequently, however, the West Midlands Local Government Association in reviewing its Regional Planning Guidance turned against urban residential extensions as it believed that the 'provision of homes on the urban fringe would further encourage an outward movement of people and thus jeopardise regeneration aims' (Niven 2001, p. 10). No wonder the local authorities were criticised by the local branch of the CPRE for an inconsistent approach to greenfield land release.

Furthermore, when it appeared that one of the major employment sites identified in the West Midlands would take longer to come to fruition than expected, another 50 hectares of land north east of Coventry was added to the draft Warwickshire Structure Plan to serve that same purpose. Ironically, however, the independent Inspector who reported in 2000 on the inquiry into the separate Coventry Unitary Development Plan concluded that the City Council was over-optimistic in seeking to concentrate 1300 new dwellings in the city centre over the following decade and recommended that more greenfield land should be allocated for housing so that the city centre figure could be reduced by 220 on account of ownership and financial constraints (*Planning* 2000b).

These examples highlight the apparently different value systems applied by local politicians to employment and housing encroachment on to greenfield land. Although at first sight, demand for peripheral residential development may be viewed as the unfortunate outcome of an Anglo-Saxon culture that perpetuates an idyllic rural myth, in truth, it is part and parcel of the wider processes of urban decentralisation and economic development. Since demand for new residential development is primarily derived from the economic fortunes of potential purchasers, it is thus essential to take a rounded view of greenfield development pressure and not to separate it from other land-use demands in a locality.

Supply factors

Agricultural land in the green belt is normally traded at the agricultural land prices, with perhaps some additional hope value to represent the possibility of its eventual release for development in the distant future. In contrast, land allocated for residential development will be traded at residential land prices. The difference between these two sectors can be quite staggering.

Fig. 7.3 Aerial view of greenfield development at Tamworth, West Midlands.

For instance, in the South East of England, the average value of 1 hectare in spring 1999 was £1 370 000 if traded as bulk residential building land, but only £8000 if traded as mixed agricultural land. In the less pressured North West, the respective figures were £630 000 and £7005 (Inland Revenue Valuation Office 1999).

In the UK, owing to the existence of a well-developed and well-understood planning system, no intermediate market of any significance exists between land intended to remain in agricultural use and that likely to receive planning permission for residential development (Goodchild & Munton 1985). Indeed, from an economist's perspective, development planning creates rental gaps between sectors that reinforce sectoral divisions in the land market (Keogh 1985). The reallocation of land in a development plan (or through the unexpected granting of planning permission) from one sector of the market to a more valuable one, in which demand for development exists, creates the chance to capture the difference in value between the two. This difference is commonly termed development value.

If it were possible to buy 1 hectare of land in the South East at £8000 in the agricultural land market, have it reallocated for residential development and sell it for £1 370 000 in the residential land market, a gross return of 170 times the original sum invested would be achieved. This aspiration ensures that the potential supply of land for greenfield development is driven primarily by the sheer scale of the development value that can be realised from transferring the land from one sector of the market to another. In reality, however, it may take many years and great effort before reallocation happens or planning permission is granted.

As Chapters 5 and 6 explained, the political nature of the planning system ensures that many decisions on the release of greenfield land for housing are both protracted and highly contested. Whereas brownfield development is often dependent on the resolution of problematic ownership and physical constraints, in the case of greenfield development, conflicts centre on both the release of land itself and the distribution of benefits that flow from that release. Competition among landowners, developers and planning authorities to capture the greater share of development value is critical to understanding the greenfield residential development process.

Statutory planning encourages owners of agricultural land to seek its transfer for residential development through involvement in the planning process, especially as no lasting method to tax development value has ever been agreed between political parties. As this is an expensive and time-consuming process, many greenfield landowners are prepared to enter into options or conditional contracts with housebuilders who then take on responsibility for promoting land release through the planning system. Although this is an uncertain and lengthy exercise, empirical evidence would suggest that options and conditional contracts still allow landowners to capture the bulk of development value, even if the developer has had to work hard to secure residential planning permission[1].

Indeed, as planning restrictions have tightened over the years, land prices have become an increasingly significant element within development appraisals. From research into major greenfield residential developments of between 400 and 5000 dwellings, Meikle *et al.* (1991) estimated the average dwelling cost in the South East of England at that time to be £117 000, of which land costs accounted for just over one-third. As Table 7.1 shows, these figures allowed for developers' overheads but not developers' profit.

Obviously, land as a proportion of total costs will vary from region to region according to the extent of development pressure. In an excellent example of an actual development appraisal of a greenfield residential site, one Scottish developer showed how the residual land value of £1 215 000 was only slightly above the developer's minimum acceptable profit of £1 200 000 (Gill 1991). However, taking account of tax and overheads, the landowner's net profit stood at £705 000, while that of the developer, who took responsibility for almost all the work to bring the development to fruition, was reduced to £520 000. The full figures are shown in Table 7.2.

In his second example, Gill (1991) considers the financial implications of additional costs of £250 000 for resolving abnormal ground conditions and £200 000 for meeting the planning gain requirements of the local authority. He seeks to show that these additional costs should properly have no impact on the developer's net profit but should reduce that of the landowner

Table 7.1 Typical breakdown of housing development costs for a three-bedroom house of 80-m² floor area in the South East of England in early 1990s.

Development component	Cost per dwelling	%
Land cost	£40 000	34.2
Housebuilding costs	£35 000	29.9
Housing site costs	£9 000	7.7
Off-site infrastructure costs	£6 000	5.1
Community facilities	£4 000	3.4
Developers' overheads	£23 000	19.7
Total costs	**£117 000**	**100.0**

Source: Meikle *et al.* (1991).

Table 7.2 Greenfield development appraisal 1: No abnormals and no planning gain requirement. Details of development: 10 acre (5 ha) housing site in Crieff, Scotland.

Income	50 detached units	@ 150 000		7 500 000
Expenditure				
Building	50 units at 1500 sq ft	@ 56.50 per sq ft	4 237 500	
Abnormals				
Cost of planning gain				
Professional and legal fees		2.55%	191 250	
Local authority and NHBC charges		0.40%	30 000	
Sales and marketing costs		3.35%	251 250	
Interest charges		5.00%	375 000	
Minimum acceptable dev profit		16.00%	1 200 000	
Total costs			6 285 000	6 285 000
Residual land value generated				1 215 000
Developer's return				
Development profit				1 200 000
Allocated overhead			375 000	
Group interest allocation			25 000	
Pre-tax profit				800 000
Corporation tax		35%	280 000	
Developer's profit				520 000
Landowner's return				
Land value				1 215 000
Existing use value			15 000	
Fees and interest			25 000	
Pre-tax profit				1 175 000
Capital gains tax		40%	470 000	
Landowner's profit				705 000

1 sq ft is about 0.09 m².
Source: Gill (1991).

from £705 000 to £446 250. The detailed calculations are shown in Table 7.3. Since this is dependent on planning gain requirements being known to the developer prior to site purchase, Gill (1991) argues strongly that such requirements should be flagged in advance in development plans, wherever possible.

From these apparently dry calculations, some very interesting questions arise that reach to the heart of the competition among landowners, developers and planners to capture the greater share of development value. If

Table 7.3 Greenfield development appraisal 2: Poor ground conditions but planning gain requirement. Details of development: 10 acre (5 ha) housing site in Crieff, Scotland.

Income	50 detached units	@150 000		7 500 000
Expenditure				
Building	50 units at 1500 sq ft	@56.50 per sq ft	4 237 500	
Abnormals			250 000	
Cost of planning gain			200 000	
Professional and legal fees		2.55%	191 250	
Local authority and NHBC charges		0.40%	30 000	
Sales and marketing costs		3.35%	251 250	
Interest charges		4.75%	356 250	
Minimum acceptable dev profit		16.00%	1 200 000	
Total costs			6 716 250	6 716 250
Residual land value generated				783 750
Developer's return				
Development profit				1 200 000
Allocated overhead			375 000	
Group interest allocation			25 000	
Pre-tax profit				800 000
Corporation tax		35%	280 000	
Developer's profit				520 000
Landowner's return				
Land value				783 750
Existing use value			15 000	
Fees and interest			25 000	
Pre-tax profit				743 750
Capital gains tax		40%	297 500	
Landowner's profit				446 250

Source: Gill (1991).

landowners stand to make such huge returns for apparently so little effort, how much of that return can be extracted by the state in the form of planning gain? Does this become easier or more difficult in the case of major developments, such as new settlements, where the developer might need to negotiate separately with several landowners? How can one be sure that the cost of any planning gain is actually borne by the landowner, rather than the developer in the form of reduced profit or the house purchaser in the form of higher prices or lower quality? If planning restrictions have so increased returns to landowners, should not the corollary of further restrictions on greenfield development be some special sort of tax on those sites where development is actually allowed?

We thus contend, in turning our attention to how best local planning authorities should manage greenfield development pressures, that the crucial decisions in greenfield land policy concern not merely the release of land for development but the financial implications, for landowners, developers and the state, of any releases that do take place.

Management of greenfield development pressure

In March 2000, John Prescott, the Deputy Prime Minister and Secretary of State for the Environment, Transport and the Regions, in introducing the revised PPG 3 on Housing to the House of Commons, proudly announced the end of what he described as the 'predict and provide' approach to housing land allocation and its replacement by an alternative method described as 'plan, monitor and manage'. While this change in terminology may appear no more than astute civil service semantics, in truth, it reflects a gradual shift in policy towards greenfield development pressure that had occurred over the previous two to three decades.

For when the comprehensive town and country planning system was introduced in 1947, its prime strategic emphasis lay not in restricting greenfield development as a whole, but rather in directing it to preferred locations such as new and expanded towns. Certainly, with the formal introduction of green belts into Government policy from 1955, the outward expansion of conurbations and other selected towns was checked. On a regional level, however, green belts were regarded as but one side of a wider policy. On the other side, the planning system sought to provide enough greenfield land to meet regional housing demand either in specified growth areas such as the notorious Area 8 on the borders of Berkshire, Hampshire and Surrey, in new towns such as Milton Keynes, Redditch and Warrington, or in the numerous greenfield expansions that took place up and down the country, as the economy prospered and owner-occupation grew.

Until the overwhelming needs of urban regeneration began to capture the policy agenda from the late 1970s onwards, strategic planning thus saw its role not as limiting the demand for greenfield housing but rather as managing that demand by directing it to preferred locations. In implementing this strategic management of greenfield development pressure, the planning system was partnered by both public and private development agencies. In the public sector, new town development corporations and local authorities played an important role in providing publicly funded housing on greenfield land. As significantly, a shared interest emerged during these years between a planning system that sought to provide for housing demand while redirecting it to preferred locations, and a speculative housebuilding industry, whose corporate basis, identity and organisation was predicated on the unproblematic conversion of greenfield land into owner-occupied housing estates.

Although this shared interest appeared to have been carried forward into the 1980s, with a series of government circulars and pronouncements that appeared to require the planning system to continue to meet housing demand, the increasing emphasis on redirecting housing development pressure towards sites within existing towns and cities meant that policy gradually shifted from managing greenfield development to resisting it. Later in the chapter, we explore how resistance has now become the dominant discourse in responding to greenfield development pressure. In this section, however, we consider what remains of the instruments of management. Our focus is first on the continued relevance or otherwise of green belts, secondly, on the ever-growing use of planning gain as a method to extract wider benefits from whatever greenfield development is allowed, and thirdly, on the increasing importance attached to sustainable greenfield design.

Green belts

As Elson *et al.* (1993) revealed, green belt coverage paradoxically doubled during the Thatcher years. Thus by 1997, approved green belts in England covered 1.65 million hectares or 13% of land area (DTLR 2001a). Although no green belts have been introduced in Wales, almost 165 000 hectares of land are covered by the five Scottish green belts (Scottish Office 1991). According to Tewdwr-Jones (1996), green belts thus represented one of the last bastions of the pre-1979 planning system to have remained unscathed by the Thatcher reforms.

In England, there are five official purposes of including land within green belts:

- To check the unrestricted sprawl of large built-up areas.

- To prevent neighbouring towns from merging into one another.

- To assist in safeguarding the countryside from encroachment.

- To preserve the setting and special character of historic towns.

- To assist in urban regeneration, by encouraging the recycling of derelict and other urban land (DOE 1995b).

Elson *et al.* (1993), in their major study of the effectiveness of green belts, found that the first four purposes were generally well understood and had operated successfully, although they drew attention to the need to clarify the relationship between the protection of historic centres and the restraint of development on their periphery. Urban regeneration, they suggested, might sometimes require the release of green belt land for major employment development and would, in any case, be more dependent on efforts to encourage the reuse of urban land than the mere denial of peripheral development opportunities.

According to Elson *et al.* (1993), green belts have had six main benefits. They have first prevented the worst excesses of scattered development and instead managed the process of decentralisation into clear physical form. 'What they have not done is greatly to affect the pace and rate of decentralisation. In short they are "shapers" not "stoppers"' (Elson *et al.* 1993, p. 138). Secondly, they have thus contained patterns of development to its most economic form, at least in terms of demands made on sewer runs, public transport routes, school provision and other demands historically made on public expenditure. Thirdly, they have helped separate urban areas, protect valued gaps and retain much valued identity. Fourthly, green belts have helped protect valuable agricultural land and keep open the possibility of aggregate extraction near major centres of demand. Fifthly, they have retained accessible and pleasant recreation land close to where people live and finally, by their very clarity in policy, they have discouraged speculative planning applications and reduced bureaucracy.

Criticisms of green belt policy are also well summarised by Elson *et al.* (1993). They revolve around three main areas: the economic costs of containment (which we discuss in Chapter 9), the over-prescriptive application of green belt policy preventing even minor forms of development within green belts, and negative side effects, both in terms of over-intensification within existing urban areas and 'leapfrogging' of development beyond green belts. As the DOE (1995b, para 2.8) recognised: 'If boundaries are drawn excessively tightly around existing built-up areas it may not be possible to maintain the degree of permanence that Green Belts should have.' At some point, the dynamic nature of the urban development process will grind to a halt against the static wall of a green belt. It is to this issue that we now turn in more detail.

Whether or not green belt boundaries are drawn tightly in the first place, some measure of flexibility is needed to adjust them when available land within the inner boundary is eventually exhausted. Otherwise, as Elson *et al.* (1993) remark, development may simply be diverted into deeper countryside, increasing distance travelled and commensurate carbon dioxide pollution. However, over the years, ministerial statements and circulars that have stressed the inviolability of the green belt and indicated that it could be amended only in exceptional circumstances have aggravated this predicament. As a result, there is now a substantial gap between public perceptions of, and support for, the concept of green belts and what might actually be needed to ensure sustainable urban development.

In Cambridge, for example, buoyant economic growth during the 1980s and 1990s meant that the green belt, originally devised in the 1950s to protect the city's perceived identity as a true university town, 'begun to act less as a protective shield and more as a tourniquet' (Studdert 2001, p. 56). The diversion of housing growth beyond the green belt transformed small villages into detached suburbs, increasing the car dependence of their new residents who still looked to Cambridge itself for employment and leisure activities. Regional Planning Guidance for East Anglia to 2016 now suggests that over the 15-year period, it will be necessary to accommodate as many households in the Cambridge subregion as currently exist in urban Cambridge. The Guidance proposes a sequential approach in which attention should focus on peripheral development around Cambridge, once the limited supply of brownfield sites within the city has been exhausted and before approval is given for a new settlement elsewhere.

However, since peripheral expansion is so constrained by the tight inner boundary of the Cambridge green belt, it will require a major outward movement of that boundary for any significant contribution to be made by the city to meeting its own housing requirements. Such an opportunity may well be provided by the proposed relocation of Cambridge Airport, the release of which would allow a planned extension of the city to take place on its least sensitive eastern side (Studdert 2001). As the case of Cambridge illustrates, a dynamic local economy is more happily reconciled with the concept of an adjustable rather than a permanently fixed green belt. It may thus be better to instil expectations within the general public that green belts are designated for a period of say 15–20 years at a time, than for politicians to create the dangerous illusion that such designations will last forever.

Yet 'because of the potential political explosiveness of any reappraisal of green belt policy, no serious national discussion on the topic is taking place' (Elson 1999, p. 156). According to Elson (1999), green belts are best employed as an exceptional measure in areas of high development pressure to channel growth to nearby areas where it may be more acceptable. Elsewhere, the growing use by local authorities of strategic gaps and green wedges could well be more appropriate than further extensions of green belts, since such local planning tools need not be regarded as permanent in the green belt sense but can instead have the same duration as other policies in the plan (Elson & Nichol 2001).

Although they found that many strategic gaps were quite narrow, Elson and Nichol (2001) suggested that they could still offer the physical and psychological benefits that derive from retaining open land close to where people live. Even as a local tool, strategic gaps can help prevent coalescence between separate settlements and protect their separate identities. Green wedges, as an alternative form of local restraint, are intended to penetrate urban areas and may provide opportunities for new greenways and cycle systems leading out into the countryside. Their designation can be based on the environmental quality of land and not just its location.

Since the principles of sustainable development may well require the use of land currently designated as green belt for sustainable urban extensions, Elson (1999) argues for a more sophisticated approach to urban growth management, in which more thoughtful and sparing use is made of green belts as a restraint tool, with strategic gaps and green wedges employed instead where justified by local circumstances. More radically, Leedale (2001) contends that it would be preferable to start new development plans with a clean sheet by first determining which are the most sustainable locations for new peripheral housing and only then applying local gap and green wedge notations, where they are necessary. He fears that, unless the weight accorded to such essentially local designations as strategic gaps remains below that of green belts, it will become increasingly difficult to secure sustainable forms of housing development anywhere on the edge of existing settlements.

In the north of Newcastle, however, almost 500 hectares of land was removed from the green belt in the late 1990s as part of the revised Unitary Development Plan for the city. The intention was both to provide additional development capacity within the city's boundary and to facilitate an innovative implementation linkage between greenfield development on the periphery and brownfield redevelopment within the existing city. The consortium responsible for the development of 80 hectares of the released land known as Newcastle Great Park subsequently agreed with the planning authority to link the phasing of greenfield housing development with the rate of brownfield development elsewhere within the city. On this basis, if the ratio of brownfield to greenfield development in the city as a whole were to fall below 60/40, then the consortium, which includes the housebuilders Bryant Homes and Leech Homes, agreed itself to develop potentially profitable brownfield sites for housing and to cover the costs of any compulsory purchase action taken by the local authority to assemble them.

This example illustrates how even in a northern city with a hesitant housing market, potential exists to capture wider benefits on the release on green belt land for development. Elsewhere, the greater the development pressure and the longer it is resisted, then the more lucrative the financial benefits that are likely to arise from the release of green belt land. In the absence of a national system for the taxation of development gain, we now turn our attention to the attempts of local authorities to capture a share of the financial benefits from greenfield development, whether or not previously designated as green belt.

Planning gain

In recent years, planning gain has become an increasingly important means by which local planning authorities have sought to manage development pressure through capturing more and more of the financial benefits that derive from the reallocation of greenfield land for development. Planning gain can be defined as the provision by a developer of some additional benefit, not necessarily related to the immediate development, offered to, or more usually requested by, a local planning authority (Adams 1994). Although in popular use, the term is not found in relevant legislation. Section 75 of the Town and Country Planning (Scotland) Act 1997 refers to planning agreements. However, in England and Wales, when Section 106 of the Town and Country Planning Act 1990 (previously Section 52 of the Town and Country Planning Act 1971) was amended by the Planning and Compensation Act 1991, planning obligations replaced the term planning agreements, south of the border.

According to Campbell *et al.* (2000), the use and scope of planning obligations significantly widened during the 1990s. They calculated that, between 1993 and 1998, the proportion of English planning permissions accompanied by planning obligations rose by about 40%. This they attributed to the austere financial environment in which local authorities now operate. As a result, planning obligations are now widely employed as an important mechanism by which financial responsibility for the provision of off-site infrastructure, facilities and services can be shifted from government to building producers and consumers. As discussed in Chapter 4, they are now also regarded as an essential means to secure affordable housing development.

While Campbell *et al.* (2000) suggested that only about 1.5% of English planning applications as a whole have a planning obligation attached to them, this proportion rose to almost 17% in the cases of major forms of development and to almost 26% for major residential development. From a sample of over 500 separate planning obligations, they found an important change in the nature of planning obligations from an earlier emphasis on on-site works such as environmental enhancement and the provision of open space towards off-site infrastructure such as major highway improvements in the locality.

At a more general level, developers were increasingly expected to contribute to civic amenities, public art, commuted sums for park and ride schemes and other forms of wider community benefits, rather than merely to reduce the impact of the specific development. The rationale for planning obligations has thus been broadened from that of merely seeking to mitigate development impacts and remove development constraints to 'the amelioration of more diffuse social, economic and environmental impacts and to the pursuit of wider policy objectives' (Campbell *et al.* 2000, p. 766).

As might be expected, the growing dependence of local authorities on planning gain as a substitute for funding expenditure that might in the past have been met from the public purse has created an implicit and occasionally explicit linkage between planning decisions and the provision of local infrastructure and other services. At one level, this puts corporate pressure on the planners within local authorities to secure the best financial deal from new development for other parts of the organisation, in the form, for example, of new schools and roads. More significantly, however, the capacity to extract planning gain from development has become an increasingly influential consideration not only once development has been agreed in principle, but also at the earlier stage of choosing between development alternatives.

For, as Campbell *et al.* (2000, p. 773) reported from their research:

> several officers noted that both the designation of sites in the development plan and the preparation of planning briefs was influenced by the propensity to extract planning gain. One implication of this, for example, is that larger, greenfield sites would tend to be favoured for residential development over smaller sites or sites in brownfield locations.

Since there are much greater opportunities for funding facilities and services from developers' contributions in the thriving regions of Britain than in those experiencing economic decline, it is apparent that the far broader use and scope of planning gain by the late 1990s contributed to the case for well-managed and large-scale greenfield development in prosperous parts of the country.

For, as Grant (1998b) points out, under certain market conditions especially, the additional cost of planning gain on greenfield development can be passed back into the land price rather than forward to house buyers. Campbell *et al.* (2000) show this changing relationship diagrammatically (see Fig. 7.4),

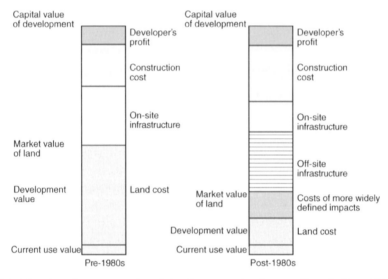

Fig. 7.4   The changing construction of development value (source: Campbell *et al.* 2000).

suggesting that the practice of planning gain is now so well-entrenched that landowners increasingly expect to adjust prices downwards to cover the costs of off-site as well as on-site infrastructure provision. This is one reason why developers are prepared to accept obligations to fund services and facilities that, as Evans and Bate (2000) point out, can be only tenuously related to the proposed development. In Chapter 9, we investigate in more detail the circumstances in which the cost of planning gain may or may not be passed back to the original landowner.

Although, as Ennis (1996) reminds us, developers will often negotiate hard both to resist local authority demands for planning gain and to limit the scale of provision, in the end they often go along with such demands in order to speed up the planning process and secure local authority support. Whereas much of the early literature on planning gain concerned its alleged lack of morality and legitimacy (see, for example, Heap & Ward 1980; Property Advisory Group 1981), developers take a far more practical approach to extending the scope of planning obligations, whenever necessary to secure a speedy permission and avoid a lengthy appeal (Ennis 1996). Campbell *et al.* (2000) offer a more positive view of the benefits of planning obligations to developers, suggesting, for instance, that a housing development providing places in a new primary school for residents' children will be more attractive to house buyers and more lucrative to developers than one reliant on overcrowded school capacity in the general locality.

There has been much discussion of whether the practice of planning gain should be replaced by standard development impact fees (see, for example,

Grant 1998b; Evans & Bate 2000). The DTLR (2001d), in a consultation paper issued as part of its fundamental review of the planning system, favoured a more flexible approach of standardised tariffs for different kinds of development that would be set locally through the plan-making process, while still leaving some room for variation on a site-by-site basis.

Our concern here, however, is not to evaluate alternative methods to collect planning gain but rather to show that the financial implications of planning decisions for local authorities are no longer a tangential issue but now reach to the heart of the greenfield/brownfield debate. The more local authorities become dependent on planning gain (or whatever alternative method is preferred to enable them to share in development value) then the stronger will be the pressure upon them to favour new development where that value is at its greatest. A contradiction may therefore exist between local political resistance to greenfield encroachment and an authority's financial interest in maximising the potential for planning gain by allocating large greenfield sites for development.

Sustainable greenfield design

In earlier chapters, we argued that although new housing development on greenfield land can be designed to accord with sustainability principles, traditional practices in the speculative housebuilding industry present a significant barrier to the implementation of sustainable residential development. In particular, most of the industry is primarily concerned with immediate marketability of individual house types and has little commitment to the sustainability impact of these products in the long term, let alone to the creation of residential communities or their relationship to existing urban areas.

In a Scottish context, Moir *et al.* (1997) claim that new housing, even in the countryside, need not jar with the existing landscape but can be designed to be in harmony with, and even to contribute to, the enhancement of the local landscape. This can be achieved, they suggest, if effective design control is applied by local authorities and accepted by developers. More controversially, they argue that such an approach would encourage a shift away from traditional strongly held protectionist stances against new development in some parts of rural Scotland to more flexible, even permissive approaches to housing in the countryside.

In the past, local planning authorities have faced significant challenges in seeking to influence the practices and products of the speculative housebuilding industry to accord more fully with the principles of sustainable development. Now, however, the policy context is rapidly changing with central government exhorting local authorities to adopt design policies that will enable both greenfield and brownfield development to be managed in a more sustainable way. At a local level, such policies are becoming an increasingly important mode of response in those regions experiencing intense development pressure.

In Kent, for instance, all the local authorities have come together to produce a new Design Guide that seeks, in contrast to most such guides of the past, to move beyond aesthetic and highway considerations and instead address a much fuller range of sustainability issues (Raymond 2000). This new guide is intended to demonstrate how innovation and innovative techniques in relation to highway design, water demand, community safety, construction materials and mixed-use forms of development can be used to promote sustainability objectives. Such a pro-active attempt to influence the design and form of new development and not merely its location, emerged as a policy response to the poor quality of many recent developments in Kent, which were dominated by highway layouts, lacked convenient facilities and led to increasing dependence on the private car.

The Urban Task Force (1999), while setting out how the achievement of design excellence was essential to delivering an urban renaissance, also commented that this fresh commitment to urban design should apply not just to existing towns and cities but to greenfield sites as well. This theme was taken forward by the Deputy Prime Minister and Secretary of State for the Environment, Transport and the Regions, John Prescott, who, in introducing the new PPG 3 to the House of Commons, pointed out that well-designed, attractive and sustainable new housing need not consume endless hectares of beautiful countryside (Prescott 2000).

To emphasise the increasing importance of well-designed residential environments within Government policy guidance, a companion guide to PPG 3 entitled *By Design: Better Places to Live* was published jointly by the DTLR and the Commission for Architecture and the Built Environment (DTLR/ CABE 2001). This illustrated how key principles of urban design could be applied to create sustainable residential development at both brownfield and greenfield locations by:

- Making more efficient use of land.

- Promoting better accessibility to local facilities and public transport.

- Supporting crime prevention and community safety.

- Creating more socially inclusive communities.

- Promoting energy efficiency.

Two related Government publications also demonstrated how good design principles needed to be applied as much to greenfield as brownfield locations. Of these, the *Urban Design Compendium*, published by English Partnerships and the Housing Corporation (Llewelyn-Davies 2000), aimed to unravel the design qualities of successful urban areas, while *By Design: Urban Design in the Planning System: Towards Better Practice* (DETR/CABE 2000) explored how better urban design could be achieved through best practice in planning.

This increasing political commitment to higher-quality urban design in its broadest sense was reinforced in both the Urban and Rural White Papers published in 2000. The Urban White Paper called for good-quality design to be second nature for new development and emphasised its importance in achieving social, economic and environmental sustainability in new housing schemes (DETR 2000b). Interestingly, the Rural White Paper was more specific on this point, commenting that:

> New housing is not always well-designed or attractive. Poor housing can change the character of a settlement, particularly in a village setting. New housing needs to be sympathetically sited and built in a style and use of materials which blend in with the rest of the village .... Creating better-designed places is a central message of our new planning guidance for housing (PPG 3).
>
> (DETR/MAFF 2000, p. 54)

A forceful array of policy guidance and best practice advice has thus emerged that suggests that the poor standard of greenfield housing design evident in the past is likely to prove less acceptable in the future. However, such good intentions still need to be translated into practical results. As a demonstration of what can be achieved in sustainable forms of development on greenfield land, construction of the Duchy of Cornwall's new urban village known as Poundbury on 160 hectares on the edge of Dorchester is now well advanced. Development began in 1993 in accordance with the masterplan designed by Leon Krier and approved by the Prince of Wales in his capacity as Duke of Cornwall and sole landowner. Much of the press attention has focused on the architectural details of the development that seek to reflect the traditional Dorset vernacular in terms of traditional market scale, pattern, design, materials and decoration.

Unlike most speculative housing estates, however, Poundbury (see Fig. 7.5) has been designed to be a community in its own right with a mix of different land uses and tenures in close proximity. Each of its four urban quarters will provide local education, employment, shopping and leisure facilities. Over a 20-year period, Poundbury is intended to reach an eventual population of about 5000 people accommodated in a design form that contrasts sharply with the standard suburban estate of the twentieth century and instead draws its inspiration from more fine-grained traditional approaches to urban layout. The success of Poundbury, however, is not dependent only on its design approach but also on four important institutional factors, namely, the single landowner, a sympathetic local authority, a clear masterplan and extensive public consultation (Prince's Foundation and English Partnerships 2000).

Fig. 7.5   Poundbury, Dorchester.

Although it can be argued that the way these four institutional factors came together was unique in Poundbury's case, Thompson-Fawcett (2000) suggests four reasons why the project could be replicated elsewhere. First, the development has been financially viable with the returns increasing with time. Second, the traditional forms of architecture employed have been proved to have strong market appeal. Thirdly, Poundbury has demonstrated that social housing can be developed to a high quality and with architectural variety, even within Housing Corporation guidelines. Finally, the use of a building design code has allowed a wide variety of design solutions to be produced even within the local vernacular tradition. While Poundbury is certainly not typical of much British housing development, its success and broad appeal thus presents an important challenge to long-established practices in both the speculative housebuilding industry and the planning system.

For sustainable residential development to be achieved on greenfield land, an effective institutional environment needs to be in place for controlling and influencing the processes and products of the development industry. Unfortunately, however, the past weakness of the planning system in relation to the housebuilding industry and its lack of integration within a broader land policy agenda have convinced many politicians at local level that the best response to greenfield development pressure is not that of management but increasingly that of resistance. It is to this alternative that we now turn.

Resistance to greenfield development pressure

Under the Planning and Compensation Act 1991, central government devolved more responsibility for strategic decisions on new housing requirements in England to structure and unitary planning authorities. In many instances, the withdrawal of immediate central supervision of housing land allocations provided authorities with the long-desired opportunity to reduce the amount of greenfield land they allocated for housing development. In this section, we first draw on some recent examples to demonstrate how resistance to greenfield development pressure is fast becoming the dominant discourse in housing land policy, especially in the South of England. We then investigate whether the introduction of a greenfield development tax would reinforce such strategic planning policies by reducing the incentive of landowners and developers to bring forward greenfield development proposals.

Playing housing numbers

A pattern is now emerging, at least in southern England, of local planning authorities using their new-found freedom to reduce their future housing land allocations below those recommended by regional planning guidance. In some cases, such reductions have been implemented in defiance of recommendations from independent structure plan panels. Only rarely does the Secretary of State appear willing to use his reserve powers of intervention in such cases. Although many technical arguments are put forward by local authorities to justify decisions to reduce housing land allocations, at heart they reflect growing opposition to greenfield housing development and a belief that past emphasis on managing development pressure should be replaced by a policy of increasing resistance.

As a prelude to this discussion, it should be noted that numbers of new housing units proposed in final regional planning guidance are usually higher than those proposed in the draft guidance and reflect the recommendations of public examination panels as amended by the Secretary of State. In East Anglia, for instance, the number of new housing units proposed up to 2016 in the final Regional Planning Guidance (RPG) is 207 900 in comparison with 204 500 in the draft, while in the South East, a final figure of 780 000 was inserted by the Secretary of State compared to a draft figure of 666 000 (Counsell & Bruff 2001). In the latter case, the panel had initiated much controversy (see Chapter 1) and incurred the wrath of the Secretary of State by recommending a figure of 1.1 million, which he refused to accept.

In other regions, where the regional planning process was less advanced, panels had recommended that the draft figures up to 2016 of 373 000 for the South West and 251 700 for Yorkshire and the Humber be increased to 407 000 and 263 700 respectively[2]. Only in the East Midlands and the North East had panels recommended reductions in the proposed housing numbers contained in the draft RPG (Counsell & Bruff 2001). In most cases, therefore, the regional planning process may well serve to increase proposed housing numbers above those preferred by local authorities, although not necessarily to the levels proposed by independent panels. The real battle begins, however, once regional planning guidance is used to inform structure and unitary plan preparation.

In the South West, for example, Somerset County Council resolved in early 1999 to provide land for only 44 800 new dwellings over the period 1991 to 2011, despite higher figures of 50 000 for the county in regional planning guidance and 50 700 recommended by the structure plan panel. In this case, the technical justification appeared to revolve around the Council's perception that the panel had misunderstood economic signals and allowed for higher labour market growth than necessary. A few months later in the adjacent Avon structure plan area, the independent Structure Plan Panel Report was published, recommending that new housing figures for the period 1996 to 2011 be increased from 43 000 proposed by the local authorities to 54 300.

In nearby Gloucestershire, at about the same time, the County Council resolved to adopt a revised structure plan, which made provision for only 50 000 new homes in the county over the period 1991–2011 in comparison with 53 000 recommended in regional planning guidance and 55 000 by the Structure Plan Panel. Predictably, the Secretary of State's decision not to intervene in the Gloucestershire case was hailed by the CPRE as a welcome signal but lamented by the HBF as a threat to the credibility of the independent examination process. Since the Secretary of State had earlier in the same year failed to prevent the housing numbers in the Devon/Plymouth area, located deeper in the South West, being reduced from 79 000 in regional planning guidance to 75 800 in the relevant structure plan, housebuilding interests in the South West were becoming increasingly frustrated by the flexibility devolved to local authorities.

In the South East, however, the Secretary of State intervened to force West Sussex to provide for an additional 12 800 homes in its structure plan for the period up to 2011, on top of the 37 900 proposed by the County Council. When taken to the High Court by West Sussex in 1999, the Secretary of State was found to have acted lawfully and the decision was upheld. In Essex, the Structure Plan Panel reporting in the same year, recommended that housing provision in the county over the structure plan period be increased from 69 600 to 76 000 and that the inner boundary of the green belt be modified to find further housing sites. More recently in 2001, Kent County Council resolved to provide land for only 4700 new homes a year over the structure plan period in contrast to the higher annual figure of 5700 set out in recently published regional guidance.

Almost on a monthly basis, these examples of resistance to greenfield development pressure are repeated in those parts of the country considered most attractive by the housebuilding industry. Where local authorities successfully reduce the numbers of new homes required in planning documents, that reduction is almost invariably attributed to greenfield rather than brownfield provision. Indeed, alongside the prevalent desire to reduce housing numbers as a whole, local authorities are increasingly keen to place an ever-greater proportion of development on brownfield sites.

In Leicestershire, for example, when the new county structure plan was placed on deposit in 2000, the proportion of new homes to be built on brownfield sites was increased from 50% recommended in draft regional planning guidance to 55%. In fact, as Table 7.4 shows, the Secretary of State, in finalis-

Table 7.4 'New style' RPG: proportion of new dwellings intended to be built on brownfield land or provided by conversions.

English region	Draft RPG produced by regional planning body		Final RPG issued by Secretary of State	
	Date	Proportion	Date	Proportion
East Anglia	August 1998	40%	November 2000	50%
South East	December 1998	60%	March 2001	60%
South West	August 1999	36%	September 2001	50%
Yorkshire and the Humber	October 1999	60%	October 2001	60%
East Midlands	November 1999	45%	February 2002	60%
North East	December 1999	60%	April 2001*	65–70%

*Proposed changes to draft.
Source: Counsell (2001) as updated from DETR web site.

ing 'new style' regional planning guidance, has given every encouragement to this latter tendency by regularly raising the proportion of new dwellings required to be built on previously developed land or provided through conversions above the draft figures previously submitted by the regional planning bodies (which consist largely of local authorities within the particular region acting collectively).

In a Scottish context, Walton (2000) suggests that the rules of the housing planning process set by government fail to take satisfactory account of likely 'windfall' development (the technical term for those sites that unexpectedly become available for redevelopment during the plan period). He claims that: 'the consistent underestimation of the contribution made by windfall sites has resulted in local authorities unnecessarily allocating large areas of open countryside for housing' (Walton 2000, p. 402).

Although Walton (2000) points out that the different planning requirements south of the border do not make his detailed Scottish analysis immediately applicable in a English context, his logic of seeking to limit greenfield development as far as possible by exploiting brownfield opportunities to the full is one that strikes a chord with much current planning thinking both in central and local government. The Secretary of State's reluctance to intervene in most of the above decisions of planning authorities that ignore regional planning guidance or recommendations from independent panels derives primarily from their shared desire to resist greenfield development.

Yet, as Essex *et al.* (1999) point out, fragmented land ownership, redundant listed buildings, contamination and other site problems mean that it should not be assumed that urban windfall sites will continue to come forward at the same rate as in recent years. Indeed, since many of the easy urban sites have already been developed, those that remain are more likely to require some form of public intervention to ensure their development. On this basis, resistance to greenfield development pressure is unlikely to succeed in the long term unless it is matched by more determined efforts to ensure that a compensating supply of housing land is made available on brownfield sites.

Irrespective of the success of future brownfield policies, however, fundamental questions remain about the demand implications of a policy of resistance to greenfield housing development. In Chapter 9, we suggest that urban containment policies may have significant side effects in terms of housing markets and that these will be exacerbated if planning policies seek increasingly to resist the allocation of greenfield land for development, without taking commensurate action on the demand side. In this context, we next consider whether the introduction of a greenfield development tax would be a useful supporting mechanism in seeking not only to resist pressure for greenfield development but also to reduce it.

Greenfield development tax

In 1998, the Civic Trust proposed the concept of greenfield housing levy, payable on the grant of planning permission for all housing development on sites where no built development has existed since 1947. If the levy were to be set at 10% of development value, the Trust estimated that approximately £250 million would be raised annually in England. This could then be channelled back into urban regeneration, most probably through regional development agencies (Civic Trust 1998). In principle, a greenfield levy thus has two potential purposes: first, to act as a direct disincentive to greenfield development and secondly, to apply the money raised to assist brownfield redevelopment. As Evans and Bate (2000, p. 7) comment: 'The two elements offer a neat connection between greenfield and brownfield development which give an inherent appeal to this mechanism in principle.'

However, this confusion of purpose masks a contradiction in the practicality of any greenfield tax. If it is intended to reduce greenfield development, then only limited funds will be raised for redirection to brownfield redevelopment. More worrying, if it is intended to raise funds for brownfield redevelopment, then as Evans and Bate (2000, p. 8) point out: 'A perverse incentive would be set up to encourage greenfield land release as a fund-raising device for brownfield land recycling.' However, according to the Civic Trust (1998), the prime purpose of a greenfield levy would indeed be to encourage urban revitalisation and more quality urban housing rather than merely stop greenfield development.

The Urban Task Force (1999) called for further research into whether any greenfield tax would be likely to change behaviour and reduce development, be absorbed into reduced land values, and raise resources to promote better use of urban land and buildings. Subsequently, Needham (2000) offered a theoretical review of the effects on land taxation and development charges on land use. He argued that, in order to have a significant effect on land use, any such tax would need to be huge and, as a result, no owner would be willing to supply land for development. Alternatively, a tax at the politically realistic rate of 10% of market value would have only a small effect on prices and a negligible effect on land use. He concluded that land taxes and charges could not be effective as an instrument of planning, unless they were applied very selectively, for example to reduce the amount of land devoted to car parks.

Previous British experience of attempts to tax development land value suggests that only small sums are actually raised at relatively high administrative costs. This is partly because private owners held land off the market in anticipation of political change leading to the abolition of the tax while, as the Urban Task Force (1999) points out, developers slowed down their activity and diverted resources into the financial markets. The present political consensus around planning gain and other established forms of taxation may well hold out a better prospect of influencing land markets than proposals to introduce wholly new taxes.

Evans and Bate (2000) thus recommend the extension of value added tax (VAT) at the full 17.5% rate to all new house construction on greenfield sites, apart from that built by registered charities or for social housing. They suggest that this would have most impact where development pressure is limited and land values are low, but they argue that this is precisely where brownfield development is most desirable. On the financial side, they calculate that such a tax would produce over £900 million annually, about half of which could be directed to VAT adjustment in favour of building repair, maintenance and refurbishment and the other half to urban regeneration more generally.

Subsequently, the Fabian Society (2000) concurred that the full rate of VAT should be levied on new housebuilding in designated greenfield locations and calculated that this would produce some £1 billion for regeneration schemes. Critically, the Society argued that such a tax would have little impact on house selling prices but would instead result in lower values paid by developers for greenfield housing land. However, if this were to reduce the incentive of owners to supply greenfield land for development, it might well contribute to house price inflation, unless consumer demand for new housing products were also to fall.

The concept of a greenfield development tax should be distinguished from the more general notion of 'land value taxation' that derives from the work of Henry George in the nineteenth century and is carried forward today by such organisations as the Henry George Foundation and the Land Value Taxation Campaign. Land value taxation, or site value rating as it is sometimes called, is commonly defined as a tax on the annual market rental value of land, disregarding buildings and other improvements.

Proponents of land value taxation often allege that it will help reduce urban sprawl by bringing back into productive use vacant urban land that is currently kept off the market by speculators (Roakes 1996). However, the likely strength of this indirect effect on the demand for greenfield land could depend on many factors, not least of which would be the extent of actual encouragement offered by land value taxation to more intensive forms of urban development, especially in cities with high rates of vacancy (Wyatt 1994).

If land value taxation could provide a more effective means to capture development value than the previous legislative attempts of 1947, 1967 and 1975 or the current more informal system of planning gain, as Law and Mills (2000) contend, it might act directly either to increase or reduce the supply of greenfield land. For, on the one hand, while the rate of greenfield development may be accelerated if owners of land with development potential are encouraged to sell more quickly to developers, on the other, such owners may be left with little desire to see their land released for development in the first place. Such alternative scenarios suggest that, as a mechanism to control urban sprawl, land value taxation could be even more unpredictable than a greenfield development tax.

In this context, however, it is important to remember that the original concept of land value taxation as conceived by Henry George was intended as a taxation not a land policy measure. As Wyatt (1994, p. 1) explains:

> His 'single tax' movement was based on the belief that LVT could completely substitute for all other forms of government taxation, and that this would remove the unearned surplus accruing to landowners and redistribute unearned private wealth to the society at large. The notion had populist anti-monopoly adherents over the years.

Only more recently have some environmentalists suggested that land value taxation might also help control urban sprawl, although the arguments here remain ambiguous and controversial.

The variety of potential impacts that could arise from seeking to reduce greenfield development pressure through the taxation system rather than merely by restrictive planning policies, highlights the need for all such forms of intervention in land and housing markets to be appraised in economic as well as political terms. For while it may well be possible to resist development pressure in a particular locality, and allow it to be diverted to neighbouring localities, the greater the area over which any attempt is made to hold back the tide of development, then the harder it becomes to succeed without detrimental side effects.

At a regional or national level, it cannot be assumed that brownfield land necessarily provides a ready substitute for greenfield land, without more active public sector intervention in urban land markets than has been the case in the recent part. Thus, any evaluation of the policy of resisting greenfield development pressure can be undertaken only in the light of the success or otherwise of attempts to promote brownfield redevelopment, which we discuss in detail in the next chapter. Before then, however, as the next section explains, it is worth remembering that in some limited parts of the UK, greenfield development pressure is not resisted but actively encouraged and accommodated.

Accommodation of greenfield development pressure

A rare reaction among local authorities these days is to seek, for social or economic reasons, to encourage and exploit greenfield development potential. In the past, authorities such as Sheffield have tried to ensure the provision of executive housing on their urban peripheries in order to broaden the scope of the local housing market and reinforce their policies to attract new employers to the city. More recently, authorities in the North East of England sought to provide in regional planning guidance for a greater number of houses than commensurate with government population predictions as part of their overall strategy to promote a more dynamic economy and healthy living environment. However, the independent panel report concluded that such an approach would necessitate undue modification of the green belt and cut the overall housing provision from 119000 to 111000 up to 2016, while suggesting that more could be accommodated on brownfield sites than the proportion of 60% put forward in the draft RPG (Counsell & Bruff 2001). Subsequently, the Secretary of State indicated that he wished to see even this figure raised to at least 65%.

On this point, the Urban Task Force (1999, pp. 217–18) commented that:

we do not accept the argument of certain northern planning authorities that the way to overcome low demand for housing in their area is to build on the surrounding greenfields, rather than tackling the regeneration of their urban heartlands. The release of such land will simply exacerbate their long term problems.

It is indeed ironic that authorities in locations with the least development pressure appear the most willing to accommodate greenfield development.

In their study of new housing in the Scottish countryside, Moir *et al.* (1997) note that a number of planning authorities, especially in the remoter rural areas, were prepared to adopt a relaxed approach to housing in the country-side. Such a permissive approach to small-scale development was taken to encourage economic or community revitalisation, especially in those loca-tions where the settlement pattern was already dispersed and where it was considered that new development could be readily absorbed into the local landscape.

In England, a rural exceptions policy has similarly permitted small-scale social housing on greenfield land since the late 1980s. More generally, from her work on sustainable housing strategies in rural Gloucestershire, Wil-liams (2000) argues that new housing development could help regenerate rural areas that have long suffered from social and economic decline. She points out the benefits that new housing development can bring to rural areas in terms of expanding opportunities to provide local employment and services. As she explains, this approach requires considered use of such techniques as accessibility analysis and catchment area analysis, but it does point to the fact that new development potentially has advantages as well as disadvantages.

Conclusions

As Warren Evans (1997, p. 90) points out: 'There was nothing in the Labour Government's 1947 planning legislation to suggest that it would operate as a rationing system for development land.' In many parts of the UK, however, greenfield development pressure is increasingly seen not as the outcome of broader social and economic processes requiring careful management, still less as an opportunity to create more sustainable patterns of living than in the past, but rather as an immediate and potent threat to rural amenity. In such locations, resistance to what is now perceived as a potentially over-whelming tide of further development is regarded as the most appropriate strategy both to preserve what remains of that amenity and to protect the interests of those fortunate enough to have arrived before the barriers against further greenfield development were strengthened.

Rationing of development land is thus widely practised, creating a high-price land market in many localities. For as we have shown in this chapter, the current controversies over greenfield development are not simply matters of land use but critically concern how the potential benefits from development are distributed. It could, for example, be argued that the growing practice of planning gain and its possible future codification into standardised tariffs, represents a conspiracy between planner and developer to deprive the land-owner of significant development value. However, since development value is largely attributable to planning restrictions in the first place, the tighter those restrictions become, then the more planning gain there is to be extract-ed from landowners without necessarily reducing their absolute returns.

It should be remembered, of course, that resistance to greenfield develop-ment in the name of amenity protection is not necessarily comparable with environmental protection. In Germany, for example, municipalities are re-quired to prepare their own landscape plans, establish the current state of the local environment and landscape, define objectives for nature conservation and landscaping, and indicate how they might be implemented. In assessing development proposals, 'The approach is an ecological one chiefly concerned with maintaining ecosystem functions, rather than a cosmetic one chiefly concerned with maintaining amenity. In this, it differs fundamentally from the traditional emphasis in Britain' (Wilding & Raemaekers 2000, p. 217).

This is because, in Germany, where new development is seen to be harmful to the existing ecological balance, specific compensatory works are required either within the development site or nearby to ensure that local ecological systems are at least maintained and maybe enhanced. In view of the ecologi-cally barren nature of much of the so-called greenfield land that the British planning system now goes to great length to protect, it may be worth reflect-ing whether a more ecologically based approach to development opportuni-ties could actually enhance environmental systems, even if at the expense of visual amenity.

Indeed, it is possible that the planning system could achieve more in sus-tainability terms, if it concentrated its attention on improving the quality of new housing that is actually produced, and dropped its apparent obsession with limiting the quantity of development. For, if urban containment comes to be regarded in British popular and political thinking, not as one possible approach to planning but rather as the entire embodiment of the planning system, then the broader potential of planning to influence the development process as a whole could be put at risk, should containment ever fall into public disrepute.

However, while it can thus be argued that the tide of development pressure can never be permanently held back, our concern here is not to press for immediate and substantial release of greenfield land, not least because the current structure of the British housebuilding industry would be likely to waste the opportunity to create sustainable patterns of development. Instead it is important to identify the contradictions involved in current housing land policy and draw attention to the urgent need to match greenfield restrictions with realistic policies to ensure greater brownfield redevelopment. It is thus to the potential of brownfield land that we turn in the next chapter.

Notes

(1) Of course, if developers were willing and able to purchase agricultural land years before the likelihood of planning permission arises, and retain it over this lengthy period, they, rather than the landowner, would be able to capture the bulk of development value. There is, however, little evidence that this approach is common among developers today. Nevertheless, as Chapter 5 explained, potential still exists for developers to benefit from any inflationary increases in land prices between the time when options are exercised or conditional contracts for the freehold purchase of land are completed after the grant of planning permission and the eventual selling date of the finished dwellings.

(2) Final RPGs for South West and for Yorkshire and the Humber were published in late 2001, some months after the analysis by Counsell and Bruff (2001) had appeared. New housing provision in the South West is set at an annual rate of 20 200 new dwellings over the period from 1996 to 2016 or a total of 404 000, which is slightly below the panel recommendation of 407 000 but still substantially above the draft figure of 373 000. For Yorkshire and the Humber, an annual figure of 14 765 new dwellings is set for the period 1998 to 2016, which equates to 265 770. This is above both the panel recommendation of 251 700 and the draft figure of 263 700.

8

Brownfield Housing Development

Brownfield redevelopment is now at the heart of the UK Government's urban land policy. By 2008, it is intended that 60% of all new homes in England should be constructed on previously developed land or provided through the conversion of existing buildings. In this chapter, we critically examine whether, over a prolonged period of time, such substantial concentration on brownfield redevelopment is realistically capable of implementation. Since only a small proportion of future homes is expected to be built directly by the public sector, the Government is crucially dependent for the success of its policy on influencing the strategies and actions of speculative housebuilders, registered social landlords (RSLs) and others. Brownfield land policy thus presents a classic test of the extent to which agencies beyond the immediate control of government machinery can be persuaded to implement government policy and, more generally, of whether and how land and property markets can be influenced by the state.

The chapter begins with a quantitative assessment of brownfield development potential. Although headline figures of recent performance may appear to provide grounds for optimism in meeting the 60% brownfield target, we argue that caution is needed in interpreting past trends. Moreover, since uncertainty surrounds estimates of future supplies at both the national and local levels, we contend that the institutional measures by which brownfield development potential can best be realised deserve as much, if not more, attention than the precise calculation of that potential.

This leads on to the second part of the chapter, which investigates how the brownfield redevelopment process is impeded by specific constraints, such as planning, physical and ownership difficulties. These constraints mean that, while towns and cities can appear to the general public to contain numerous brownfield sites capable of residential development, the practical suitability of brownfield land for development may well be limited, unless the state acts to ensure that such supply-side constraints are overcome.

Yet irrespective of any such action, housebuilders will not be persuaded to switch their activities increasingly to brownfield sites unless they perceive a demand for their products. The third part of the chapter therefore considers the nature of recent demand for new housing at brownfield locations and examines how it might be broadened. We suggest that in contrast to greenfield locations, successful marketing of brownfield development is likely to be less dependent on the images created by housebuilders and more dependent on the capacity of urban policy-makers to promote and create thriving towns and cities.

The chapter therefore concludes by calling on policy-makers to focus not simply on the development potential of each vacant and derelict site but more fully on the broader urban context within which such sites are located. While there are now welcome signs of a renewed and more substantive policy commitment to urban areas, significant policy challenges lie ahead if brownfield redevelopment is ever to provide the location of first choice for the majority of new house purchasers.

Brownfield development potential

How much new housing can be accommodated on brownfield sites? At the turn of the twenty-first century, this is perhaps the most important question in the minds of those responsible for the development of urban land policy in the UK. This section approaches the question from three different directions. We first examine past trends extracted from *Land Use Change Statistics* (LUCS), secondly consider future supplies indicated by the *National Land Use Database* (NLUD) and finally reflect on the nature and potential contribution of *Urban Capacity Studies* (UCS). However, before embarking on this review, it is important to recall the precise substance of the Government's target and of other views on what proportion of new housing could be accommodated on brownfield land.

In 1995, the Conservative Government announced that it wished to see half of all new homes in England built on reused sites (DOE 1995c). After much controversy, the incoming Labour Government resolved in 1998 that a more ambitious commitment should be made. Accordingly: 'The national target is that by 2008, 60% of additional housing should be provided on previously-developed land and through the conversion of existing buildings' (DETR 2000a, para 23). Officially, this target applies only to England. Although planning policy in Scotland and Wales far prefers the reuse of vacant and derelict land to greenfield development, no official target for brownfield development has been set.

Among those who considered even a 60% target too low, perhaps the most authoritative voice was that of the UK Round Table on Sustainable Development (1997) which argued for a 75% aspirational target in England and for similarly challenging targets in Scotland, Wales and Northern Ireland. The CPRE (1997b, c) along with other environmental groups supported this more ambitious target. In contrast, however, the Town and Country Planning Association (1997) consistently questioned the wisdom and practicality of raising the English target from 50% to 60%.

Close examination of the precise wording of the Government's target reveals three interesting features. First, it makes no distinction between previously developed land in urban and rural areas. In 1995, for example, although 53% of all new dwellings in England were built on previously developed land, almost 13% of these were located in rural areas and just under 41% in urban areas (DETR 1998d). Redevelopment of mineral, landfill and defence sites for housing in rural areas therefore contributes to the target, even if such sites are located in open country. It is thus not surprising that House of Commons Environment, Transport and Regional Affairs Committee (1999) argued that the Government should 'aim to concentrate development on brownfield sites in appropriate urban locations. Accordingly as we have frequently recommended, it should set a target for the re-use of brownfield sites in urban areas' (Recommendation (w) of 11th report).

Secondly, new dwellings produced through the conversion of existing buildings contribute to meeting the Government's 60% target. No annual statistics are available for such conversions; instead, the Government estimates that they add about 3% to the proportion of new dwellings built on previously developed land. Alternatively, in comparison with the previous Conservative Government's target of 50% of all new homes to be built on reused sites, it could be said that incoming Labour Government raised the figure to only 57% and not 60%.

Finally, the policy focus on the *relative* proportion of brownfield redevelopment and conversions creates the paradoxical possibility that Ministers can claim success, even if the *absolute* amount of land recycled falls, for example, as a result of a slowdown in housebuilding. This suggests that too much concentration on targets and potential capacities may serve to distract attention from what needs to be done in practice to promote more brownfield housing development.

Land Use Change Statistics

Land Use Change Statistics (LUCS) have been produced for England since the mid-1980s. They now provide a valuable time series that enable changes between the most important urban and rural land uses to be tracked. From the data, brownfield redevelopment can be monitored in two ways:

- The proportion of **land** used for new dwellings that was previously developed.

- The proportion of **new dwellings** built on previously developed land.

When the 3% estimated allowance for the conversion of existing buildings to residential use is added to the proportion of new dwellings built on previously developed land, a third statistic is created against which progress towards the Government's 60% target can be monitored. Figure 8.1 shows the trends for the three statistics since they have each been available.

A difference of approximately six percentage points is immediately noticeable in Fig. 8.1 between the 'land' and 'dwellings' rates of recycling. This is because the density of new residential development on previously developed land (at 28 dwellings per hectare, on average) is higher than development on land that was not previously developed land (at 22 dwellings per hectare,

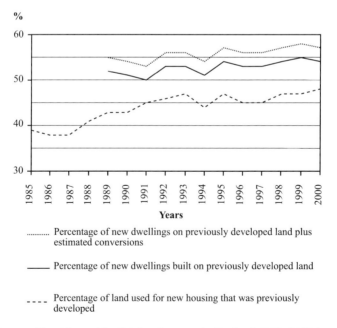

Fig. 8.1   Reuse of land for residential development in England 1985–2000 (source: DTLR 2001a).

on average). Recent policy advice discourages developments at less than 30 dwellings per hectare and encourages those of between 30 and 50 dwellings per hectare (DETR 2000a). If successfully implemented, this could make a significant difference to future rates of recycling.

An impression can be drawn from LUCS that recycling trends are proceeding in the right direction and that it is only a matter of time until the 60% target is reached. Unfortunately, such an impression is false. Certainly, the proportion of housing land supplied from previous development increased from 39% in 1985 to 48% in 2000. However, most of this improvement took place up to 1992, since when the rate has remained largely unchanged. Again, the proportion of new dwellings built on previously developed land in 2000 – 54% – was very close to the 1992 figure of 53%.

More worryingly, however, for policy-makers are the *absolute* figures on the reuse of brownfield land for new housing development that tend to be obscured beneath the headline attention accorded to *relative* proportions. In 1988, of the 7730 hectares of land used for residential development, 41% or 3169 hectares was previously developed. Taking this 1988 figure as an index base (as recommended by LUCS), it is apparent that the absolute total of previously developed land used for new housing actually declined during the 1990s, to such an extent that the 1998 figure of 2898 hectares of previously developed land used for new housing was only 91% of the 1988 figure, a decade previously. Figure 8.2 shows this *absolute* decline in the reuse of

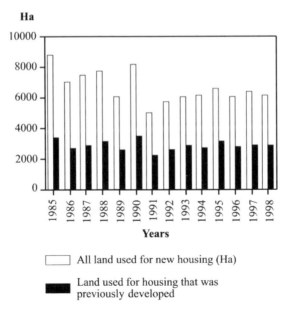

Fig. 8.2 Total hectarage of previously developed land used for new housing in England 1985–98 (source: DTLR 2001a).

previously developed land for housing over this period. This is converted into an index (with 1988 = 100) in Fig. 8.3, which also shows, for the purposes of comparison, the upward movement in the *relative* proportion of land used for new housing that was previously developed.

Over-reliance by policy-makers on improvements in relative proportions may thus produce good headlines, while serving to obscure real deterioration in absolute figures. At one level, Figs 8.2 and 8.3 provide an interesting illustration of the need to regard headline statistics with some degree of scepticism and delve instead for the reality beneath them. At another level, however, the figures cast serious doubt on whether even the apparent improvement in the proportion of previously developed land used for new dwellings can be sustained in the future in a period of growth rather than decline in housebuilding. For while almost 220 000 new dwellings were started in England in 1988, by 1999/2000, this figure had slumped to just under 149 000 new starts (DETR 1999c, 2000e). What may have happened in the mean time is that any apparent improvement in rates of land recycling was due more to a decline in the industry's demand for land and less to the success of policy measures. If so, it is all the more important not to assume that the current policy emphasis on brownfield development can be sustained in any future period of housing growth without radical changes in the wider institutional environment.

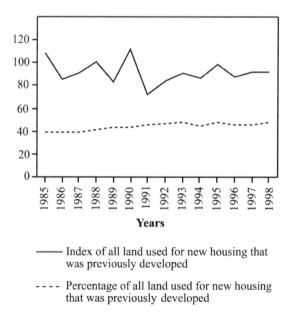

Fig. 8.3   Index of total hectarage of previously developed land used for new housing in England 1985–98 (source: DTLR 2001a).

Fig. 8.4   Winwick Park, Warrington: new 300-unit development on former hospital site.

At a regional level, LUCS reveals noticeable variations between recycling rates in different English regions. Over the period 1993–1997, London achieved the highest proportion of new dwellings built on previously developed land, at 85%. The next highest recycling rates were found in the North West, West Midlands, South East and Eastern regions, with the lowest rates recorded in the East Midlands and South West. Bibby and Shepherd (1999) suggest that regional variations can be attributed to urban structure, economic structure and economic buoyancy. The more urbanised an area, then the greater the overall potential for brownfield redevelopment. However, whether and at what pace brownfield sites come forward for redevelopment will depend on the rate of structural economic change in the area. Even so, brownfield opportunities are most likely to be taken up in economically buoyant locations. This latter factor, they suggest, explains why much lower proportions of brownfield housing than commensurate with rates of urbanisation have been recorded in Newcastle upon Tyne and Sheffield, and much higher proportions in Hertfordshire and Surrey.

National Land Use Database

To provide a more accurate indication of future brownfield supply, a National Land Use Database (NLUD) for England was launched in 1998, drawing on information contributed by local authorities. Significantly, the NLUD is not limited to land and buildings already vacant but seeks to make some assessment of important redevelopment opportunities likely to arise in the future, even if still in current use. It therefore categorises entries under five headings:

- Previously developed land that is now vacant.

- Vacant buildings.

- Derelict land and buildings.

- Other previously developed land or buildings, currently in use, allocated for any development in an adopted plan or having planning permission for housing.

- Other previously developed land or buildings, currently in use, where there is known potential for redevelopment, even though the sites do not have any planning permission or a plan allocation.

Provisional results for the five categories were published in 1999 and finalised in 2000. The finalised results are shown in Table 8.1. From this, it is apparent that some 57 710 hectares of previously developed land were identified in England as either unused or, if in current use, as having potential for redevelopment. Of these, 27 320 hectares (47% of the total) were considered suitable for housing. On past density rates, this area was estimated to have potential for 733 530 dwellings, although if the Government's proposals to raise residential densities are successfully implemented, a much greater provision of new homes could be provided on the identified land.

To put the NLUD results into context, on the basis of the 6165 hectares that LUCS found to have been consumed for all residential development in England in 1998, the 27 320 hectares identified by the NLUD represents about 4.5 years' supply of land. Such simplistic analysis, however, should certainly not be taken to imply that the NLUD has already pinpointed enough brownfield land to meet all housing requirements for nearly the next five years! This is because, as we argue below, some sites may be problematic to develop and take many years to come to fruition, while others may eventually be used for non-residential purposes. As importantly, at the local and regional levels, the location of the potential supply identified by the NLUD is unlikely to match the location of future demand for new housing.

On a regional basis, for example, much of the vacant and derelict land identified in the NLUD was concentrated in the industrial heartlands of the North

Table 8.1 Previously developed land with redevelopment potential in England in 1998 (hectares).

Government office region	Vacant and derelict land			Currently in use		All previously developed land that is unused or may be available for redevelopment
	Previously developed vacant land	Derelict land and buildings	Vacant buildings	Allocated in a local plan for any use or with planning permission for housing	Known redevelopment potential but with no planning allocation or permission	
North East	1 330	1 660	160	620	340	4 120
North West	2 830	3 400	700	800	640	8 370
Yorkshire & the Humber	3 130	3 850	610	640	700	8 930
East Midlands	1 110	2 330	430	910	840	5 610
West Midlands	1 650	1 560	290	630	910	5 040
East of England	1 130	2 460	510	1 610	1 240	6 950
London	470	530	290	1 120	410	2 820
South East	1 760	1 310	850	3 420	2 400	9 740
South West	1 440	2 240	470	1 210	750	6 110
England	**14 860**	**19 340**	**4 310**	**10 960**	**8 240**	**57 710**

The totals are those given in the original document. Inaccuracies are presumably due to rounding errors.
Source: National Land Use Database (2000).

East, North West and Yorkshire and the Humber, with relatively little found in London and the South East. This regional disparity was partly offset by the relatively large proportions of land in the South East currently in use but either with planning permission or allocated for redevelopment or considered to have redevelopment potential even if currently without planning status. Even so, it is interesting to note that the Urban Task Force (1999), which took into account early data from the NLUD, concluded that, under then current policies, the South East (outside London) was likely to accommodate only 39% of its projected household growth between 1996 and 2021 on recycled land. According to the Urban Task Force (1999), while London was considered capable of achieving the highest national recycling rate over this period of 81%, the rate was not predicted to exceed 49% in two other regions under development pressure (Eastern and the South West).

There is a welcome recognition within the NLUD (which some of the most extreme opponents of greenfield development tend to ignore) that not all vacant, derelict and potential redevelopment land within towns and cities is suitable for housing. Indeed, residential development is considered appropriate on less than half of the total supply identified by the NLUD. For if sustainable urban communities are to be promoted, land also needs to be provided for new employment, shopping, leisure and community uses within towns and cities, not to mention quality open space. Indeed, Turok (2001) cautions against the growing temptation to accommodate more and more households within cities at the expense of allocating sites for job creation. Such unbalanced development may not only create poor residential environments but may also serve to limit employment opportunities for their occupants.

Moreover, even sites now considered suitable for housing may eventually be developed for other purposes. As the Civic Trust (1998) found, of the 54 brownfield sites originally identified as having potential for residential use in an earlier 1986 survey, only 29 had actually been developed for housing by 1998, while 10 had been used for other purposes including industry, retailing and leisure. More ominously, 15 still remained vacant by 1998.

It is thus tempting but erroneous to regard the potential supply of brownfield sites identified by NLUD as a fixed stock, gradually to be whittled down to zero. In reality, it provides a snapshot of a continuous flow that needs to be properly monitored. Perhaps the most important aspect of the NLUD was therefore the announcement that the survey would be repeated in 2001 and thereafter undertaken annually. Over a period of time, this exercise will enable a more rigorous assessment to be made of the potential flow of land into the development process. What is surprising is that such data have never before been collected in England when, in contrast, a Scottish Vacant and

Derelict Land Survey (SVDLS) was initiated in 1988, updated in 1990 and undertaken on an annual basis since 1993.

For trend data, the SVDLS now provides a very useful indication of the flows into and out of land dereliction and vacancy. This is summarised in the 'components of change analysis' set out in Table 8.2. From this, it is apparent that, while there has been a recent reduction in the stock of vacant and derelict land in Scotland, this represents the combined effect of a greater 'outflow' of vacant and derelict land brought into use and a lesser 'inflow' of land that becomes newly vacant or derelict. Translating this to an English context, it is important to regard the first NLUD merely as a base survey that cannot possibly hope to identify all potential redevelopment land in the first instance. What will become important over the years is whether and at what rate the 'outflow' of land into development exceeds the 'inflow' of land that becomes vacant, derelict or potentially available.

Here again, SVDLS provides some detailed information on a whole range of factors (previous and preferred uses, contamination, ownership, etc.) that affect the speed at which sites flow into and out of the available stock. Of particular interest is the length of time sites in the SVDLS have lain vacant or derelict. Of the land included in SVDLS 2000 for which relevant information was known (all but 900 of the 11 310 hectares identified in the survey), 34% had lain vacant or derelict prior to 1981, a further 35% had become vacant or derelict between 1981 and 1990, another 18% between 1991 and 1995, and only 13% since 1996. The critical and indeed disturbing question for policy-makers is therefore not how much vacant or derelict land exists at any point in time but rather why so much of it remains vacant or derelict for so long. We argue below that the answers are to be found in a detailed analysis of market conditions and development constraints at a local and site-specific level. Without this detailed knowledge, aggregate analysis of potential land supply provided by the NLUD and the SVDLS should be regarded as simply the initial step in an evaluation process and certainly not as definitive information on which to base policy judgements.

Urban Capacity Studies

Aggregate statistics of potential brownfield land supply are valid only so far as they are based on detailed site-specific knowledge. All local planning authorities in England are now required by PPG 3 to undertake Urban Capacity Studies (UCS) in order to determine how much additional new housing can be accommodated within their urban areas (DETR 2000a). UCS are intended to evaluate development options in respect of residential density, parking

Table 8.2   Vacant and derelict land in Scotland: components of change analysis 1996–2000 (hectares).

	1996	1997	1998	1999	2000
Year start					
Stock of derelict land brought forward	8 778	8 482	7 858	7 787	7 251
Stock of vacant land brought forward	4 944	4 619	4 612	4 425	4 434
Total vacant and derelict land brought forward	**13 722**	**13 101**	**12 470**	**12 212**	**11 685**
Inflows					
Land becoming derelict	192	228	542	460	363
Land becoming vacant	234	382	369	479	184
Total inflows	**426**	**610**	**911**	**939**	**547**
Outflows					
Derelict land reclaimed	293	616	468	764	301
Vacant land brought into use	395	374	355	537	299
Derelict land removed from register for definitional reasons	329	98	288	146	171
Vacant land removed from register for definitional reasons	50	79	106	59	35
Derelict land removed from register owing to naturalisation					64
Vacant land removed from register owing to naturalisation					12
Total outflows	**1 067**	**1 167**	**1 217**	**1 506**	**882**
Other adjustments					
Unexplained change in derelict land	134	–138	143	–86	83
Unexplained change in vacant land	–114	64	–95	126	–123
Total other adjustments	**20**	**–74**	**48**	**40**	**–40**
Total net flow	**–621**	**–631**	**–258**	**–527**	**–375**
Year end					
Stock of derelict land carried forward	8 482	7 858	7 787	7 251	7 161
Stock of vacant land carried forward	4 619	4 612	4 425	4 434	4 149
Total vacant and derelict land carried forward	13 101	12 470	12 212	11 685	11 310

Source: Scottish Vacant and Derelict Land Surveys 1996–2000, as refined by Scottish Executive.

provision, layout and housing mix. A practical guide on how best to assess urban housing capacity, drawing on research and case study experience, was later published by the DETR (2000f) to help planning authorities meet the requirements of PPG 3.

Since it would be almost impossible to investigate potential housing capacity in England throughout the length and breadth of the country, UCS tend to involve the selection of representative areas, in which constraints are analysed, detailed design work undertaken and different scenarios tested. For example, Llewelyn-Davies investigated the housing potential of 50 small infill sites in London by comparing three design approaches (Crookston 1998). The three approaches were:

- Applying the current Unitary Development Plan (UDP) policies and standards on car parking, privacy distances and density.

- Adopting a site-specific design-led approach to issues of density and privacy, while reducing the requirement for off-street parking to one space per unit. This increased site capacities by 50% over those permissible under UDP controls.

- Taking the same design-led approach as the second option, but eliminating the requirement for off-street parking altogether. This increased site capacities by 100% over those permissible under UDP controls.

Such an inventive approach to re-thinking long-established planning standards has not necessarily been typical. Indeed, the Urban Task Force (1999, p. 213) complained that: 'In practice, capacity studies have generally failed to consider alternatives to existing planning policies, design standards, housing densities and parking provision, or to challenge traditional thinking about consumer preferences. This had led to unduly limited and restrictive approaches to development.'

Despite some commendable examples, UCS remain formulative in their methodologies and tentative in their implications for traditional planning standards and controls. The representative nature of any small area sampled for detailed design work, and the extent to which the conclusions from any such small-area design can be 'grossed-up' to an urban area as a whole, are both open to question. Moreover, there are those who argue that to be realistic, design-led approaches to urban capacity must be supplemented by some hard-headed financial analysis. Oxley (1998, p. 8), for example, suggests that: 'Estimates of urban housing capacity should consider the potential costs and the potential returns from housing development. Thus, house prices, rents,

Fig. 8.5 Brockwell Park, South West London: classical style development of former primary school site.

land prices, and building costs need to be considered as well as the financial assistance available to social housing developers.'

Nevertheless, as Bibby and Shepherd (1999) maintain, the realism of the Government's brownfield development target is critically dependent on the ability of capacity studies to squeeze more development out of existing urban areas. Detailed site-specific studies offer an advance on traditional and much criticised 'windfall' approaches (Walton 2000) that often make artificial assumptions about the extent to which previous supply rates of unforeseen brownfield land can be rolled forward to the next plan period. Yet, as Rudlin and Falk (1999, p. 136) argue: 'Future sources of vacant land are difficult to predict – maybe supermarkets will close due to home shopping or car parks become surplus to requirements due to policies to reduce car use.'

Apart from the simple device of raising the density of new development, Rudlin and Falk (1999) identify seven sources of increased urban housing capacity, which they argue can be achieved without incurring the curse of town cramming. These sources (with Rudlin & Falk's own national estimates of extra homes produced) are:

- Redevelopment of older council estates built at very low densities, producing at least 22 000 extra homes.

- Redevelopment of surface car parks, producing up to 200 000 extra homes.

- Conversion of outdated commercial properties, such as obsolete office blocks, to residential use, producing more than 100 000 extra homes.

- Identification of existing housing areas by backland development of garage courts and back gardens and by building on small areas of open space, producing around 280 000 extra homes.

- Making better use of empty homes, by bringing back into use the 250 000 that have been empty for more than a year.

- Turning empty and under-used space over shops into residential accommodation, producing between 1 and 1.5 million extra homes.

- Subdivision of larger houses, the yield from which would depend on the extent to which planning controls are relaxed and owners are willing to subdivide.

Rudlin and Falk (1999) put forward these ideas, of which some are indeed radical and controversial, to indicate how the urban environment could be restructured to meet a 75% recycling target, rather than the current 60% target. Linking back to our earlier discussion of the case for and against compact cities set out in Chapter 3, many may question whether the kind of urban environment envisaged by Rudlin and Falk is realistic, let alone desirable. At this stage, however, their suggestions simply illustrate how the concept of urban capacity is a moving feast and that the results of urban capacity studies very much depend on the assumptions made of likely institutional and policy change.

As this section has shown, it may take some years to produce reliable time series data on brownfield land supply and to resolve what changes to the urban fabric are and are not acceptable in the name of increased housing capacity. We therefore move on to review what is already known about the main barriers to the flow of brownfield sites through the development process.

Brownfield development constraints

Brownfield development is often portrayed as more problematic than greenfield development, owing to specific constraints in the development process. In this section, we consider the extent and significance of three particular barriers to brownfield development, namely planning, physical and ownership constraints.

Planning constraints

The House Builders' Federation (1999) alleges that the operation of the planning system obstructs their members' attempts to develop marketable brownfield sites in urban areas. Specifically, the HBF identifies six significant planning constraints to brownfield redevelopment:

- No automatic presumption in favour of developing suitable brownfield sites.

- Unrealistic protection of potential housing sites for future employment use.

- Outdated development plans, particularly in urban areas.

- Inappropriate planning gain requirements.

- Local resident opposition to development that can exceed that on greenfield sites.

- Delay and inconsistency in planning appeal decisions.

The Urban Task Force (1999) likewise called for the planning system to be streamlined and speeded up, with unnecessary regulations dropped and outdated land-use allocations abandoned. Subsequently, the DETR (2000f) advised local planning authorities to consider if their existing reservations of urban employment land were actually realistic, especially where they prevented the reuse of previously developed land for housing or mixed-use development. This accords with the comment of the Urban Task Force (1999, p. 202) that: 'Too many local planning authorities are still practising rigid adherence to employment land allocations, for sites with no demand, and in some cases, no suitability for modern employment uses.'

Potential local opposition to brownfield redevelopment should not be underestimated, especially in those parts of urban areas that 'are perceived as over-developed, or overcrowded by their residents, where valuable open space has been lost, traffic is congested, and air, noise and light pollution are having a detrimental effect on the quality of life' (Williams *et al.* 1996, p. 93). For example, in Bradford-on-Avon, Taywood Homes' proposal for 82 dwellings, five shops, three restaurants and a new town square on the riverside site of a 2.25-hectare former rubber factory was opposed by a coalition of local community organisation and the national pressure group, Save Britain's Heritage, on the grounds that it would exacerbate traffic problems within an already congested town centre (*Planning* 1999). Despite the local controversy, however, the developers successfully gained planning permission in 1999.

In another case in Aberdeen, the local authority issued a planning and design brief for a redundant school site to guide potential developers bidding for the land. A local housebuilder who followed the brief closely was successful in agreeing the purchase of the site, subject to planning permission. However, when the planning application was submitted in accordance with the local authority brief, intense local opposition was generated to the proposed housing scheme on the grounds of alleged over-development. The local authority then refused the housebuilder's planning application, rewrote the brief to ensure lower density development and eventually sold the site to a competing developer.

The Town and Country Planning Association (1997) believes that the new urban agenda is likely to make residents more rather than less determined to defend existing urban amenity and protect themselves against what might be viewed as over-intensification. On this basis, the TCPA suggests that developers should expect objections to any additional traffic or parking generated by new urban housing. Nevertheless, it remains debatable whether the Bradford-on-Avon and Aberdeen examples, and indeed the HBF's more general accusations about the operation of the planning system, are representative of the broad experience of those actually trying to promote brownfield housing development. Indeed, Syms (2001) discovered from extensive research into the views of 230 stakeholders in the urban regeneration process (the vast majority of whom were based in the private sector) that: 'The overall impression gained from the questionnaire responses, seminars and interviews was that the decision makers involved in redevelopment were generally satisfied with the way in which applications were handled by local authorities' (Syms 2001, p. 10).

Empirical support for this comes from the Civic Trust (1999) whose research compared 29 brownfield sites that had been developed for housing over the period 1986 to 1999, with 24 that either remained vacant or had been developed for other purposes. It found only three sites where an unsupportive planning regime partially accounted for lack of housing development.

In contrast, 'A supportive political and planning context was seen as the strongest factor in achieving successful housing development on sites in our survey' (Civic Trust 1999, p. 14).

From research into brownfield housing development in Strathclyde, Llewelyn-Davies (1996) concluded that there was scope to make public sector processes for brownfield housing more efficient and 'developer-friendly'. Equally, however, its report was scathing about the poor quality of much of the private residential development proposed or undertaken on brownfield sites in the area, commenting that degraded environments deserved higher-quality not lower-quality housing design. Since then, design quality has certainly become a far more significant consideration in the planning system (DETR/CABE 2000) and is likely to emerge as perhaps the most contentious planning constraint on future brownfield development.

Physical constraints

By definition, brownfield sites come with the physical legacy of their own previous use (Syms 2001). Typical problems may include the presence of substantial underground obstructions, such as old foundations or machinery bases, and redundant services. New development on brownfield sites must also be carefully woven into the existing urban fabric. Vehicular access, for example, may be hard to provide unless adjoining land can be purchased to provide necessary visibility splays for drivers at road junctions. Thus, even apart from the threat of contamination, Syms (2001) emphasises that it is important to appraise the physical characteristics of brownfield land in terms of site size, nature of the soil and subsoil, topography and relief, and prospective site attractiveness.

Although public funding towards derelict land reclamation has long been concentrated on bringing derelict sites back into developed use, Llewelyn-Davies (1996) argues that it may sometimes be more cost effective to reclaim potentially expensive sites for recreational use. Indeed, where existing local provision of urban open space and recreational facilities is limited, reclamation of derelict land for these purposes rather than for housing may well contribute more effectively to sustainable development. It should not therefore be assumed that redevelopment is the only beneficial use to which contaminated land can be put.

Despite the potential array of physical constraints to brownfield housing development, attention has tended to focus on the issue of contamination. An excellent review of the nature of land contamination and the alternative methods of treatment is provided by Parliamentary Office of Science and Technology (1998). Here, we concentrate on its implications for brownfield development potential.

In his research on housebuilders' attitude to brownfield risk analysis, Fulford (1998) found that the type and extent of contamination were the highest-ranked potential risks, as viewed by the respondent developers. Unfortunately, however, the word 'contaminated' was applied generically by housebuilders, irrespective of the type of contaminants on site. This uncertainty within the industry over the specific nature of contamination may help explain why Syms (1997) discovered that housebuilders, and to a lesser extent housing associations, were reluctant to divulge information about the contamination history of development sites to potential purchasers and tenants.

The Environment Act 1995 introduced a new statutory regime, based on the 'polluter pays' principle for determining legal liability for the remediation of contamination. However, the extensive grounds of appeal within the Act against remediation notices created severe doubt as to whether the new legislation will provide a speedy mechanism to resolve dispute liability. In practice, it is intended that the treatment of contaminated land will normally be resolved through the planning process, when redevelopment applications are made. Even so, both valuation uncertainties and the land-value aspirations of previous users can be particularly problematic constraints in the case of contaminated land (Adair & Hutchison 2000; Syms 2001).

In recent years, some excellent case studies have demonstrated that, although contamination may well add significant costs to a development project and length of the development process, it does not represent an absolute constraint on brownfield reuse. For example, Fulford (1998) provides 10 case studies of successful residential development on brownfield land. Such development was also complete or well under way on nine of the ten case studies investigated by Syms and Knight (2000). From their case studies, they identify four overarching lessons applicable to all brownfield redevelopment:

• The need for a comprehensive site investigation, of which the historic study of land use forms an essential part.

• The need for a comprehensive written and photographic record, including waste-handling notes, of all remediation works.

• The need for validation to demonstrate compliance with the remediation strategy and the achievement of its goals.

- The need for factually correct and readily assimilated information on past uses, site investigations and remediation works to be made available to purchasers and tenants (Syms and Knight 2000).

As this suggests, the most significant challenge to residential development posed by contamination is not necessarily its presence or degree, but rather the lack of an effective institutional framework for remediation activities in which all parties can have confidence. As the Urban Task Force (1999, p. 238) concluded: 'With the obvious exception of nuclear waste, the problem of contamination is not primarily technical, although more research is undoubtedly needed to make the remediation process more efficient and equitable. In almost all cases, it is essentially a problem of finance and/or perceived legal risk.'

Ownership constraints

According to Breheny and Ross (1998, p. 23):

> Alongside issues of contamination and access, the difficulty of site assembly is seen as a major constraint on the development of urban sites. Sites that have the potential for development are often in multiple ownership. In many cases, ownership is difficult to determine. When it is determined, owners are often reluctant to sell land – usually because of an expectation of higher gains in the future.

While the Urban Task Force (1999) also drew attention to the fragmented and complex land ownership patterns in many inner urban areas, Adair *et al.* (1998) argued forcibly that disjointed land ownerships and multiplicity of tenurial rights act as a serious deterrent to private investment in urban regeneration projects.

Adams *et al.* (2001a) suggest that ownership constraints derive from the distinctiveness of land as a commodity, the imperfect nature of the land market, the behavioural characteristics of landowners and the institutional context for land ownership, exchange and development. On this basis, they contend that an ownership constraint can be said to exist if development is unable to proceed because the required ownership rights cannot rapidly be acquired through normal market processes.

Five main types of ownership constraints can thus be identified:

- Ownership itself may be unknown or unclear.

- Ownership rights may be divided: the power of freehold owners to sell development land with immediate vacant possession may be restricted by lesser rights in the same land.

- Ownership assembly may be required for development.

- Owners may be willing to sell but not on terms acceptable to potential purchasers.

- Owners may be unwilling to sell.

As Fig. 8.6 shows, each of the types can be further subdivided into more precise categories.

A	Ownership unknown or unclear	A.1	Title deeds incomplete or missing
		A.2	Ownership in dispute
B	Ownership rights divided	B.1	Land held in trust
		B.2	Land subject to leases or licences
		B.3	Land subject to mortgages or other legal charges
		B.4	Land subject to restrictive covenants
		B.5	Land subject to easements
		B.6	Land subject to options or conditional contracts
C	Ownership assembly required for development	C.1	Ransom strips
		C.2	Multiple ownership
D	Owner willing to sell but not on terms acceptable to potential purchasers	D.1	Restrictive terms or conditions of sale
		D.2	Unrealistic expectations of prices
E	Owner unwilling to sell	E.1	Retention for continued current use for: * Occupation * Investment * Making available to others on non-profit basis
		E.2	Retention for control or protection
		E.3	Retention for subsequent own development
		E.4	Retention for subsequent sale * Indecision *(terms of sale unresolved)* * Postponement *(delayed sale advantageous)* * Uncertainty *(unsure of present value or potential)* * Speculation *(hoping for future rise in value or potential)*
		E.5	Retention for no specified purpose: inertia

Fig. 8.6 Classification of ownership constraints in the development process (source: Adams *et al.* 2001a).

In their study of 80 large redevelopment sites in four British cities, Adams *et al.* (2001a) found that such ownership constraints disrupted plans to use, market, develop or purchase 64 of the sites between 1991 and 1995. Altogether, 146 individual ownership constraints, or 1.8 per site, were found. As Table 8.3 shows, divided ownership rights proved the most prevalent form of constraint. However, since most existing leases on potential redevelopment sites were of short-term duration, their impact was limited. The need for ownership assembly was the most disruptive type of constraint. Multiple ownership of land, in particular, proved hard to resolve without the prospect of lucrative commercial development and/or state acquisition or intervention.

About half of the 146 ownership constraints identified by Adams *et al.* (2001a) were resolved before the end of their research. Unknown or unclear ownership proved much easier than on average to resolve, and divided ownership rights slightly easier to resolve. In contrast, owners willing to sell but not on terms acceptable to potential purchasers proved harder to overcome. Constraints were primarily resolved because such action was essential to enable proposed development or marketing to proceed. Other less important means of resolution were changes in ownership strategy, and mediation, arbitration or resort to law. Only 5% of constraints were resolved by actual or threatened state acquisition or intervention.

The work of Adams *et al.* (2001a) concerned the full range of brownfield development opportunities and was not limited merely to those with housing potential. However, ownership constraints can prove particularly problematic for brownfield housing, owing to the extensive land needs of residential development. According to the DETR (2000a), in such circumstances local authorities should be prepared to facilitate brownfield housing development by making a compulsory purchase order (CPO), if developers find it impossible to assemble land by negotiation.

Unfortunately, as the Urban Task Force (1999) pointed out, there are five main obstacles to the successful use of compulsory purchase in the assembly of land for urban regeneration. First, specific resources are not available to assist local authorities with the cost of compulsory purchase. As a result, many authorities are prepared to contemplate compulsory purchase only where they have previously entered into a 'back-to-back' deal with a prospective developer who contracts to cover an authority's CPO costs in full.

Secondly, the Urban Task Force highlighted the bureaucratic nature of, and protracted time scale inherent within compulsory purchase procedure. As an earlier research study for the DOE (1996e) demonstrated, the average time

Table 8.3   Extent of disruption caused by ownership constraints.

		Minor		Significant		Very significant		Total	
		No.	%	No.	%	No.	%	No.	%
A.1	Title deeds incomplete or missing	8	80	1	10	1	10	10	100
A.2	Ownership in dispute	2	50			2	50	4	100
A	**Total: Ownership unknown or unclear**	**10**	**71**	**1**	**7**	**3**	**21**	**14**	**100**
B.1	Land held in trust								
B.2	Land subject to leases or licences	13	62	4	19	4	19	21	100
B.3	Land subject to mortgages/other legal charges	2	67	1	33			3	100
B.4	Land subject to restrictive covenants	6	50	2	17	4	33	12	100
B.5	Land subject to easements	4	44	3	33	2	22	9	100
B.6	Land subject to options or conditional contracts	1	33	1	33	1	33	3	100
B	**Total: Ownership rights divided**	**26**	**54**	**11**	**23**	**11**	**23**	**48**	**100**
C.1	Ransom strips	1	17	2	33	3	50	6	100
C.2	Multiple ownership	3	15	5	25	12	60	20	100
C	**Total: Ownership assembly required for development**	**4**	**15**	**7**	**27**	**15**	**58**	**26**	**100**
D.1	Restrictive terms or conditions of sale	3	75	1	25			4	100
D.2	Unrealistic expectations of price	3	16	13	68	3	16	19	100
D	**Total: Owner willing to sell but not on terms acceptable to potential purchasers**	**6**	**26**	**14**	**61**	**3**	**13**	**23**	**100**
E.1.1	Retention for continued current use for occupation	1	17	2	33	3	50	6	100
E.1.2	Retention for continued current use for investment	3	100					3	100
E.1.3	Retention for continued current use for making available to others on non-profit basis					1	100	1	100
E.2	Retention for control or protection								
E.3	Retention for subsequent own development	1	13	5	63	2	25	8	100
E.4.1	Retention for subsequent sale: indecision	1	33	1	33	1	33	3	100
E.4.2	Retention for subsequent sale: postponement								
E.4.3	Retention for subsequent sale: uncertainty			5	100			5	100
E.4.4	Retention for subsequent sale: speculation			4	100			4	100
E.5	Retention for no specified purpose: inertia	1	20	2	40	2	40	5	100
E	**Total: Owner unwilling to sell**	**7**	**20**	**19**	**54**	**9**	**26**	**35**	**100**
	Totals	**53**	**36**	**52**	**36**	**41**	**28**	**146**	**100**

Source: Adams *et al.* (2001a).

taken from the preliminary stage to the payment of compensation was 8 years for Highways CPOs, 6 years for Planning CPOs and 4 years for Housing CPOs. In summary, compulsory purchase is a complex, time-consuming and bureaucratic process, leading to higher costs (DETR 1999d).

Thirdly, the Urban Task Force called for simplification of compulsory purchase law and practice, arguing that the multitude of legislation, policy guidance and case law on compulsory purchase causes confusion to practitioners and is prone to restrictive interpretation by lawyers. Associated with this, the fourth identified weakness concerned the loss of necessary skills and experience at the local level, owing to the infrequent use of compulsory purchase in the previous two decades.

Finally, the Urban Task Force highlighted the widespread perception that compensation for the compulsory purchase of commercial property is inadequate, since it does not take account of the forced nature of the transaction. This, it believed, was reflected in added owner hostility to the process, which served only to further delay the outcome. Research has also shown that the manner in which compulsory purchase is implemented can be insensitive and highly disruptive to existing businesses and others in current occupation within proposed redevelopment areas (Imrie & Thomas 1997).

In its Urban White Paper, the Government promised to bring forward legislation, when parliamentary time allows, to simplify, consolidate and codify compulsory purchase law, speed up its procedures and make compulsory purchase simpler and more equitable (DETR 2000b). Although it subsequently confirmed this intention in a detailed consultation paper on compulsory purchase and compensation (DTLR 2001e, see Chapter 10), published at the same time as the Planning Green Paper, any claim that such legislation would immediately resolve ownership constraints to brownfield development is perhaps over-ambitious, since compulsory purchase is likely by its very nature to remain a costly and confrontational process.

As an alternative approach, Adams *et al.* (2001b) have put forward the concept of an Urban Partnership Zone (UPZ), in which existing landowners would be entitled to participate alongside the local authority and a chosen development partner in a joint venture redevelopment company. Combined with greater planning certainty and other benefits, this innovation would enable the development process to operate more rapidly without immediate compulsory purchase. UPZs would thus provide a practical means to encourage those who already hold ownership rights in an area to participate in any redevelopment.

UPZs would be much broader in scope than the Business Planning Zones proposed in the Planning Green Paper (DTLR 2001b) since the latter appear intended merely to address potential planning constraints in a small number of largely high-technology development clusters. In contrast, UPZs would seek to resolve widespread market failure in urban land assembly through the provision of an institutional framework designed to encourage negotiation and compromise between intending developers and existing landowners. This process would take place within a clear masterplanning framework that itself carried the status of outline planning consent. By thus offering a more flexible means to tackle ownership constraints to urban redevelopment than the blunt instrument of compulsory purchase, UPZs could make a significant contribution towards securing the much greater emphasis on brownfield housing development that the Government wishes to achieve.

Of all the recognised constraints within the development process, ownership has long remained the most elusive. Even if ownership constraints to brownfield redevelopment are actually resolved, the time and resources this process consumes may generate a negative reputation for brownfield sites that serves to switch the spatial pattern of development in favour of greenfield sites. Since greater brownfield development is likely to involve increasing disruption to historic patterns of urban land ownership, it is contended that institutional reform to deliver smooth and rapid resolution of ownership conflicts demands as much attention from policy-makers as the design of an effective planning system or the remediation of contamination.

Brownfield housing demand

Having identified the main constraints to the smooth flow of brownfield housing sites through the development process, it is important to consider the nature of demand for brownfield land. This can be subdivided into the well-established categories of user, developer and investor demand (Adams 1994; Keogh 1994). By users, we mean those who occupy the products of the residential development industry, either as purchasers or as tenants. By developers, we concentrate here on the speculative housebuilding industry, while noting the important role of RSLs in brownfield redevelopment. By investors, we refer primarily to those who might consider residential property an alternative form of investment to their traditional interest in commercial or industrial property. Following discussion of these 'actor-orientated' perspectives, the concept of urban villages is explored as an illustration of how demand for brownfield housing development can be stimulated by appropriate institutional measures.

User demand

Most brownfield sites are either surrounded by or located close to existing housing areas. Those already living in these areas may provide an immediate demand for brownfield housing, provided it is priced competitively compared to the existing stock in that neighbourhood. In some towns and cities, however, low demand for housing is a growing problem. According to government figures, in 2000, there were around 470 000 homes in the social rented sector and 375 000 in the private sector located in unpopular neighbourhoods or in areas of low demand (DETR 2000e).

Detailed research on abandoned urban neighbourhoods in Manchester and Newcastle found that in the worst affected areas, even good-quality, modernised homes had been abandoned and house prices had fallen almost to zero (Power & Mumford 2000). These areas are certainly not typical of brownfield locations but they do highlight the importance of effective market demand. It should not therefore be assumed that developers will be interested in brownfield sites simply because their supply of greenfield land diminishes.

Nevertheless, the main concern here is not to assess the strength of existing local demand for new housing at brownfield locations but to consider whether new forms of demand can be generated to match the policy intention of concentrating more and more housing development on brownfield sites. In the language of the Urban Task Force can the English be persuaded to forego their decentralist tendencies and rediscover their traditional urban roots? There is now some evidence from residential development undertaken in city centres in the 1980s and 1990s to indicate which social groups are most likely to return to central locations.

An early study by Cameron (1992) looked at the occupants of newly developed housing in Newcastle city centre in the late 1980s. Although some of the developments were built for rent, most were developed for sale. The research found that those living in new city centre housing were quite different from the city average both in terms of age and household size. The central accommodation was more likely to be occupied by young single adults while, in contrast, few families with children and few elderly people were present. Although this occupancy pattern was particularly strong in the owner-occupied housing, it was also found to a lesser extent in the social rented sector. The owner-occupiers were predominantly white-collar workers, with over 60% having come from outside the city boundary. Cameron (1992, pp. 8–9) concluded that: 'even in a relatively depressed area such as Tyneside, there is a demand from a high-income, non-local population in high status employment for inner area housing in this type of location.'

In subsequent research on housing development completed in Manchester and Liverpool city centres between 1988 and 1996, Couch (1999) found a preponderance of student occupiers in the new accommodation. In Liverpool, student housing accounted for 69% of the 2574 residential completions over this period, while in Manchester, it was responsible for 55% of the 3592 completions. In both cities, owner-occupied development dominated the remainder of the new city centre housing, with a social structure similar to that recorded by Cameron (1992) in Newcastle.

Although 80% of the 3.8 million new households expected to form in England between 1996 and 2021 are predicted to contain only one person, the Urban Task Force (1999) argued that it would be mistaken to rely on particular social groups to repopulate the city. Instead, policy-makers should recognise how individual needs change through life and seek to persuade much broader groups of the population to reconsider urban living. The report suggested that:

> For many people, the crunch comes with having children. An urban environment previously perceived as diverse and stimulating starts to appear unsafe. Schools and health services become more important. While it is therefore accepted that, at this stage in their life cycle, many people will continue to move to more suburban or small town environments, we must look to persuade more families to stay. This means looking beyond the design, planning and building of the urban environment at the role played by health, education, security and social services.
>
> (Urban Task Force 1999, pp. 35–6)

Hall, P. (1999) controversially suggests that while higher urban densities can be imposed in the buoyant market of inner London, in many of the less favoured midland and northern cities it will be necessary to work with people by giving them the kind of densities they understand and like. Although this may appear to some to be a patronising view, it is important to remember that, while occupier demand for brownfield housing may remain strong in London and the centres of other major cities, elsewhere it may well need to be nurtured by responsive and supportive public policies. In fragile market locations, where much of the available brownfield land is likely to be concentrated, market demand will thus primarily be structured by the extent to which urban regeneration policies succeed.

Developer and investor demand

According to the Urban Task Force (1999, p. 221) 'Whatever the finan-

cial constraints on greenfield development, developers will only develop
brownfield sites if there is a sufficient demand at a price which generates a
reasonable return.' In the past, brownfield development was too often seen
as a minority pursuit by the speculative development industry, conducted
either by specialist companies or by the specialist subsidiaries of the volume
housebuilders. As a result, the Civic Trust (1999) found that only 13 of the 54
potential brownfield housing sites identified in the earlier 1986 survey had
been developed by the private residential sector by 1999. This was attributed
to three reasons: an apparent lack of market demand at some locations, a lack
of brownfield development skills in much of the speculative housebuilding
industry and the preference of local authorities and other public agencies to
work with housing associations on brownfield sites.

As we explained in Chapter 5, attitudes towards brownfield redevelopment
are changing rapidly in parts of the speculative development industry, with
some innovative companies leading the way in responding to the brownfield
challenge. What is more, although grants and subsidies from the public sector remain necessary in many locations, in London and the more prosperous
provincial locations, it is apparent that some companies are now making
very good returns from brownfield redevelopment without the need for public sector financial support. Nevertheless, the broader institutional environment within which development takes place appears critical to the success
of brownfield housing projects.

In this context, Adair *et al.* (1998) who compared the characteristics and attitudes of private investors and non-investors in urban regeneration found
that the creation of confidence and the reduction of risk were critical to
greater private sector investment and development in urban regeneration
areas. The preferred mechanism to facilitate the flow of private sector finance into urban regeneration, according to the investors interviewed, was
a single regeneration agency with visionary planning and land assembly
powers. Partnership between the public and private sectors was seen as an
increasingly acceptable development structure. Although financial support
from the public sector needed to be simplified and better directed, the report
suggested that non-financial instruments, such as guaranteed minimum
standard of infrastructure, clarity in public policy and processes, simplified
planning processes and land assembly, were equally if not more important.

Although most of the respondents in the Adair *et al.* survey were involved
in commercial and industrial development rather than housebuilding, the
message that private sector investment and development in urban regeneration areas is highly dependent upon a supportive policy context applies as
much to residential as to other forms of development. As housebuilders are

much less in control of their own financial destiny if they choose to build on brownfield sites within urban areas than on greenfield ones at the urban periphery, developer demand for brownfield land is highly dependent on a favourable institutional environment.

In short, although there is emerging evidence of increased innovation within the speculative housebuilding industry in respect of brownfield develop-ment, the extent to which innovative brownfield practice will become the norm rather than the exception in the industry will depend on the success of the type of risk-reduction and confidence-building measures recommended by Adair *et al.* (1998). In this context, it is worth considering how the inno-vative concept of urban villages can help reinforce demand for brownfield residential development.

Urban villages

In 1989, the Urban Villages Group, comprising influential developers and other property professionals, was established by Business in the Community at the request of the Prince of Wales. Its subsequent report (Aldous 1992) launched the concept of urban villages with the following characteristics:

- Entirely new urban communities, with mixed uses and mixed tenures.

- About 40 hectares in size (ideally) with all buildings within 10 minutes' walk of each other.

- Designed to minimise car use and promote walking, cycling and public transport.

- High-quality environment and landscaping, with central public space or square.

- Generous community facilities provided beyond those normally justified by commercial return.

- Long-term management by community development trust representing village's developers, residents and businesses.

Among urban villages developed or under development are those at Crown Street in Glasgow (see Fig. 8.7), Ancoats in Manchester and West Silvertown in London Docklands. The Government's Millennium Communities initia-tive, of which the Greenwich Millennium Village was the first step, took

Fig. 8.7   Crown Street, Glasgow.

up the concept of the urban villages, although progress on schemes after Greenwich was more problematic than originally anticipated. Nevertheless, the Urban Task Force commended the initiative and recommended that a series of government-sponsored demonstration projects be undertaken to illustrate how an integrated design-led approach to area regeneration could be achieved in different types of urban neighbourhood.

Practical experience in the development of urban villages has been evaluated by a number of authors including Higgins and Karski (2000) and Thompson-Fawcett (2000). Taking as one example the West Silvertown scheme in London (see Fig. 8.8), it is apparent that the integrated development of urban villages can offer significant advantages, for both the occupier and developer, over sporadic development on a number of unrelated brownfield sites. When fully developed, West Silvertown will be home to some 5000 people living in a mixed-use and mixed-tenure community, built to a masterplan that demands high-quality urban design and ensures the provision of a new school, village hall, community centre, open space and other facilities. The development, which is taking places on 11 hectares of previously derelict land in the London Docklands, includes 777 houses and apartments built for sale by Wimpey, 140 affordable units built by the Peabody Trust and a further 95 units built by the East Thames Housing Group.

Apart from its obvious locational advantage of being within close travelling distance to the centre of London, a development of this scale and character

Fig. 8.8   West Silvertown Urban Village, London Docklands.

offers the chance to create a sustainable and mixed residential community within the urban fabric that can more than rival the perceived advantages of many greenfield developments. Critically, the public authorities (in this case, the London Docklands Development Corporation working closely with the local Newham Borough Council) took the initiative to ensure the availability for mixed development of a large urban site that was offered by open competition within a clear planning and urban design framework.

The experience of urban villages in general, and of West Silvertown in particular, would suggest that a crucial factor in fostering both user and developer demand for brownfield housing development in many urban locations is likely to be an effective but shared division of responsibilities between the public and private sector for creating and bringing forward brownfield sites that are capable of out-performing greenfield ones in their attractiveness both to house buyers and to the industry.

Conclusions

This chapter has not assumed that brownfield residential development is intrinsically more sustainable than greenfield development, since that depends on their precise nature and on the institutional context within which they each take place. Although brownfield housing development is now far more commonplace than in the early 1990s, the available statistics, when closely examined, indicate that the overall amount of previously developed land reused for housing has not significantly increased since the late 1980s. Meanwhile, substantial supplies of vacant and derelict land remain within towns and cities, although we simply do not know what proportion is well located and is capable of early housing development. In time, national monitoring of available urban land supplies might provide a valuable time series in England on such important factors.

In this context, it is important to regard any such supplies of land not as a fixed stock gradually to be whittled down to zero but rather as the current outcome of a series of flows into and out of the productive built environment. On this basis, it is reasonable to expect the flow of land into vacancy and dereliction to continue, and maybe to increase, as social and economic change gathers pace. However, as future sources of redundant urban land, and the speed at which they enter the cycle of vacancy or dereliction, must remain matters of speculation, policy attention needs to concentrate instead on the institutional processes by which such land is endowed as quickly as possible with redevelopment potential.

Bearing in mind both the Scottish experience and the now numerous case studies of brownfield development, two important conclusions emerge from the early part of the chapter. The first is that many potential urban housing sites appear to remain vacant and derelict for long periods of time before they are eventually brought into use. Secondly, and perhaps closely related, development constraints can be significant in slowing the progress of brownfield sites through the development process. Of these constraints, although planning delays and land contamination tend to attract policy-makers' attention, those attributable to land ownership may well be of equal if not greater concern.

The later part of the chapter demonstrated how dependent brownfield housing redevelopment has so far been on certain social groups and specialist types of developers. To promote 60%, let alone 75%, of new homes on brownfield sites in a housing upturn would require brownfield development to become a mass housing movement and not merely a specialist activity. This has far-reaching policy implications since it is unlikely that brownfield sites will ever compete on equal terms with greenfield sites, without an active and interventionist policy environment. In this context, while there is a role for fiscal and other incentives to underpin occupier demand for brownfield housing, the main policy focus to achieve greater brownfield land development needs to be upon the creation of development opportunities that are themselves viable, and in particular on those wider forms of investment, both public and private, most likely to transform towns and cities into more attractive places in which to live.

Although 'favourable market conditions' and 'a good location for housing' were common features of successful brownfield housing developments according to the Civic Trust (1999) survey, they were outweighed in importance by the presence or absence of a supportive planning and political context for brownfield redevelopment. As this indicates, a favourable policy environment can nurture and sustain market confidence by helping to create or enhance attractive housing locations. In the context of market cycles, active policy intervention can also ensure that brownfield sites are available and ready for development at the start of an upturn. Such windows of development opportunity, which may be relatively short in fragile market locations, must not be missed by delays in bringing sites forward.

The final two chapters of the book will thus seek to draw together the main policy challenges involved in locating new housing development. We suggest it would be mistaken, indeed highly complacent, for the Government to assume that the 60% target for new homes to be provided on previously developed land and by the conversion of existing buildings can be achieved or bettered through the mere continuation of policies whose record in shifting overall market patterns during the past decade has been at best mixed, and at worst ineffective. Equally, policies that merely seek to cram every vacant and derelict urban site with as much housing as possible need to be avoided since they are unlikely to offer much prospect of a sustainable urban future.

Thus, on matters of housing location, the policy stakes are now high. If government policy fails to deliver the promised level of brownfield redevelopment, while constraining greenfield development, or worse still, produces poor-quality development that lasts only a generation, then the costs of policy failure will be substantial, to individuals, communities and the public purse. As Lord Rogers of Riverside, the Chairman of the Urban Task Force, concluded, 'achieving an urban renaissance is not only about numbers and percentages. It is about creating the quality of life and vitality that makes urban living desirable' (Urban Task Force 1999, p. 7).

9

The Economics of Planning and Housing Development

In his review of the British planning system since 1947, Cullingworth (1997) laments the fact that, in general terms, economic analysis plays only a very limited role in land-use planning debates. He highlights, in particular, the dearth of economic studies of the operation of the planning system and draws attention to the lack of economic analysis of the merits of alternative development patterns. This theme has been picked elsewhere by a number of commentators. Several authors, for example, are highly critical of the failure to account for changing economic circumstances at various stages in the production of household projections (Bramley & Watkins 1995; Baker & Wong 1997; Bramley 1998a, 2000; Jones & Watkins 1999). This critique is supported by a number of empirical studies. For instance, Bramley *et al.* (1998) highlight the need to consider the impact of economic factors on household formation rates, Champion *et al.* (1998) indicate that economic variables influence out-migration from urban areas, and Meen (2000) shows the effect of economic influences on the volume of household moves. The need for economic analysis also finds general support in other recent contributions to the planning and development debates (Meen *et al.* 1997, 2001).

Elsewhere, commentators have highlighted the limited economic perspective in the subnational elements of the planning system. Coopers and Lybrand (1985), for instance, were critical of the lack of economic content in land availability studies. Maclennan argued, more generally, that housing market planning and monitoring could be improved by adopting an economic mode of analysis. He emphasised the need to explore price effects on demand, tenure choice and locational preferences on the basis of a sound conceptualisation of the economic structure of local markets (Maclennan 1986, 1992; Hancock & Maclennan 1989).

Several of these gaps, notably the comparative analysis of alternative development patterns, have been addressed in some detail elsewhere in the book (see Chapter 3). Other issues, including the weaknesses of household projection and the limitations of local market studies, have been discussed in the context of the limitations of the residential planning process. In this chapter, however, we adopt a more explicit economic focus and concentrate in detail on two particular issues.

The first part of the chapter explores the impact of the planning system on the housing market. The discussion seeks to determine the impact of planning intervention on a range of market outcomes including the price, quantity, quality and density of new housing development. It also considers how these outcomes might impact on different groups of actors, including developers, existing landowners and new purchasers. The section concludes with reflections on the extent to which planning intervention contributes to societal and environmental goals by steering market activity.

The second part of the chapter examines the economics of planning gain. In this section, two key issues are addressed. First, building on earlier discussion in Chapters 2 and 7, we assess the economic case for using planning gain as a means of requiring developers to provide an element of affordable housing within development sites. Secondly, we try to determine the extent to which the cost of planning gain will impact on different groups including developers, landowners and house purchasers. It is argued that the distribution of these impacts will inevitably have an effect on the ability of planners to negotiate the development of adequate levels of social and affordable housing.

Both parts of the chapter are based largely on the standard textbook comparative static analytical framework that is characteristic of the neo-classical school of economics. In the final section we consider the limitations of this mode of analysis and reflect on the potential value of applying the tools of behavioural social science, or institutional economics. Some of the implications of our discussion for issues in housing development are explored and areas for further research are identified. In concluding the chapter, we also consider the implications of the gaps in knowledge for the development of policy-based resolutions to the conflicts surrounding housing development.

Market efficiency and planning intervention

On the basis of their model of perfect competition, neo-classical economists are able to demonstrate mathematically that unfettered markets will allocate society's scarce resources efficiently. Here 'efficiency' is used in the Pareto optimal sense. This means that the allocation of resources arrived at through market processes cannot be redistributed in such a way that some individuals will be made better off without worsening the position of others. This outcome, however, is achieved only under perfect competition and, as such, is dependent on a number of key assumptions. These include the assertion that actors will engage in rational behaviour based on perfect information and foresight. In reality, however, there are no perfectly competitive markets. All markets diverge from this ideal and are prone to 'market failure'. Market failure might result from the problems associated with the provision of public goods, the treatment of externalities or the inequitable distribution of resources (Adams 1994). The need to correct market failure provides the rationale for government intervention in land markets. Despite this, economic analyses of the land market have tended to be based on the specific application of the perfectly competitive framework.

The standard neo-classical model of the land market can be traced to the seminal work of Alonso (1964) and Wingo (1961). These models, their application and subsequent extension now make up a voluminous theoretical and empirical literature that seeks to explain the patterns of urban land use, as well as household and business location decisions (see Ball *et al.* 1998 for a review). The basic proposition of these models is that, in a competitive land market, the value of land will decline with distance from the city centre. Land may be used for residential, commercial, industrial and agricultural uses and will be more profitable in particular uses in certain locations.

The attraction of this model is its tractability and mathematical elegance. This elegance is predicated on a number of simplifying behavioural assumptions. For example, the 'quality' of land is assumed to vary only in respect to its proximity to the urban core. There is no differential associated with brownfield or greenfield sites, for example. In addition, the economy comprises perfectly competitive goods and factor markets. In this context, land is allocated according to its value in the production process. Producers are profit maximisers who possess perfect information and foresight and make rational choices.

The model starts from the assumption of a uniform homogeneous, featureless plain. The outcome from the operation of the market is a pattern of urban land use that allocates land in the urban core to high-value commercial activities and land at the greater distance from the city to agricultural uses. This is considered to be the optimal pattern of land use and, in the technical sense, is economically efficient. Despite its apparent limitations, the model can be used to provide insights into the long-term nature of change in urban areas. By extension, for example, it might be used to show that increased incomes and lower per unit construction costs will lead to suburbanisation (Jones & Leishman 1998).

The weaknesses of the model relate to its divergence from reality and, in particular, the extent to which the conditions of perfect competition are breached in land and property markets (Adams 1994). Land and housing markets do not operate efficiently. Housing markets are characterised by imperfect information, high search and transaction costs, and stock hetero-geneity (Maclennan 1982). The housing system features high levels of public sector intervention in the form of grants and subsidies to both producers and consumers.

Development land, even for housing, is heterogeneous not homogeneous. It is traded infrequently in a series of linked submarkets. Transaction costs limit the ease of market entry and exit and reduce liquidity. Submarkets are not merely geographically defined, but are also product differentiated. In residential land, separate submarkets exist for bulk land, small housing sites and sites suitable for flatted development. The number of buyers and sellers for land as a whole, let alone each submarket, is limited (Adams *et al.* 2001a). The peculiarity of land and housing, as economic goods, impacts upon the operation of the market. The imperfections in the market are likely to ensure that price signals will be transmitted only slowly to buyers and sellers or never at all. This can make the attainment of equilibrium elusive, even in the long run.

In addition, land markets often have public good characteristics, and specific uses have external effects that spill over on to others (Keogh 1985). This provides the economic rationale for planning intervention in the market. Through development controls, the planning system seeks to constrain the activities of individuals, by correcting externalities. Although it is intended that there should be minimal impact on the behaviour of market participants where there are no adverse social or economic consequences associated with their actions, planning intervention certainly distorts the pattern of land values that one might expect to arise in a perfectly competitive system. The measurement of the extent of this impact and the analysis of its distributional effects has been the subject of considerable research effort in the UK.

The impact of planning constraints on housing markets

At a superficial level at least, mainstream economists tend to apply the analytical framework developed from welfare economics as a tool for assessing the wider impacts of the planning system (Maclennan & Gibb 1993). This framework usefully focuses on the private and social impacts of the system as well as both the costs and benefits associated with intervention. As such, this analytical approach encourages us to think about the benefits derived from planning intervention in the widest sense. It suggests that we need to look at both positive and negative impacts when evaluating the efficacy of market intervention through development control. However, in reality, economists (and other critics) tend to focus on the costs imposed on the individual household. The discussion of benefits and of social benefits, in particular, is often perfunctory.

In short, neo-classical economic analysis suggests that the development control system will lead to higher land and house prices, higher densities for new development, smaller dwelling and lot sizes and reduced quantities of new housing provision (Bramley *et al.* 1995). All these impacts tend to be seen as costs, which are ultimately passed on to the house buyer. The negative impacts can be demonstrated elegantly with recourse to basic microeconomic theory. Standard comparative analysis contrasts outcomes under market equilibrium conditions with and without planning restrictions on the supply of new housing. This is shown diagrammatically in Fig. 9.1.

In the first part of Fig. 9.1, the market is in equilibrium and the price of housing (P_0) and the quantity traded (Q_0) is set at the level established by the intersection between the demand (D_0) and supply (S_0) schedules. This is a world without planning in which supply is assumed to be relatively price-elastic. This means that new housing output is fairly responsive to changes in price levels. An exogenous change in demand levels, caused for instance by changes in household income levels or, more topically, by the increasing

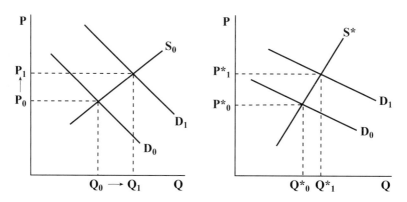

Fig. 9.1 Price and quantity effects of planning intervention.

rate of household formation, would lead to a rightward shift in the demand schedule from D_0 to D_1. Under the standard assumptions of the neo-classical framework, price and output will adjust to a new equilibrium level where D_1 and S_0 intersect. This change in demand has had both price and quantity effects, since both the market price for housing and the quantity of homes provided has risen, from P_0 to P_1 and from Q_0 to Q_1 respectively.

In the second part of Fig. 9.1, we introduce the influence of planning constraints on housing supply. New homes cannot be built without planning permission and planning permission is rationed. This need to seek planning permission inhibits the extent to which new homes can be provided instantaneously. This implies that the quantity of new housing supplied will be less sensitive to price changes, less elastic. This translates into a more steeply sloped supply schedule (S^*). Under these conditions, when a demand shock takes place, there is a much larger increase in the price of housing (P^*_0 to P^*_1) and comparatively little expansion in the quantity of new homes provided (Q^*_0 to Q^*_1).

In the interests of simplicity, this analysis ignores distinctions between short-run and long-run market adjustment processes, and assumes instantaneous adjustment to any change in demand or supply-side conditions. It also ignores the possible impact that shortages of skilled labour and other development lags might have on the speed of supply-side adjustment, and on the differences between the price elasticity of supply in the short run and the long run (see Bartlett 1989 or Meen 1998 for a discussion). These, of course, are potentially important influences on the capacity of the market to adjust but, nevertheless, this simple comparative static analysis illustrates the differences in the price and quantity of housing provided in a market with planning, compared to a market without planning.

A number of studies have sought to provide both evidence of this (largely negative) impact of the planning system on the housing market and an assessment of the scale of the impact on a range of market outcomes. To some extent these studies seek to shed some light on whether the costs of planning intervention might be a price worth paying. In addition to measuring the price and quantity effects discussed above, the studies also consider the extent to which the planning system might also impact on the density and type of new development. Unfortunately, the range of methods used and variations in the focus of the projects make direct comparison of the research findings difficult. There are, however, some worthwhile insights (and interesting debates) generated by this series of academic studies.

The earliest of these studies were essentially descriptive and were not explicitly grounded in a mainstream economics framework (see Dawkins &

Nelson 2002 for a review). Using data from a survey of developers, Hall *et al.* (1973) showed that the ratio of land prices to house prices (for a constant density unit) had risen steadily. In the London area, for example, the ratio increased from around 10% in 1960 to between 25% and 38% in 1970. The authors concluded that these increases are partly attributable to the effects of national and local planning policy and not increases in demand. The study also cites work by Denman (1964) as evidence of the impact of planning on densities. They show that, although land prices per acre increased between 1939 to 1959, the ratio of plot price to land price remained constant because of the reduction in house size. Thus, as price per acre increased, houses were constructed on smaller lots and at higher densities (Dawkins & Nelson 2002).

In a seminal polemic, Evans adopts a more explicit neo-classical economics mode of analysis. This provides the basis for a summary of a range of insidious effects of planning intervention in land and housing markets (Evans 1991; see also Evans 1988). Evans notes that land in agricultural use near the city of Reading might cost around £2000 per acre (about £4000/hectare) compared with between £500 000 and £1 million (£1–2 million/hectare) when planning permission has been granted. Although he acknowledges that the price difference is not so great elsewhere in the country, he maintains that the difference in other regions is also substantial. Evans also goes on to describe a number of trends in design, layout and house building, which collectively have led to intensification of land use and the significant contraction of open space within the urban environment.

In defence of planning, however, it is possible to pose questions about the quality and generalisability of some of the evidence reported. The nature of Evans' work is such that there is no rigorous investigation the nature, scale or causes of the post-planning outcomes. The analysis side-steps the possible impact of a range of other influences including local land and housing market conditions, social and demographic trends, and institutional factors. The discussion also ignores the extent to which planning regimes may impose different levels of restraint on the operation of the market (Bramley 1998b). Although Evans' assertions about the effects of planning are supported by fairly selective anecdotal evidence drawn from the South East, the paper provides a robust introduction to the debate about influence of planning on development.

A number of subsequent studies seek to re-examine the issues raised by Evans (1991). These studies tend to be based on more rigorous programmes of empirical research. Although there is debate between the main contributors about the validity of the models and research methods used, as a whole this body of research provides less emphatic but, perhaps, more compelling evidence of scale of the negative effects introduced in Evans' work.

In one of the earliest empirical studies, using data from 1984, Cheshire and Sheppard (1989) undertook a comparative analysis of two local housing markets. As case study areas they chose Reading, in the South East, a market with strong constraints on new development, and Darlington, in the North East, a market with a less restrictive planning regime. Following methods established in the US zoning literature, they used a standard econometric modelling procedure, known as the hedonic house price function, to isolate the impact of different attributes on house prices (see Fischel 1990 and Podogzinski & Sass 1991 for further details of this approach and its application to zoning debates).

The hedonic model can be interpreted as measuring the value of a range of individual physical dwelling attributes, as well as neighbourhood and locational characteristics. Cheshire and Sheppard also used the model to shed light on the impact of the planning system on house prices. Although the study was undermined, in part, by the use of asking prices rather than actual transaction prices and by debates surrounding the validity of hedonic estimation procedures, the main conclusion was that the impact of the planning system was passed on mainly through higher densities and not through vast increases in price. The results suggest that plot sizes and the area of the towns would respectively have been 65% and 50% larger in the absence of planning controls because, with lower prices, house purchasers would have been able to buy larger homes. The price effects of the local planning regimes were shown to be between 2% and 12% depending on house type.

In a more recent paper, Cheshire and Sheppard (1996) update their analysis using data from 1993. In this research they focus on the distributional consequences of planning, and in particular ask what the consequences might be for a household in Reading if the planning regime was relaxed to the lower levels of constraint found in Darlington. The research showed that the reduction in housing costs would lead to a rise in household income of approximately £640 per annum at the urban periphery and approximately £775 per annum in the urban core.

A team of researchers based at Cambridge also present findings on this issue. This evidence is based on a series of research projects and academic papers (Gerald Eve 1992; Jackson *et al.* 1994; Monk *et al.* 1996; Monk & Whitehead 1996, 1999). This body of work adopts a more qualitative approach than that used by other economists, and combines a comparative static analysis with empirical research based on a behavioural social science methodology. The empirical work is based on two separate projects, funded respectively by the DOE and the Joseph Rowntree Foundation.

The first of these, the DOE study, examines the extent to which land supply, and the operation of the planning system, impacted on house prices in Britain during the 1990s. The study sought to identify whether the planning system had merely constrained supply or whether it had led to a reorganisation of that supply. The analysis was based on national and regional trends and a series of local case studies of Wokingham, Reigate, Beverley and Barnsley. The Rowntree study examines land supply within a local market. It seeks to explore the differential effects of planning constraints at local level, and to examine the extent to which land allocations in one area can act as a substitute for land in another area where tighter constraints have been imposed. The research focuses on South Cambridgeshire and Fenland.

The price effect arguments introduced by Evans find rather more empirical support from this research. The results show that prices are much higher at the margins of urban areas when compared with agricultural land and that the inflationary impact of planning is also reflected in differentials between areas. The Gerald Eve (1992) study, for example, shows that, as a result of land constraints, prices increase by 35% to 45% in the South East, while the Rowntree work suggests land prices are 200 times greater than agricultural land in highly constrained areas compared with 60 times greater in less constrained areas (Monk & Whitehead 1996). Furthermore, the temporal dimension of this research suggests that the planning system tends to exacerbate price increases at times of economic growth. Taken together with the failure of the system to help increase output at times of low market activity, the planning system adds to the volatile, cyclical nature of British housing markets. In addition, the research points to the negative role of the planning system in narrowing the densities and types of dwellings produced.

A series of papers by Meen (and others) introduce a temporal dimension to the analysis (Meen 1998; Meen & Andrew 1998; Meen et al. 2001). This research, based on a time-series econometric model, can be deployed to examine the way in which the housing market responds to different economic conditions. Specifically the simulations can be used to investigate what might happen if we make different assumptions about supply-side conditions in the market and about the price elasticity of supply (PES), where the PES is sensitive to the level of planning constraints.

The model shows that, with a PES of around 0.3, when demand expands the price effects will be much larger than changes in quantity supplied. This balance changes only when the PES is raised to levels much higher than those in the UK. Although the PES of 0.3 is lower than those estimated by Malpezzi (1996) and Bramley and Watkins (1996b), which were between 0.9 and 2.1, and 0.8 respectively, the simulation results do not change much even when the highest of these estimates is used. The apparent lack of responsiveness of housing development, however, cannot be wholly attributed to the influence of the planning system. For this reason, research by Meen and Andrew (1998) is used to provide more direct estimates. This shows that the cumulative effect of reducing new housebuilding by 25% (approximately 40 000 units) of its current level for ten years, and thus reducing the overall availability of homes, would be a 2% increase in house prices. Although these findings are interesting, the authors make it clear that, as the models were not developed with the purpose of simulating the impact of planning constraints on prices, the results are unlikely to be as reliable as those generated by other models constructed specifically for the purpose.

In research funded by the Joseph Rowntree Foundation, Bramley developed such a purpose-built model. This work focuses on the relationship between the amount of land available for housing, the nature of the local planning regime and the quantity and price of new housing supplied (Joseph Rowntree Foundation 1994). This programme of research is arguably the most sophisticated and comprehensive attempt to quantify the impacts of the planning system on the housing market (DOE 1996a). Bramley's approach involved estimating a number of key relationships on data for a cross-section of 90 English local planning authorities in the South, South West and Midlands. Summary measures of planning policy and constraints are used as inputs into models. The estimated equations are used to provide a framework for a range of policy scenarios, which are discussed in a series of related outputs. The issues examined include supply-side responsiveness and the effect of mortgage tax relief on the housing system (Bramley 1993a); the impact of land release policies and planning agreements on new housing supply (Bramley 1993b) and on housing quantity and density (Bramley *et al.* 1995); and estimation of the determinants of in-migration and new household formation (Bramley & Watkins 1995).

The results of this research suggest that the price and quantity effects are relatively modest. It is helpful to refer back to Fig. 9.1 to visualise the scale of the effects. With fairly low levels (say 15%) of additional land released for new construction, the price effects will be less than the quantity effects. This implies a relatively flat supply schedule. After a few years, even with a substantial increase in land supply, prices would have fallen by only 5% while the output of new housing would have increased by only 10%. If the land allocated for housing were doubled, the reduction in prices would be less than 10% in the long term.

Significantly, however, Bramley shows that the level of planning intervention may have important impacts on density. Although density is not sensitive to price changes, Bramley *et al.* (1995) suggest, by using composite
measures of planning policy constraints, that there will be a 4.7 homes per
hectare decrease in density for every one standard deviation change in policy.
Although this statistical device is difficult to imagine in practice, it implies
that local planning policies have a major impact on densities.

On the basis of this research, the Joseph Rowntree Foundation's *Inquiry into
Planning for Housing* comes to the general conclusion that 'large land releases are ineffective and environmentally damaging ways to reduce prices'
(Joseph Rowntree Foundation 1994, p. 30; also quoted in Evans 1996, p. 583).
Evans (1996) questions the validity of these findings and the conclusions
drawn from them on several grounds. For instance, he highlights theoretical
problems relating to the structure of the model and, in particular, the assumptions about the equilibrium state of the market upon which the model
is predicated (see also Bramley 1996 on this issue). He moreover highlights
the weak statistical relationships between some of the variables and, importantly, argues that, because the models' simulations are rolled forward
from data from a single period (1988), there are questions about whether the
relationships estimated remain stable over time. Overall, Evans suggests
that, in aggregate, these features have the effect of lowering the estimates of
the impact of planning on price levels. As such it is possible that Bramley's
evidence diverges from that of Evans and the Cambridge group because of
the inherent limitations of the modelling approach.

These criticisms are partly addressed in more recent research where Bramley
extends the geographical and temporal coverage of his data set (see Bramley
& Watkins 1996a; Bramley 1998b, 1999). The new data set covers 162 local
authority areas and allows models to be developed for two points in time: one
in 1988 at the peak of the boom and the other in 1992. These newer estimates
continue to emphasise quantity effects over price effects. The simulation
model shows that with a one-third increase in land available for new housing provision, prices will fall by only 4% while new output will increase by
around 9%.

In a more recent extension of this research, Leishman and Bramley (2001)
follow a similar approach in order to derive a model for local authority areas
in Central Scotland, where constraints on land availability are generally less
pronounced than in Southern England. The results from this analysis are
similar to those discussed above. The policy simulations show that, with
a 50% reduction in the supply of land, private completions would fall by
around 13% after 2 years and by almost 27% after 3 years, while average

house prices would increase by 2% after 2 years and almost 4% after 3 years. On the other hand, if land supply were to be doubled, this might lead to increases of 15% and 36% in new completions, and reductions of 2% and 4% in prices after 2 and 3 years respectively.

Notwithstanding the criticisms of Bramley's work, there are two important conclusions to be drawn from this research. First, and arguably the most important finding, is that the level of land released through the planning system for private housebuilding does not have a large impact on house prices. As the work of Meen *et al.* (2001) also shows, the flow of new homes is small relative to the size of the second-hand market and this reduces the impact on prices. Second, the results suggest that simply allocating land for new homes does not guarantee that it will be built on. There is a clear 'implementation gap'. As we discussed in earlier chapters, in reality, landowners and developers tend to determine the rate of take-up of land supply with regard to demand levels, the capacity of the market to absorb new development and their own business strategies.

However, as Evans (1996) suggests, these results remain specific to the nature of the model specified. Pryce (1999) uses Bramley's data set to revisit these issues. Pryce makes the interesting suggestion that the supply curve is actually backward bending (again it is useful to contrast this with Fig. 9.1 above), rather than upward sloping as normally assumed. The implication of this assumption is that new construction responds by successively small amounts as price increases. This means that, after a certain point, supply actually falls. This may occur if the value of the land held vacant is greater than the value of the land under housing development.

Pryce argues that this is consistent with the stylised facts. In a boom, where there is also likely to be a shortage of skilled labour in the construction sector, the supply response will be constrained (Ball 1996). The empirical analysis supports this explanation. It shows that for a 10% increase in land released for new development, new supply will rise by 8% and prices will fall by 5%. The scale of impact on price levels and output are larger than those estimated by Bramley. This produces a more negative picture of the impact of planning than the earlier analysis of the same data.

Overall, these studies seek to provide a partial analysis of the distributional effects of planning intervention in the housing market. Although estimates of the magnitude and distribution of the effects differ, it is clear that planning constraints lead to higher prices, and densities, restrictions in the quantity of homes supplied and convergence in the type and design of new homes. Although these results are perceived in generally negative terms, there are winners and losers. Higher purchase prices force new buyers to pay more, but existing landowners gain from higher returns through the inflated selling prices in land and housing markets. Developers' profits are dented by higher land prices and lower levels of development but are also inflated by higher selling prices. Residents derive unmeasured utility from the better urban environment associated with protected green belts but lose out through higher densities and smaller lot sizes within urban areas and at the urban fringe. Crucially, however, none of these studies is able to measure the less tangible social costs and benefits. Neither are they are able to gather systematic data, which might allow the accurate assessment of the aggregate effects of the more measurable impacts. As Breheny (1999) notes, however, the clear losers when supply is restricted are the poor!

It is also worth noting that, in general, the mode of analysis employed places some limits on the scope of the research. The comparative static model explored above allows us to theorise the impacts of imposing planning constraints on a previously unfettered market. This provides a useful theoretical guide to the likely distributional effects of planning intervention. However, the empirical research cannot replicate this comparative analysis. The planning system was in place throughout the study periods. As such it is difficult to assess the impact of planning intervention because we cannot do a 'before and after' experiment. Instead all we can usefully do is consider 'what if' (Monk & Whitehead 1999). We can merely observe the actual market outcomes, in terms of price, output or density, and try to assess the ways in which the implementation of land-use policies might have altered the behaviour of the market institutions and their role in the process of determining these outcomes. This might suggest that behavioural or institutional modes of analysis are more appropriate than the quantitative studies that dominate the economics literature. This is an issue to which we return in the concluding section of the chapter.

The economic impact of planning gain on affordable housing development

As we note in Chapter 2, the use of legal obligations or agreements to obtain affordable homes within new housing developments has replaced traditional forms of social housing provision by the state. The agreements take the form of a contract, usually between the planning authority and developer. The use of such agreements is lawful if the contents of the contract are related to the development to which it is linked. In the USA this is known as the 'rational nexus' between the development site and the community need for which the planning gain is sought (Crook 1998).

As we indicated in Chapter 7, there are a number of concerns with the use of planning agreements and the extraction of planning gain. For instance, there has been a fear that placing policies in development plans may 'institutionalise' the pursuit of legal obligations by planning authorities (Rowan-Robinson & Durman 1993). At one stage the practice of using agreements to bargain for planning gain was considered a questionable and even disreputable practice. These concerns have diminished as attitudes to the roles of the state and market have changed. In the financial climate within which the public sector currently operates, it is now widely accepted that requiring developers to contribute to the internal and external costs of carrying out development is legitimate practice (Campbell *et al.* 2000).

Despite this, however, some doubts have continued to be expressed about the legality of agreements regarding the provision of affordable housing. In particular there are questions about whether a link necessarily exists between a private housing scheme and affordable housing (Crook 1998). In law, the link between the requirement for affordable housing and the planning application should be considered in each case and in many instances this link is not clearly established (Slater *et al.* 1999).

Although there is clearly merit in some of these concerns, these are generally outweighed by the flexibility agreements afford to the planning system and the contribution that can be made in claiming back benefits for the community. From an economics perspective what is more interesting than these concerns is the potential for taxing economic rent in order to produce these benefits. This possibility raises questions about how planning gain might impact on different groups including developers, landowners and house purchasers. It also raises questions about the extent to which planning gain might distort the level and pattern of housing development activity.

The distributional effects of securing affordable homes through planning gain

Planning agreements have the potential advantage of transferring the external costs of development to the private sector. In particular it seems likely that costs will be passed on to landowners, house purchasers or developers. As Evans (1999) explains, since it became standard practice in the 1980s to purchase an option on land and then seek planning permission, developers have imposed conditions that have lowered land prices. As such, the cost of any planning gain conceded to obtain planning permission would result in a lower price being paid to the landowner in the event of the option to buy being taken up.

Elsewhere it is suggested that, as a result of planning gain, developers will charge a higher price for the end product which will then be paid for by the home buyer (Samuels 1978; Tucker 1978). Keogh (1985) dismisses these arguments on the basis that price is determined by the market and not the developer. Indeed the inelasticity of supply means that, in the short run, prices are driven by consumer demand. As a result, planning gain will reduce the residual that exists after the costs of development have been deducted from revenue. In theory, this residual is thought to flow to the landowner. This, of course, is contingent on certain neo-classical assumptions about the conditions under which exchange takes place. For example, in a world of perfect information, purchasers of land would know the full cost of planning gain requirement at the time of purchase and would adjust their bidding prices downwards accordingly. In the real world, however, demands for planning gain may be apparent only at a later date, after a purchase has been completed.

There are also concerns about the extent to which planning agreements might restrict the overall level of development activity. This may be valid if planning gain were transformed so that it acts as a tax on development but, even then, textbook economics tells us that a tax on development profits will not restrict development activity provided normal profits can still be earned. Rather, it seems more likely that the rate of development will be constrained by the actions of landowners, who value their land holdings above the market price. Evans (1983) provides a useful example when he suggests that a farmer would not be persuaded to sell his land by an offer based on its agricultural use. He might, however, sell at its residential use value. As development tax will impact on the difference between the agricultural and residential value, it will influence the farmer's behaviour and might have the effect of pushing up the pre-tax price of land. In this case, the developer's activities are unlikely to be altered.

Comparative static analysis can be used to assess the possible distribution of the impact of planning gain. Figure 9.2 represents a slight variation on the first part of Fig. 9.1. In this figure the housing supply schedule is completely price-inelastic. This assumes a planning regime that is completely unresponsive to market forces. The area represented by the rectangle bounded by the origin, the equilibrium level of output (Q_0), the point of intersection between the long-run supply and demand schedules and the equilibrium price (P_0) depicts the level of benefit flowing to the producer (or the economic rent). The requirement for the developer to provide an element of affordable housing will have the effect of taxing the economic rent, by the amount shown in the area between P_a and P_0. Thus, the realisation of planning gain involves securing some or all of the economic rent to provide benefits for the community. The impact is passed on through reduced profit to the landowner. The

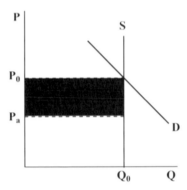

Fig. 9.2   The impact of planning gain on economic rent.

planning gain has no impact on the quantity of housing provided. As Crook and Whitehead (2002) point out, this is probably the implicit model envisaged by policy-makers when the system of planning gain was introduced. This model, however, is highly contingent on the inelasticity of supply and does not reflect the diversity of circumstances in which planning gain is sought in practice.

Under different assumptions, the same framework might be used to imply a different distribution of the costs of planning gain. The low supply elasticity estimates discussed above suggest that it is more likely that the supply curve will be upward sloping (although perhaps gently) in the long run (see Fig. 9.3). If this is the case, planning gain will have several effects. First, as the tax is incorporated into the cost of development, a leftward shift in the supply schedule to S_1 will be induced. The neutral impact on the price of housing and the quantity supplied no longer exists. Price rises pass the impact of

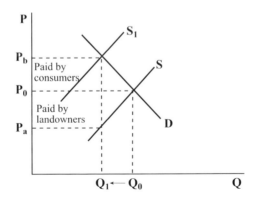

Fig. 9.3   The impact of securing affordable housing under a less restrictive planning regime.

planning gain on to consumers, and the level of new housing development falls for both market and affordable homes.

The major limitation with the preceding comparative static analysis is that it makes no allowance for differential land 'qualities' or market conditions. Most commentaries on the use of planning agreements have tended to highlight that the ability to secure affordable housing varies in different circumstances. Where development takes place on greenfield sites and the cost of development is already high, the effect of planning gain may be less easy for developers to bear. In areas where housing demand is low, and this is translated into lower prices, the capacity to secure affordable homes might also be limited. Crook and Whitehead (2002) extend their comparative static analysis to cover these issues. They show that there are indeed some conditions under which the use of planning gain to secure affordable homes will have a fairly neutral impact on house prices and the quantity of homes provided. These conditions require that levels of housing demand are high or that development sites are low cost or, of course, that both of these conditions prevail.

There are also concerns that the scope for planning agreements may vary depending on development size. It seems more likely that the requirement for affordable housing on a small site will have an adverse affect on the financial viability of the project, compared with larger sites. Consequently, emphasis tends to be placed on the use of larger development sites to meet the need for affordable housing. In addition, it is also worth noting that affordable housing has to compete with other types of planning gain, including the provision of transport infrastructure, and open space. There is some evidence that planning authorities have seen transport infrastructure as a higher priority (Slater *et al.* 1999). There are also instances where the process of negotiation will operate against the provision of affordable homes. In instances where open space may enhance the appeal of a new housing development, the non-housing alternative would tend to prevail since the provision of affordable housing could be viewed as a deterrent by some potential purchasers.

In summary, it seems that landowners and developers compete over their relative share of development profits (Ball 1981, cited in Keogh 1985). Most of the impact of planning gain appears to be transferred to the landowner rather than the developer. There is some theoretical or empirical evidence to support the assertion that planning gain reduces the incentive for development to take place. There is also some evidence that the impact of planning gain may be passed on to the house buyer. These effects, however, depend on market conditions and the size and types of development sites involved.

From a public sector perspective, it also seems possible that attempts to secure affordable homes may be displaced by other forms of planning gain.

Conclusions: comparing modes of economic analysis

This chapter has focused on the economic impact of planning intervention on the housing system. The first part of the chapter reviewed a number of theoretical and empirical contributions to the literature. These studies showed, as one might predict, that the planning system leads to higher prices for new and existing homes, higher building densities, lower levels of new housing development, and greater convergence in the type of home developed. The attempts to quantify these effects provide a wide range of estimates and, as such, provide a basis for adopting a range of political or policy stances with respect to the role of planning.

What is much more clear is that planning intervention impacts differently on different groups and, in some market contexts, developers and existing owners may benefit greatly from inflated prices (see Chapter 6). The social and environmental effects deriving from guiding and restricting development are less obvious and, given the inability to accurately measure the impacts of intervention, are almost impossible to estimate. This leaves us with little sound empirical evidence upon which to base an assessment of the overall performance of the system or its specific influence on housing development.

The second part of the chapter focuses on one specific form of planning intervention, namely the use of planning gain to secure affordable housing. As Evans (1999) points out, planning gain would not have been possible without the strict planning controls on development that have caused the price of land with planning permission to be higher than the price without it. As such, planning gain is one of the unforeseen effects of intervention in the housing market. It is partly for this reason, and because the planning system has contributed to pushing up prices, that the system has been seen as providing the institutional basis from which to secure the development of affordable homes. The use of planning gain, however, has not been without criticism. In particular, critics have focused on the distributional impact of planning gain and its potentially adverse effects on the operation of the market.

Keogh (1985, p. 223) summarises the economic arguments when he states that:

conventional economic theory offers no justification for objections to planning gain. There is scope for argument about the extent to which the distributional outcome would be desirable but, in terms of economic efficiency, planning gain appears to improve, rather than worsen, the allocation of land and other resources.

Although Crook and Whitehead (2002) appear to agree with this general statement, their analysis shows that this improvement will hold only if the impact of planning gain does not affect price and output. These conditions, however, are most likely to occur only in areas where demand for housing is high and/or the cost of sites low. In other circumstances, planning gain may have adverse distributional effects and these might exacerbate ownership constraints on development and lead to higher purchase prices. Agreements might also reduce the level of development of both market and affordable homes. These problems might be most acute where brownfield sites are being developed in low demand contexts, as is the case in many of the declining cities in the north.

In the case of both the discussion of the general economic impact of planning intervention and of the impact of planning gain, there are clear limitations associated with this sort of analysis, not least because of its partial nature. In particular, the mode of analysis deployed ignores many of the behavioural realities of the market such as the role of information imperfections in shaping actors' decisions, and the complexity of the bargaining process and the nature of exchange. It is also clear that the values of the market dominate this analysis and, as such, insufficient weight is ascribed to the broader social objectives of the system. While the work of Keogh (1985) and Crook and Whitehead (2002) provides useful insights into the distributional effects of planning agreements, the analysis is heavily influenced by the underlying assumptions about the behaviour of actors and market conditions. An alternative institutional approach may provide a framework within which to relax some of these behavioural assumptions and to switch the focus from outcomes to the process that shapes these outcomes.

The majority of studies reviewed in this chapter clearly adopt the behavioural assumptions associated with the mainstream, neo-classical school of economics. Given the broad social objectives of the planning system, there are sound reasons for applying this mode of analysis to the assessment of the distributional impacts of planning intervention in the housing system. This approach is in line with the analysis of the objectives of other public policy areas, and in effect what most economists are doing is approaching the study of planning impacts within an implicit welfare economics framework. The welfare economics approach provides a clear framework for tracking the effects of policy interventions on individuals and groups. This also provides scope to theorise the relative scale of these impacts. There is a tendency, however, for the framework to obscure the implicit value judgements that inform the analysis and to leave unqualified the conclusions drawn from these empirical studies. In addition, there is a tendency again for the models to focus on market outcomes at the expense of market process.

There is, of course, a well-established body of applied land and property market studies based on different modes of analysis. Elsewhere in this book we have touched on the insights from studies of housebuilders' behaviour and institutional analyses of the development process (see, for example, Drewett 1973; Goodchild & Munton 1985; Healey 1992; Adams *et al.* 1992; see also Adams 1994; Ball *et al.* 1998 for reviews).

However, although Rydin (1986) appeals for considered analysis of planning from the point of view of process and outcomes, in the context of this chapter, only the work of Monk and Whitehead (and the other members of their research group) seeks directly to quantify the effects of planning intervention on the housing market on the basis of a more behaviourally orientated mode of analysis. These authors conclude their most recent output with a commentary on the challenge for researchers. They note that behavioural analysis alone remains insufficient for understanding markets and for making policy decisions. They go on to say that 'the most important requisite is to be able to quantify more accurately the extent of impact on prices, outputs and outcomes arising from constraints. Only then can the costs and benefits of the planning system be properly assessed' (Monk & Whitehead 1999, p. 93). Only then, of course, can the positions held by various groups in debates about housing development be better informed.

On the other hand, D'Arcy and Keogh (1998) illustrate the potential limitations of an approach dominated by mainstream modes of economic analysis. They note that, within mainstream economics, data on market activity (or market outcomes) are generally used and interpreted at face value. Instead, it is suggested that interpretation should be conducted with reference to the institutional aspects of market process, and behaviour, that generated the data and shape the outcomes.

On balance, it seems that, given the inherent limitations of the neo-classical model, further development of alternative modes of analysis is required to enhance our understanding of the economics of planning for the housing market. Although there will remain a role for mainstream economic approaches, these must build on theoretical and technical advancements in microeconomics. In particular, these models must more effectively embrace the influences of information asymmetry, search behaviour and price formation in thin markets (Maclennan & Whitehead 1996). We may then begin more effectively to understand the role of policy intervention, spatial interactions and temporal dynamics in the operation of land and housing markets.

The research agenda must address the inherent limitations of the neo-classical model. In particular models must be less static in nature, focus on market process as well as outcomes, and be built on behavioural assumptions that have greater realism. To date, these limitations have meant that neo-classical analyses have been less able to inform policy decisions than other methodological approaches (McMaster & Watkins 2000). As such, economists have tended to opt out of the debate rather than adopt new approaches. The adoption of new methodological approaches, however, may provide a basis for addressing the dearth of economic studies of issues in planning and development, and may also open up new research questions.

10

Conclusions and Policy Implications

The location of new housing development has become one of the most intractable controversies of modern times. At a superficial level, debate is centred on the use of land and, specifically, on the use of particular parcels of land that from time to time come under development pressure. Yet, to reduce what should be a broad evaluation of the most appropriate location for new housing development to a simple choice between brownfield and greenfield land is to miss the point. For as we have attempted to show in this book, the controversies that so often seem to surround new housing development can be properly understood only in relation to the wider institutional context for individual land-use decisions. This makes it impossible to devise a truly effective housing land policy without taking full account of such factors as the structure and organisation of the housebuilding industry, supply and demand pressures in the housing market, the growing importance of sustainability and the motives and behaviour of those in political control of the planning process.

Since housing land policy represents a classic attempt by government to influence what it does not directly control, this book has essentially presented a case study of state–market relations in the production process. For while the private sector is primarily responsible for the production of new housing, it acts within a policy environment through which the state seeks to influence certain aspects of housing production, of which location is perhaps the most noticeable. Issues of policy effectiveness, and more specifically of the extent to which land and property markets can be influenced by state policy, are thus central to the discussion in this final chapter.

The importance of state–market relations in housing development can be traced back to several earlier studies of housing land policy. Rydin (1986), for example, emphasised the inter-relationship between economic structures, political structures and political ideology in shaping policy development at both the national and local levels. Although, at that time, she highlighted the incorporation of large housebuilding interests within central government policy formulation, she also identified the significance of anti-development interests in protecting the green belt and maintaining the overall philosophy of urban containment.

Home (1985) commented on the importance of the price and supply of housing land to housebuilders' profitability. He suggested that, of all the various inputs to the housing development process, land was the most susceptible to political pressure. In this context, however, research by Hooper *et al.* (1989) on prosperous market areas in the South East of England contended that the planning system had a reasonable track record in responding to higher completion rates or household projection figures by altering the planned release of development land. Although the form and extent of state intervention in the housing development process may well change, as the relative power of competing interests shifts and new agendas such as sustainability come to the fore, it is apparent that many of the themes of this book have generated controversy over past decades and will no doubt continue to be debated in the years ahead.

In the next section, we therefore summarise the main political and market factors that have become fundamental to understanding the institutional context for new housing. The chapter then moves on to consider some important policy challenges for the future, arguing strongly that it will remain impossible to resolve the controversies of housebuilding by focusing merely on matters of land use. Instead, a more holistic approach is required in which a broader concept of land policy is itself well embedded within an urban policy agenda. Indeed, since current disputes about new housebuilding are only superficially about land use, we contend that they will not be resolved effectively until policy for new housing successfully addresses a much wider range of land policies than mere matters of use.

Political and market context

People come together to influence the housing market as both consumers and voters. As consumers, they have been living in smaller households while demanding higher standards of space and better quality environments, at least within the home itself. Whether by choice or necessity, they have participated in a process of urban decentralisation that is apparent in the interwoven dispersal of housing, employment, retailing and other activities from the centre to the periphery of urban areas and from larger to smaller settlements. Over the years, housing consumers have switched tenure increasingly into owner-occupation, although it remains unclear whether this switch has been generated more by personal choice and greater economic prosperity or by political encouragement in the form of taxation or other incentives. Nevertheless, all these trends point to increased consumer demand for housing space, especially at decentralised locations.

By living off this demand, the housebuilding industry has been able to concentrate its attention, at least in the past, on managing uncomplicated forms of production at uncomplicated locations. Indeed, until recently, most of the skills and experience in the industry have been gained primarily through the relatively unproblematic conversion of greenfield land to new housing estates, so meeting consumer demand at decentralised locations. To what extent is location of new housing production preferred by the private sector open to positive as well as negative influences from the state? For, while it is relatively easy for policy-makers to shut off the supply of greenfield land, at least in the short term, it is much more difficult to ensure that brownfield land is widely used instead in the housebuilding industry. For housebuilders, the immediate challenge is whether to respond to supply constraints on greenfield land by reducing overall production or by seeking innovative means to develop new urban housing markets and products. How far then can the imposition of tighter state controls on one form of private housing development serve to encourage the alternative production of more acceptable forms elsewhere?

Although there is considerable evidence that the more innovative housebuilding companies have already shown a willingness and determination to adapt their strategies to deliver high-quality brownfield development, at least in the more prosperous parts of the country, it is perhaps too early to say whether such innovation will permeate the industry or country as a whole. Regional differences in economic and housing market performance may well militate against innovation in less prosperous areas. Debate therefore concerns how far the majority of the industry will choose to adapt traditional strategies or whether a new structure of provision in housebuilding will be necessary to deliver greater brownfield development, with fresh entrants and more innovative companies achieving dominant positions.

In this context, if housebuilders as a whole are to be convinced of the wisdom of developing brownfield sites, the state needs to reassure consumers that urban housing markets are robust enough to ensure the future of their investments. In the language of the Urban Task Force (1999), if the English are to be persuaded to forego their decentralist tendencies and rediscover their traditional urban roots, a wholesale urban renaissance needs to be created though innovative and holistic approaches to urban policy.

Fig. 10.1 New apartments by Persimmon Homes in Southampton demonstrating the challenge of fitting brownfield development into the existing urban fabric.

Yet, while it is possible for politicians to rely very largely on planning control when they wish to stop development, a more sophisticated range of policy tools is necessary to create development, especially within established urban locations. If new housing is to continue to be very largely delivered by the private sector, the state may need to find more effective ways to influence production so as to ensure that a regular and extensive flow of high-quality development is forthcoming at brownfield locations. Such an approach may not be wholly compatible with the increasing state dependence on the private sector for affordable or social housing provision.

Although the statutory planning system has been used successfully to restrain greenfield development, it has made only a limited direct contribution towards the explicit promotion of brownfield development. Instead, the state has relied primarily on non-statutory approaches to stimulate such interest, of which two are worth highlighting. First, in a small number of locations, active intervention by urban development corporations and other specialist agencies has shown what the public sector can achieve in assembling and preparing brownfield sites for housebuilding. Such action has usually been accompanied by environmental improvement and infrastructure provision in the wider locality. However, in quantitative terms, only a small proportion of urban housing markets have been covered by such initiatives.

Secondly and more widely, financial assistance has been made available to housebuilders on a site-by-site basis to make otherwise unprofitable development profitable. Known as 'gap funding', this assistance has been directed both to the remediation of contamination and other difficult site conditions and to underpinning development viability in fragile market locations. Unfortunately, however, since the European Commission took a dim view of the anti-competitive nature of gap funding in December 1999, it is likely to be much harder to obtain in future, except in the assisted areas of the UK.

As voters, people play a different role in the housing development process through the way in which they use and are used by politicians to resist new housing development. Reports of concerted public opposition to greenfield and occasionally to brownfield development are common in the press, but it is rare indeed to find public opinion lobbying in favour of the development of a particular housing site. Of course, those who might in future occupy proposed new housing do not yet have the necessary interest in a disputed site to organise themselves into an effective pressure group to bring about its development. Ironically, those who have recently consumed new housing at greenfield locations can often be the most militant in their opposition to further encroachment on neighbouring undeveloped areas. Moreover, it cannot be assumed that urban residents are necessarily compliant in their acceptance of increased residential densities within existing towns and cities. Planning battles, against what local residents perceive as inappropriate development, can be just as intense within cities as on their periphery.

Inevitably, politicians of all political persuasions soon discover that far more votes are to be gained from being seen to stop development than being seen to create it. This is aggravated by a strongly protectionist countryside and environmental lobby that consistently encourages national and local politicians not to resolve housing land issues, but instead to use them as vote-generators. It is thus ironic that, as no lasting method to tax development value has ever been agreed between political parties, the statutory planning system also encourages owners of agricultural land to seek its allocation for residential development through participation in the planning process.

Clearly, those who are successful stand to make huge gains, although experience would suggest that many are unsuccessful or have to wait a long time before their land is allocated for development.

Although the planning system was originally intended not to ration the overall supply of development land but rather to direct demand to locations where development was considered appropriate, it has increasingly been captured by anti-development interests seeking to ensure progressively tighter restrictions on the ability of the housebuilders to meet demand at greenfield locations. Research reported in Chapter 9 suggests this has led to higher prices and densities, reductions in the quantity of homes supplied and convergence in the type and design of new homes.

Nevertheless, since these unintended side effects are not distributed evenly, planning constraints create their own winners and losers. New house buyers, for example, obviously have to pay more for property, while existing owners gain from higher returns through the inflated selling prices. Developers' profits can be inflated by higher selling prices, but dented by higher land prices and lower levels of development activity. Again, while some residents derive unmeasured utility from the improved urban environment associated with protected green belts, others lose out through higher densities and smaller plot sizes within urban areas and at the urban fringe. Nevertheless, since these effects are all hard to measure without systematic data, it is difficult to accurately assess the aggregate effects of even the more measurable impacts.

Although town and country planning was originally conceived as a means by which to shape the future, its focus, at least in respect to new housing, has increasingly narrowed over the years. Any concern with lively or well-designed residential communities has tended to give way to debates over the quantities of land to be allocated for new housing. This concentration on land use rather than on place-making in the broader sense has put the planning system on the defensive and allowed it to be more easily captured by those interests primarily concerned with protecting the value of their properties and immediate environments. Although at the turn of the twenty-first century there are now hopeful signs in both the *New Vision for Planning* produced by the Royal Town Planning Institute (2001) and the Green Paper on *Planning: Delivering a Fundamental Change* published by the DTLR (2001b) that a broader view of planning may be starting to emerge, reliance on the statutory system alone for the future delivery of quality housing development is likely to remain misplaced.

Earlier in the book, we pointed out how the contested nature of sustainability means that a variety of urban forms have the potential to deliver sustainable development. We have consistently argued that those who suggest that brownfield development is necessarily always sustainable and greenfield development necessarily always unsustainable have either misunderstood the concept or are seeking to capture it for their own ends. Amenity protection, for example, is not necessarily synonymous with environmental protection. In certain circumstances, large-scale development on greenfield land may well offer the best opportunity to deliver local sustainability.

Too often, however, green belts have been seen as an inviolable component of the planning system and in the public's mind have been mistakenly linked to the protection of greenfield land as a whole. If the concept of sustainability is to include some measure of economic prosperity, it is apparent that green belt boundaries need to be adjustable rather than permanently fixed in order to respond to dynamic change in the local economy. Those who argue for ever-increasing proportions of new housing to be built on brownfield sites should remember that such development can face increasingly high marginal costs and may well produce unacceptable town cramming. Urban compaction, even if desirable, should not require immediate building of new dwellings on every last brownfield site, irrespective of the cost or at the expense of other desirable land uses. While sustainable brownfield development is to be welcomed, not all brownfield development is necessarily sustainable.

In the past, the planning system appears to have paid too much attention to matters of quantity and location and not enough to quality. It is possible that, in future, the planning system could achieve much more in sustainability terms if it dropped its apparent obsession with the quantity and mere location of development and concentrated instead on improving the quality of new housing. In this context, it is now widely acknowledged, at least in the academic literature, that the key to making development sustainable is not simply where it is located, but also how it is designed and managed.

Among the essential characteristics of sustainable development appear to be compactness, mix of uses and interconnected street patterns, strong public transport networks, environmental controls and high standards of urban management. However, since the state has most control over land use, it has retreated into regarding sustainability primarily as a matter of location, when, with effective institutional mechanisms in place, a more rounded approach could be adopted that might focus instead on delivering sustainable development, whether located on greenfield or brownfield land.

At the same time, the increasingly restrictive financial climate in which local authorities have had to operate has also undermined the ability of the planning system to raise the quality of new residential development. Such financial restrictions have not only led to shortages of available expertise, especially in design and development, but have limited the ability of local authorities to participate as a partner in the development process, making them ever more reliant on planning gain secured from housebuilders for the provision of essential residential infrastructure. The subservience of the state to the market has further ensured that the speed of decision-making, which can be easily measured, has been prioritised above the quality of decisions, which is far more intangible to evaluate.

As we have contended in this book, sustainable compact cities can be achieved only if the process of development is better managed and the products of development are of high quality. This has significant repercussions for private investment and public policy. Within the private sector, institutional change may well be needed to deliver that greater level of innovation essential to the successful implementation of more problematic forms of development than traditionally produced by the industry. Whether the housebuilding industry has the institutional capacity to modify current practices and procedures to emphasise brownfield development is itself an important research question.

Within the public sector, government may need to become more directly involved in the development process in order to encourage better practice in the industry. For example, tighter building regulations imposing higher standards of design and energy efficiency would be to the competitive advantage of those builders already keen to achieve such standards and would tend to undermine those who have shown little interest in improving in this area. Again, if some kind of sustainability audit were required at the time of a planning application, it would put those housebuilders who have begun to take sustainability more seriously at a competitive advantage.

Nevertheless, these are minor examples in comparison with what the Government could achieve through a more holistic urban land policy. As the experience of urban villages shows, an effective division of responsibilities between the public and private sectors for creating and bringing forward brownfield sites is likely to be crucial to stimulating user and developer demand at brownfield locations. The importance of supportive political and public action to the success of brownfield development, for example, was highlighted by the Civic Trust (1999). As Gibb *et al.* (1995) contend, partnership between local planning authorities, local communities and prospective developers is likely to become more the norm for major housing development at both greenfield and brownfield locations, with the public sector playing an increasingly important co-ordinating role.

Yet, despite public pronouncements which suggest an apparent improvement in rates of brownfield land recycling during the 1990s, our analysis of the relevant statistics revealed that the overall amount of previously developed land reused for housing has not significantly increased since the late 1980s. It would appear that the strength or weakness of the housebuilding industry's demand for land as a whole has been a much more important influence on the extent of brownfield recycling than previous policy measures.

The Urban Task Force (1999) suggested that the Government was unlikely to meet its 60% recycling target without significant changes in the policy environment. As the earlier Parliamentary Office of Science and Technology (1998) report argued, a 'business as usual' approach cannot deliver the 60% target, especially as many of the easiest brownfield sites had already been developed, leaving a legacy of more problematic sites. Although preventing development at greenfield locations remains a relatively simple and rewarding activity for politicians, it would appear that the state still lacks the essential tools to bring about a substantial switch to brownfield development. Moreover, while greenfield development has been increasingly restricted by the statutory planning system and brownfield development promoted at selected locations through urban policy, remarkably little co-ordination has been evident between these two policy instruments. In the remainder of this chapter, we therefore set out the case for a broader view of land policy to be well embedded within the emerging urban policy agenda.

Towards a new urban land policy

According to the Urban Task Force (1999, p. 25) 'An urban renaissance should be founded on the principles of design excellence, economic strength, environmental responsibility, good governance and social well-being.' If this holistic vision is to be achieved, it will require effective urban policies that aim to tackle the economic, social, environmental and political aspects of urban decline in an integrated manner. This was certainly the intention behind the Urban White Paper (DETR 2000b), which aimed to draw together the Government's response to the Urban Task Force and chart a future direction for English towns and cities.

The White Paper seeks to create better-designed, more attractive and environmentally sustainable urban places, while putting equal if not greater emphasis on the delivery of higher-quality urban services and especially on ways of enabling local people to be more directly involved in determining the future of their own towns and cities and of ensuring more effective local and regional leadership. In terms of urban land policy, brownfield development must therefore be set within an overall approach that emphasises the importance of creating liveable cities, stimulating demand, building confidence and making sites available.

Although there may well be a short-term role for fiscal and other incentives to underpin occupier demand for brownfield development, this would suggest that the main policy focus for urban housing development needs to be on the creation of brownfield development opportunities that are themselves viable and, especially, on the wider public and private sector investment required to transform towns and cities into more attractive places in which to live. Much higher standards of urban design, for example, are likely to be necessary in the future than in the past, both to instil greater urban confidence and to resolve potential conflicts within mixed-use schemes.

If property markets are to be convinced about the security and liquidity of capital invested in brownfield housing, a strongly interventionist approach may well be needed to ensure and foster consumer demand in the many areas as yet untouched by even the most innovative housebuilding companies. While the importance attached to good schools, safe streets and pleasant developments is readily apparent, what role can and should land play within this new urban policy? To help answer this, we now turn to a well-known classification of land policy instruments and consider how they might each help switch the balance of development from greenfield to brownfield housing.

In the grand visions of future urban renaissance, land issues tend to be dealt with implicitly in the sense that they are subsumed within those broader policies intended to achieve design excellence, economic strength, environmental responsibilities, good government and social well-being. According to Lichfield and Darin-Drabkin (1980, p. 11) '*land policy* and *land policy measures* can be defined as that part of *development policy* and *development policy measures* which are related to the *role* of land in the *implementation* of urban and regional plans' (original emphasis). This, they argue, provides a much sharper understanding of land policy than many earlier treatments that have commonly branded as land policy all government policies to do with land.

Lichfield and Darin-Drabkin (1980) exclude from their consideration development plan-making, rural land reform, natural resource policies, economic development and general taxation measures. Their particular concern with the way in which land resources are deployed in the implementation of development policy leads them to suggest that land policy measures can be classified in the six ways that are shown in Fig. 10.2. This table also indicates

Land Policy Measure	Illustrative Powers	Primary Emphasis
	Direct Control over Development	
1. Control over specific development without taking land	Standards and norms; permits; zoning; compulsory reparcellation	Regulatory
2. Control over specific development by taking land	By agreement or exchange; by compulsory purchase; pre-emption or sale; forced dedication	Developmental
3. Control over specific development by direct public-authority participation	Infrastructure; statutory functions; general development	Developmental
	Fiscal Control over Development	
4. Influence over general development by fiscal measures	Land profit taxes; property taxes; transfer taxes; municipal income tax; municipal sales tax; death/inheritance tax; wealth tax; subsidies; price and sales controls	Financial
5. Influence over specific development by fiscal measures	Infrastructure charges; taxation of vacant land; taxation based on development scheme; conditional loans and subsidies; transport pricing policy	Financial
	General Influence over Development	
6. General influence on the land market	Indicative planning; co-ordination of development; information on land holdings; information on land transactions	Information and guidance

Fig. 10.2 A classification of land policy measures (source: Lichfield & Darin-Drabkin 1980; Healey *et al.* 1988).

the primary emphasis of each type of measure, as specified by Healey *et al.* (1988) who subsequently applied the Lichfield and Darin-Drabkin classification in their substantive study of the role of land-use planning in the meditation of urban change.

Since an urban renaissance will demand a wholesale transformation of the way in which urban land and property are used, managed and developed in many locations, financial and developmental land policy measures must take their place alongside new forms of regulation and better information and guidance in an integrated land policy. In short, if the planning system is to play a more creative role in facilitating brownfield development then it must form part of a broader land policy. This is because it cannot be assumed that brownfield land will necessarily provide a ready substitute for greenfield land, without more active public sector intervention in urban land markets than has been the case in the recent past. Such active intervention may be required, for example, to ease the passage of urban land and property to those development interests most likely to contribute to the achievement of an urban renaissance. On this note, it is worth examining the potential role of each of the land policy measures identified in Fig. 10.2.

Regulatory measures

Regulatory land policy measures seek control over specific developments without taking land. They can be enforced by standards, norms, permits or zoning. Although development control is still the most prominent form of regulation in British land policy, it is by no means exclusive. It would be possible to use other forms of regulation already in existence to make it uncongenial for brownfield land to be kept vacant and not fed into the development process.

Under Section 215 of the Town and Country Planning Act (1990), for example, local authorities can serve what are generally known as wasteland notices, requiring owners of land deemed to be detrimental to the amenity of an area to undertake specified action to remedy its unsightly appearance. Similarly under the Environment Act (1995), appropriate persons can be required under statutory notices to remedy land contamination. As has previously been mentioned, a much greater emphasis on energy efficiency and other environmentally friendly measures in the building regulations would serve the cause of sustainability, irrespective of whether new homes were constructed on greenfield or brownfield sites. More sophisticated integration of the entire regulatory regime for the use, development and management of urban land may well be essential if the alleged capacity of existing urban areas to absorb higher levels of brownfield development is to be fully exploited.

Financial land policy measures

Financial land policy measures seek to influence development or specific forms of development through fiscal means. At the general level, Lichfield and Darin-Drabkin (1980) note that fiscal measures can have a significant impact on the development process and thus on the implementation of urban and regional plans through their effect on the price and quantity of land transacted in the market.

As we noted in Chapters 7 and 9, planning gain has served as an increasingly important financial land policy measure over the past 20 years or so. The growth and effectiveness of planning gain have been extensively documented in research, with searching questions asked in particular about their potential contribution to the provision of affordable housing. While the secretive nature of planning gain has been widely criticised in the past as unethical, it is increasingly apparent that lack of openness and certainty hinders the ability of the land market to handle requirements for planning gain through the normal process of development appraisal. As a result, the cost of planning gain may in practice not always be met through reduced prices achieved on sale by landowners.

The Government now proposes to introduce a standardised approach to planning gain, with each planning authority setting out its schedule of standard tariffs through the local planning process (DTLR 2001d). Interestingly, it suggests that tariffs might be applied differentially in certain areas with, for example, the development of a difficult brownfield site qualifying for a reduction or even a complete waiver from the tariff. Despite all the potential practical difficulties of such an approach, the whole debate that is taking place around the future of planning gain indicates the significant contribution financial land policy measures can make to sustainable development, if well integrated into urban land policy as a whole.

In recent years, there has also been substantial debate as to how far brownfield development can be directly promoted through the tax system. The Urban Task Force (1999) looked in detail at a range of possible taxation incentives to encourage developers to assemble brownfield development sites. As part of the Comprehensive Spending Review in 2000, the Government announced that regeneration budgets would grow by an average of 15% in real terms over 5 years and that it would introduce a package of taxation measures worth a cumulative £1 billion over the same period to assist urban regeneration. Specifically, in the 2001 Budget, the Chancellor of the Exchequer introduced the following:

- An exemption from stamp duty for all property transactions in disadvantaged areas.

- Accelerated tax credits for cleaning up contaminated land.

- 100% capital allowances for creating 'flats over shops' for letting.

- Reduction of VAT on residential conversions from 17.5% to 5%.

Experience suggests that while taxation incentives can certainly help stimulate development in specific locations (Adair *et al.* 1995) there is always a danger that fiscal benefits will be capitalised into higher land values or higher rents and prices (Lizieri 1999). It is thus interesting to note that the Government has concentrated on the provision of tax subsidies rather than the introduction of new selected taxes to assist urban regeneration.

In this context, it is worth recalling that the Urban Task Force (1999) recommended that the Government prepare a scheme for introducing a vacant land tax in a way that would not penalise genuine developers but would deter others from holding land unnecessarily. In its response to the report, the Government questioned the wisdom and effectiveness of a vacant land tax, believing instead that financial land policy measures are likely to be more effective when they take the form of a financial carrot rather than a stick. Clearly, it will require some years of detailed monitoring before the impact of the latest financial carrots can be evaluated. Indeed, care is needed to ensure that financial land policy measures are well targeted and time-limited, if public resources are to be deployed efficiently in this direction.

Information and guidance

As Lichfield and Darin-Drabkin (1980) maintain, planning policies provide an important context for land market decisions. However, beyond indicative planning and the co-ordination of development, information kept in public registers on land holdings and transactions can play a useful role in accelerating market processes. Although the Land Registry in England first became open for public access in 1990, details of prices paid still remain confidential in contrast to the position in Scotland. If more efficient urban land and property markets are to be promoted, there is a strong case for ensuring that all details of land ownership are made available through an 'online' system.

This would be facilitated by comprehensive land registration and could be achieved once initiatives such as the National Land Information Service (NLIS) and the Scottish Land Information Service (ScotLIS) reach maturity. Although the arrival of electronic conveyancing may prompt the provision of some 'online' ownership information, what is required is not necessarily the further development of geographical information systems (GIS) but the political will to place ownership details (including price paid) in the public domain. In the English (but not the Scottish) context this would be a controversial innovation but one that would certainly help facilitate brownfield development.

In the wider context, it has been argued that more effective use of land registration data can improve housing monitoring systems (Leishman & Watkins 2002). Other countries appear to be ahead of the UK in their institutional arrangements to deliver such market information (Costello & Watkins 2002). As argued by Adair *et al.* (1998) in respect of investment behaviour in urban regeneration and Rhodes (1995) in relation to investment in rented housing, much better systems of information on land ownership are required to inspire market confidence.

Developmental measures

Developmental land policy measures seek control over specific developments either by taking land or by direct public authority participation. As Lichfield and Darin-Drabkin (1980) note, land can be acquired by agreement or exchange, compulsory purchase, pre-emption, sale or forced dedication. In the British context, compulsory purchase for planning purposes has been quite rare until relatively recently (Adams 1996; Raggett 1998) with reliance instead placed on acquisition by agreement.

Following the change of government in 1997 and the subsequent report of the Urban Task Force (1999), a renewed interest has occurred in the use of compulsory purchase, with official reviews of relevant law and procedures established in both England and Scotland. Subsequently, the Government prepared a procedural manual to provide a comprehensive guide to the English compulsory purchase system and to offer best practice advice to those involved in its operation. More significantly, alongside its Green Paper on the future of the English planning system (DTLR 2001b), the Government published a companion document entitled *Compulsory Purchase and*

Compensation: Delivering a Fundamental Change (DTLR 2001e). This proposed a series of reforms, including enabling powers for local authorities to undertake compulsory purchase more widely for planning and regeneration purposes, with the promise of consolidating and simplifying legislation once parliamentary time allows.

It remains to be seen how far these proposals will succeed in reducing the confrontational nature of compulsory purchase and speeding up the process. However, unless the improvements proposed in the skills and legislative base for compulsory purchase are matched by the provision of the necessary funds for land acquisition, they may have little practical impact on brownfield development, other than in already healthy markets. In this context, it is important that the Urban Task Force's call for the creation of revolving public funds for land assembly be taken seriously.

Since the greater brownfield development is likely to involve increasing disruption to the historic patterns of urban land ownership, the smooth and rapid resolution of ownership constraints is likely to demand as much attention from policy-makers as the design of an effective planning system or the remediation of contamination. Whether land is acquired through compulsory purchase or through more consensual forms of transfer such as the concept of an Urban Partnership Zone, as proposed in Chapter 8, it is probable that local authorities will have to play an increasingly pivotal role in creating suitable brownfield development opportunities and making them available to housebuilders.

During the 1960s and 1970s, the traditional use of leaseholds as the favourite method to release public land for development was extended into joint venture development partnerships (Lichfield & Darin-Drabkin 1980). If this is allied to infrastructure provision and more general development policies, the proactive use of land as an input to the development process can put planning authorities, or indeed regional development agencies, in a powerful position to determine the quality and sustainability of new development.

This is likely to be seen not as hostile but as a welcome approach by housebuilders for it takes the risk out of land acquisition and enables them to concentrate on their own production process. Land assembly, within the context of a range of integrated urban policy measures intended to enhance the attractiveness of existing towns and cities as places to live, would make a powerful contribution towards the achievement of much greater levels of brownfield development. Although planning policy can be very effective in curtailing greenfield development, as it requires the state to play only a preventative role in the development process, it certainly needs to be matched by a stronger role in the assembly and release of urban land by local authorities and other public sector development agencies. Only then will brownfield land begin to outperform greenfield land as the location of first choice for the majority of housing consumers and producers.

A final word

In many ways, the greenfield/brownfield debate has provided an effective camouflage to hide politicians from engaging in real debates about the true nature of sustainable development. Sustainability represents a significant challenge to past practices in the housebuilding industry and will not be achieved unless significant innovation is promoted within the industry itself or encouraged by state intervention. This is because sustainability is concerned not simply with the particular housing estate under construction but with its whole relationship to the surrounding community and wider urban area.

In this book, we have argued that sustainable housing development requires the state to play a more active role in the development process through ensuring the ready availability of preferred development sites, whether at greenfield or brownfield locations, and by taking the lead on those intangible aspects of housing products that are beyond the role of any particular builder (such as good schools, attractive local environments and efficient transport connections). This does not amount to a call for large-scale public sector housebuilding but quite the reverse. It suggests that the state has a legitimate role to play in the overall management and co-ordination of the development process in order to achieve greater value added in terms of design and quality in housing products and environments.

We thus contend that the achievement of much greater levels of brownfield residential development (and indeed, of brownfield development more generally) will require fundamental changes in the institutional relationship between the public and private sectors and in their respective modes of operation. Future concentration by the industry on innovation and quality in the production process for its main source of profitability would contrast with excessive past attention given to greenfield land dealing, and would probably be greatly welcomed by consumers, even if it is at the expense of some of the long-established names in housebuilding.

In this context, a much broader approach to urban land policy by the state may well facilitate the necessary restructuring within the private housebuilding industry, enabling it to deliver sustainable design and quality within the context of a guaranteed urban land supply and a resource commitment by the public sector to reversing years of urban decline and decentralisation. As this suggests, real commitment to brownfield development by both the state and the industry is thus likely to have far-reaching institutional implications, the significance of which has yet to be fully recognised by both parties.

In summary, mere reliance on a brownfield housing target coupled with increasing restrictions on greenfield development is likely to prove counter-productive in the long term, unless the state is prepared to articulate and implement a broader set of policies within which those concerned with land are well connected. For if the traditional preference of the market for green-field development is to be effectively reversed, market conditions must be created within which consumers and housebuilders will regard brownfield sites as their destination of first choice. In this context, planning policies are likely to prove ineffective unless well connected to developmental and other land policy measures that are themselves embedded within urban policy as a whole. It will be apparent that this requires a much broader agenda than has previously been recognised and, despite all the good intentions in the Urban White Paper, it remains to be seen whether the sheer scale of the task ahead has been fully appreciated by policy-makers.

References

Abbott, L. F. (1999) *Political Barriers to Housebuilding in Britain*, Industry Systems Research, Manchester.

Adair, A. S. and Hutchison, N. E. (2000) *The Valuation of Urban Regeneration Land*, Department of Land Economy, University of Aberdeen.

Adair, A., Berry, J. N. and McGreal, W. S. (1994) Investment and private residential development in inner city Dublin, *Journal of Property Valuation and Investment*, **12**, 47–56.

Adair, A., Berry, J., Deddis, W., McGreal, S. and Hirst, S. (1998) *Assessing Private Finance: The Availability and Effectiveness of Private Finance in Urban Regeneration*, RICS, London.

Adair, A., Berry, J., Gibb, K., *et al.* (2001) *Defining and classifying urban regeneration property*, report to ESRC, DTLR and RICS Foundation Steering Group, Universities of Aberdeen, Glasgow and Ulster.

Adams, D. (1994) *Urban Planning and the Development Process*, UCL Press, London.

Adams, D. (1996) The use of compulsory purchase under planning legislation, *Journal of Planning and Environmental Law*, 275–85.

Adams, D., May, H. and Pope, T. (1992) Changing strategies for the acquisition of residential development land, *Journal of Property Research*, **9**, 209–26.

Adams, D., Disberry, A., Hutchison, N. and Munjoma, T. (2001a) Ownership constraints to brownfield redevelopment, *Environment and Planning A*, **33**, 453–77.

Adams, D., Disberry, A., Hutchison, N. and Munjoma, T. (2001b) Managing urban land: the case for urban partnership zones, *Regional Studies*, **35**, 153–62.

Aldous, T. (1992) *Urban Villages: A Concept for Creating Mixed-use Urban Developments on a Sustainable Scale*, Urban Villages Group, London.

Alexander, E. (2001) Governance and transactions costs in planning systems: a conceptual framework for institutional analysis of land-use planning and development control – the case of Israel, *Environment and Planning B*, **28**, 755–76.

Alker, S., Joy, V., Roberts, P. and Smith, N. (2000) The definition of brownfield, *Journal of Environmental Planning and Management*, **43**, 49–69.

Allinson, J. (1999) The 4.4 million households: do we really need them anyway?, *Planning Practice and Research*, **14**, 107–13.

Allmendinger, P. (1999) Planning in the future: trends, problems and possibilities, in: *Planning Beyond 2000* (eds P. Allmendinger and M. Chapman), pp. 241–75, John Wiley, Chichester.

Allmendinger, P. and Thomas, H. (eds) (1998) *British Planning and the New Right*, Routledge, London.

Allmendinger, P., Barker, A. & Watkins, C. (2002) From New Right to New Left: UK Planning from 1979 to 2006. *Proceedings of the 'Southern Cross' Planning History Conference*, Auckland, New Zealand.

Alonso, W. (1964) *Location and Land Use: Towards a General Theory of Land Rent*, Harvard University Press, Cambridge, MA.

Amin, A. and Thrift, N. (1995) Globalization, 'institutional thickness' and the local economy, in: *Managing Cities* (eds P. Healey, S. Cameron, S. Davoudi, S. Graham and A. Madanipour), pp. 91–108, John Wiley and Son, London.

Anas, A., Arnott, R. and Small, K. (1998) Urban spatial structure, *Journal of Economic Literature*, **36**, 1426–64.

Andrew, M. (2001) A permanent change in the route to owner occupation?, paper presented at the *European Real Estate Society Conference*, Alicante.

Armstrong, H. (1999) A new vision for housing in England, in: *Stakeholder Housing: A Third Way* (ed. T. Brown), pp. 122–31, Pluto Press, London.

Atkinson, R. and Moon, G. (1994) *Urban Policy in Britain*, Macmillan, London.

Bailey, N. (1998) *The Deregulated Private Rented Sector in Four Scottish Cities*, Scottish Homes, Edinburgh.

Baker, L. (2000) Developer launches sustainability test, *Planning*, **1363**, 2.

Baker, M. and Wong, C. (1997) Planning for housing land in the English regions: a critique of the household projection and Regional Planning Guidance Mechanisms, *Environment and Planning C: Government and Policy*, **15**, 73–87.

Ball, M. (1981) Land use planning and suburban development – the land value question revisited, paper presented at the *Structural, Economic Analysis and Planning Conference*, Sweden.

Ball, M. (1983) *Housing Policy and Economic Power*, Methuen, London.

Ball, M. (1986) Housing analysis: time for a theoretical refocus? *Housing Studies*, **1**, 147–65.

Ball, M. (1996) *Housing and the Construction Industry: A Troubled Relationship*, Joseph Rowntree Foundation, York Publishing Services, York.

Ball, M. (1998) Institutions in British property research, *Urban Studies*, **35**, 1501–17.

Ball, M. (1999a) Chasing a snail: innovation and housebuilding firms' strategies, *Housing Studies*, **14**, 9–22.

Ball, M. (1999b) Property development: policy versus the market, paper presented at the *ESRC Cities Initiative Housing Property and Competitive Colloquium*, University of Reading.

Ball, M., Lizieri, C. and MacGregor, B. (1998) *The Economics of Commercial Property Markets*, Macmillan, Basingstoke.

Banister, D. (1997) Reducing the need to travel, *Environment and Planning B: Planning and Design*, **24**, 437–49.

Barker, P. (2000) Build houses where people want to live, and let the countryside shrink, *The Independent*, 7 March.

Barlow, J. (1995) *Public Participation in Urban Development*, Policy Studies Institute, London.

Barlow, J. (1999) From craft production to mass customisation. Innovation requirements for the UK housebuilding industry, *Housing Studies*, **14**, 23–42.

Barlow, J. and Bhatti, M. (1997) Environmental performance as a competitive strategy? British speculative housebuilders in the 1990s, *Planning Practice and Research*, **12**, 33–44.

Barlow, J., Cocks, R. and Rich, D. (1994) *Planning for Affordable Housing*, HMSO, London.

Barrett, G. (1996) The transport dimension, in: *The Compact City: A Sustainable Urban Form?* (eds M. Jenks, E. Burton and K. Williams), pp. 171–80, E & F N Spon, London.

Barrett, S. and Healey, P. (1985) *Land Policy: Problems and Alternatives*, Aldershot, Avebury.

Barrett, S., Stewart, M. and Underwood, J. (1978) The land market and the development process, *Occasional Paper 2*, School for Advanced Urban Studies, University of Bristol.

Bartlett, K. (1997) Demand, cost and quality, in: *Rethinking Housebuilding* (eds C. Bazlinton and K. Bartlett), pp. 10–14, Joseph Rowntree Foundation and York Publishing Services, York.

Bartlett, W. (1989) *The Economics of Housing Supply*, Housing Finance Discussion Paper, Joseph Rowntree Memorial Trust, York.

Batty, M. (2001) Polynucleated urban landscapes, *Urban Studies*, **38**, 635–55.

Bell, G. (1998) Expanded towns: a model for the 21st century, *Town and Country Planning*, **67**, 314–15.

Berry, J., Lloyd, M.G., McCarthy, J. and McGreal, W.S. (2002) *Fiscal Incentives for Urban Regeneration.* Report to ESRC, Universities of Dundee and Ulster.

Bevis, X. (2001) Greener vision, *Roof*, May/June, 17.

Bhatti, M. (1996) Housing and environmental policy in the UK, *Policy and Politics*, **24**, 159–70.

Bibby, P. and Shepherd, J. (1999) Refocusing national brownfield housing targets, *Town and Country Planning*, **68**, 302–305.

Bishop Associates (2001) *Delivering Affordable Housing Through the Planning System*, RICS, London.

Black, J. S. (1997) Quality in development, by design or process? *Proceedings of the Town and Country Planning Summer School*, 80–82.

Blackaby, B. (2000) *Understanding Local Housing Markets: Their Role in Local Housing Strategies*, Chartered Institute of Housing, Coventry and Council of Mortgage Lenders, London.

Blowers, A. (1980) *The Limits of Power*, Pergamon, Oxford.

Blowers, A. (1993) *Planning for a Sustainable Environment*, Earthscan, London.

Blowers, A. (1997) Society and sustainability, in: *Town Planning into the 21st Century* (eds A. Blowers and B. Evans), pp. 153–67, Routledge, London.

Boleat, M. (1997) The politics of homeownership, in: *Directions in Housing Policy: Towards Sustainable Planning Policies for the UK* (ed. P. Williams), pp. 54–67, Paul Chapman Publishing, London.

Box, J. and Shirley, P. (1999) Biodiversity, brownfield sites and housing, *Town and Country Planning*, **68**, 306–309.

Bramley, G. (1991) *Bridging the Affordability Gap in 1990: An Update of Research on Housing Access and Affordability*, BEC Publications, Birmingham.

Bramley, G. (1993a) Land use planning and the housing market in Britain, the impact on housebuilding and house prices, *Environment and Planning A*, **25**, 1021–51.

Bramley, G. (1993b) The impact of land use planning and tax subsidies on the supply and price of housing in Britain, *Urban Studies*, **30**(1), 5–30.

Bramley, G. (1994) An affordability crisis in British housing: dimensions, causes and policy impact, *Housing Studies*, **9**, 103–24.

Bramley, G. (1996) *Housing with Hindsight: Household Growth, Housing Need and Housing Development in the 1980's*, Council for the Protection of Rural England, London.

Bramley, G. (1997) Housing policy: a case of terminal decline? *Policy and Politics*, **25**, 387–407.

Bramley, G. (1998a) Signs of panic in middle England: the implications of household growth for policy and planning, *New Economy*, **5**, 168–73.

Bramley, G. (1998b) Measuring indicators of planning restraint and its impact on housing land supply, *Environment and Planning B: Planning and Design*, **25**, 31–57.

Bramley, G. (1999) Housing market adjustment and land supply constraints, *Environment and Planning A*, **37**, 1169–88.

Bramley, G. (2000) Migration and policy: where next?, in: *On the Move: The Housing Consequences of Migration* (eds R. Bate, R. Best and A. Holmans), pp. 49–53, Joseph Rowntree Foundation, York Publishing Services, York.

Bramley, G. and Dunmore, K. (1996) Shared ownership: short term expedient or long term major tenure, *Housing Studies*, **11**, 105–32.

Bramley, G. and Lambert, C. (1998) Planning for housing: regulation entrenched?, in: *British Planning and the New Right* (eds P. Allmendinger and H. Thomas), pp. 87–113, Routledge, London.

Bramley, G. and Morgan, J. (1998) Low cost homeownership initiatives in the UK, *Housing Studies*, **13**, 567–86.

Bramley, G. and Smart, G. (1995) *Rural Incomes and Housing Affordability*, School of Planning and Housing, Heriot Watt University and the School for Advanced Urban Studies, University of Bristol.

Bramley, G. and Watkins, C. (1995) *Circular Projections*, Council for the Protection of Rural England, London.

Bramley, G. and Watkins, C. (1996a) *Steering the Housing Market: New Housing Supply and the Changing Planning System*, Policy Press, Bristol.

Bramley, G. and Watkins, C. (1996b) New housing supply and the land-use planning system in Britain, paper presented at *ENHR Housing Economics Conference*, South Bank University.

Bramley, G., Bartlett, W. and Lambert, C. (1995) *Planning, the Market and Private Housebuilding*, UCL Press, London.

Bramley, G., Munro, M. and Lancaster, S. (1998) *The Economic Determinants of Household Formation*, Department of the Environment, Transport and the Regions, London.

Breheny, M. (1992) *Sustainable Development and Urban Form*, Pion, London.

Breheny, M. (1996) Centrists, decentrists and compromisers: views on the future of the urban form, in: *The Compact City: A Sustainable Urban Form?* (eds M. Jenks, E. Burton and K. Williams), pp. 13–35, E & F N Spon, London.

Breheny, M. (1999) People, households and houses: the basis to the 'great housing debate' in England, *Town Planning Review*, **70**, 275–93.

Breheny, M. and Rockwood, R. (1993) Planning the sustainable city region, in: *Planning for a Sustainable Environment* (ed. A. Blowers), pp. 150–89, a report by the Town and Country Planning Association, Earthscan, London.

Breheny, M. and Ross, A. (1998) *Urban Housing Capacity: What Can be Done?* Town and Country Planning Association and Joseph Rowntree Foundation, London.

Breheny, M., Gent, T. and Lock, D. (1993) *Alternative Development Patterns: New Settlements*, HMSO, London.

Brindley, T., Rydin, Y. and Stoker, G. (1996) *Remaking Planning*, Routledge, London.

Brown, T. (1999) *Stakeholder Housing: A Third Way*, Pluto Press, London.

Bruntland Commission (The World Commission on Environment and Development) (1987) *Our Common Future*, Oxford University Press, Oxford.

Bruton, M. J. (1980) Public participation, local planning and conflicts of interest, *Policy and Politics* **8,** 423–41.

Burall, P. (2001) Time for action, *Town and Country Planning*, **70**, 82–4.

Burton, T. (2001) Vision for the future, *Roof*, Jan/Feb, 14–15.

Calthorpe, P. (1994) The region, in: *The New Urbanism: Toward an Architecture of Community* (ed. P. Katz), pp. xi–xvi, McGraw-Hill, New York.

Cambridge Econometrics (2001) *UK Energy and the Environment*, Cambridge Econometrics, Cambridge.

Cameron, S. (1992) Housing, gentrification and urban regeneration policies, *Urban Studies*, **29**, 3–14.

Campbell, H., Ellis, H., Henneberry, J. and Gladwell, C. (2000) Planning obligations, planning practice and land-use outcomes, *Environment and Planning B: Planning and Design*, **27**, 759–75, Pion Limited, London.

Carmona, M. (1999a) Innovation in the control of residential design: what lessons for wider practice? *Town Planning Review*, **70**, 501–28.

Carmona, M. (1999b) Controlling the design of private sector residential development: an agenda for improving practice, *Environment and Planning B: Planning and Design*, **26**, 807–33.

Carmona, M., Heath, T., Oc, T. and Tiesdell, S. (2002) *Public Places, Urban Spaces: The Dimensions of Urban Design*, Butterworth Architectural Press, Oxford.

Castells, M. (1977) *The Urban Question*, Edward Arnold, London.

Champion, A. G. (1993) *Population Matters: The Local Dimension*, Paul Chapman Publishing, London.

Champion, A. G. (2000) Flight from the cities?, in: *On the Move: The Housing Consequences of Migration* (eds R. Bate, R. Best and A. Holmans), pp. 10–19, Joseph Rowntree Foundation and York Publishing Services, York.

Champion, A. G. (2001) A changing demographic regime and evolving polycentric urban regions: consequences for size, composition and distribution of city populations, *Urban Studies*, **38**, 657–77.

Champion, A. G., Green, A., Owen, D., Ellen, D. and Coombes, M. (1987) *Changing Places: Britain's Demographic, Economic and Social Complexion*, Edward Arnold, London.

Champion, T., Atkins, D., Coombes, M. and Fotheringham, S. (1998) *Urban Exodus*, Council for the Protection of Rural England, London.

Chaplin, R. and Freeman, A. (1999) Towards an accurate description of affordability, *Urban Studies*, **36**, 1949–57.

Cheshire, P. and Sheppard, S. (1989) British planning policy and access to housing: some empirical estimates, *Urban Studies*, **26**, 469–85.

Cheshire, P. and Sheppard, S. (1996) On the price of land and the value of amenities, *Economica*, **62**, 247–67.

Chung, L. (1994) The economics of land-use zoning: a literature review and analysis of the work of Coase, *Town Planning Review*, **65**, 77–98.

Civic Trust (1998) *Housing and Regeneration: How a Greenfield Levy Can Help*, Civic Trust, London.

Civic Trust (1999) *Brownfield Housing: 12 Years On*, Civic Trust, London.

Clapp, J. and Myers, D. (2000) Graaskamp and the definition of rigorous research, in: *Essays in Honor of James A Graaskamp: Ten Years After* (eds J. DeLisle and E. Worzala), pp. 341–64, Kluwer Academic Press, Boston.

Coase, R. (1960) The problem of social cost, *Journal of Law and Economics*, **3**, 1–44.

Coles, A. and Taylor, B. (1993) Trends in tenure preference, *Housing Finance*, 19 August.

Commission of the European Communities (1990) *Green Paper on the Urban Environment*, EUR12902 EN, CEC, Brussels.

Construction Task Force (1998) *Rethinking Construction*, Department of the Environment, Transport and the Regions, London.

Coombes, M. (1995) Local labour market areas in Britain: new evidence from the 1991 census, paper presented at the *ESRC Urban and Regional Economics Seminar Group Meeting*, University of Reading.

Coopers and Lybrand (1985) *Land-use Planning and Indicators of Housing Demand*, Coopers and Lybrand, London.

Corkindale, J. (1998) *Reforming Land-use Planning: Property Rights Approaches*, Institute of Economic Affairs, London.

Corner, I. E. (1991) Household demography and the effective demand for new housing, paper presented at the *European Symposium on Management, Quality and Economics in Housing and Other Building Sectors*, Lisbon.

Costello, G. and Watkins, C. (2002) Towards a system of local house price indices, *Housing Studies*, **17**, (in press).

Couch, C. (1999) Housing development in the city centre, *Planning Practice and Research*, **14**, 69–86.

Cox, P. (2000) Trends in houshold formation and migration: the policy dimension, in: *On the Move: The Housing Consequences of Migration* (eds R. Bate, R. Best and A. Holmans), Joseph Rowntree Foundation, York Publishing Services, York.

CPRE (1997a) *More Welcome Homes*, Council for the Protection of Rural England, London.

CPRE (1997b) *Official Report Points the Way Towards More and Better Housing in Towns and Cities*, Press Release 20 February, Council for the Protection of Rural England, London.

CPRE (1997c) *Urban Renewal – the Key to Green Policy*, Press Release 14 October, Council for the Protection of Rural England, London.

CPRE (1998) *Hungry Housing*, Council for the Protection of Rural England, London.

CPRE (1999) *Fair Examination? Testing the Legitimacy of Strategic Planning for Housing*, Council for the Protection of Rural England, London.

CPRE (2001) *Gaping Hole in the Government's Proposals for Planning Reform*, Press Release 12 December, Council for the Protection of Rural England, London.

CPRE/Friends of the Earth (2000) *Transport Corridors: Blessing or Blind Alley*, Council for the Protection of Rural England, London.

Council of Mortgage Lenders (various) *Housing Finance*, Council of Mortgage Lenders, London.

Counsell, D. (1999) Attitudes to sustainable development in the housing capacity debate: a case study of the West Sussex Structure Plan, *Town Planning Review*, **69**, 213–29.

Counsell, D. (2001) A regional approach to sustainable urban form, *Town and Country Planning*, **70**, 332–5.

Counsell, D. and Bruff, G. (2001) Regional planning guidance – towards a stronger approach to the environment, *Town and Country Planning*, **70**, 88–91.

Cowan, D. and Marsh, A. (2001) *Two Steps Forward: Housing Policy into the New Millennium*, Policy Press, Bristol.

Crook, A. D. H. (1996) Affordable housing and planning gain, linkage fees and the rational nexus: using the land use planning system in England and the USA to deliver housing subsidies, *Journal of International Planning Studies*, **1**, 49–71.

Crook, A. D. H. (1998) Fiscal austerity, affordable housing and the planning system: betterment tax and hypothecation. *Town Planning Review*, **69**, iii–vii.

Crook, A. D. H. and Jackson, A. M. (2001) Ambiguous hypothecation: the planning system and subsidies for affordable housing, paper presented to the *Planning Research Conference*, University of Liverpool.

Crook, A. D. H. and Kemp, P. (1996) The revival of private rented housing in Britain, *Housing Studies*, **11**, 51–69.

Crook, A. D. H. and Whitehead, C. (2002) Fiscal austerity, affordable housing, planning gain and the use of land-use planning to deliver housing subsidies, *Environment and Planning A*, (in press).

Crook, A. D. H., Hughes, J. and Kemp, P. (1995) *The Supply of Private Rented Homes*, Joseph Rowntree Foundation, York.

Crook, A. D. H., Darke, R. A. and Disson, J. D. (1996) *A New Lease of Life? Housing Association Investment on Local Authority Estates*, Policy Press, Bristol.

Crookston, M. (1998) *Design Solutions for Increasing Housing Capacity*, Town and Country Planning Association: London and Joseph Rowntree Foundation, York Publishing, York.

Cullingworth, B. (1999) Postscript: British planning: positive or reluctant?, in: *British Planning: Fifty Years of Urban and Regional Policy* (ed. B. Cullingworth), pp. 276–82, Athlone, London.

Cullingworth, J. B. (1997) British land-use planning: a failure to cope with change? *Urban Studies*, **34**, 945–60.

Cullingworth, J. B. and Nadin, V. (2001) *Town and Country Planning in the UK*, 13th edn, Routledge, London.

D'Arcy, E. and Keogh, G. (1998) Territorial competition and property market process: an exploratory analysis, *Urban Studies*, **35**, 1215–30.

Dawkins, C. and Nelson, A. (2002) Urban containment policies and housing prices: an international comparison with implications for future research, *Land Use Policy*, **19**, 1–12.

Denham, A. and Garnett, M. (1998) *British Think-Tanks and the Climate of Opinion*, UCL Press, London.

Denman, D. R. (1964) Land in the market, *Hobart Paper No. 30*, Institute of Economic Affairs, London.

DETR (1998a) *Planning for the Communities of the Future*, Cm 3885, The Stationery Office, London.

DETR (1998b) *The Government's Response to the Environment, Transport and Regional Affairs Committee on Housing*, Cm 4080, The Stationery Office, London.

DETR (1998c) *Planning and Affordable Housing: Circular 6/98*, The Stationery Office, London.

DETR (1998d) *Land Use Change in England No. 13*, Department of the Environment, Transport and the Regions, London.

DETR (1999a) *Development Plans: Planning Policy Guidance 12*, The Stationery Office, London.

DETR (1999b) *A Better Quality of Life: A Strategy for Sustainable Development for the UK*, Cm 4345, The Stationery Office, London.

DETR (1999c) *Housing and Construction Statistics 1988–1998*, Department of the Environment, Transport and the Regions, London.

DETR (1999d) *Fundamental Review of the Laws and Procedures Relating to Compulsory Purchase and Compensation*, Department of the Environment, Transport and the Regions, London.

DETR (2000a) *Planning Policy Guidance 3 (revised): Housing*, The Stationery Office, London.

DETR (2000b) *Our Towns and Cities: The Future – Delivering an Urban Renaissance*, Cm 4911, The Stationery Office, London.

DETR (2000c) *Modernising Local Government*, The Stationery Office, London.

DETR (2000d) *Government Targets Better Quality Housing Design*, Press Release 27 January, Department of the Environment, Transport and the Regions, London.

DETR (2000e) *Housing Statistics 2000*, Department of the Environment, Transport and the Regions, London.

DETR (2000f) *Tapping the Potential – Assessing Urban Housing Capacity: Towards Better Practice*, Department of the Environment, Transport and the Regions, London.

DETR (2001) *Planning Policy Guidance 13 (revised): Transport*, The Stationery Office, London.

DETR/CABE (2000) *The Value of Urban Design*, Thomas Telford Publishing, Tonbridge.

DETR/CABE (2001) *By Design, Better Places to Live: A Companion Guide to PPG 3*, Thomas Telford Publishing, Tonbridge.

DETR/MAFF (2000) *The Countryside: The Future – A Fair Deal for Rural England*, Cm 4909, The Stationery Office, London.

Dewar, D. (1998) A builder in waiting, *Planning*, **1298**, 16.

Dewar, D. (2000) Building the balance, *Planning*, **1399**, 13.

DOE (1977) *Policy for Inner Cities*, HMSO, London.

DOE (1980a) *Development Control: Policy and Practice*, Circular 22/80, HMSO, London.

DOE (1980b) *Land for Private Housebuilding*, Circular 9/80, HMSO, London.

DOE (1990) *Rates of Urbanization in England, 1981–2001*, Department of the Environment, London.

DOE (1995a) *Projections of Households in England to 2016*, HMSO, London.

DOE (1995b) *Planning Policy Guidance 2 (revised): Green Belts*, HMSO, London.

DOE (1995c) *Our Future Homes: Opportunities, Choice, Responsibility*, Cm 2901, HMSO, London.

DOE (1996a) *Household Growth: Where Shall We Live?*, Cm 3471, The Stationery Office, London.

DOE (1996b) *Housing Need: The Government's Response to the Second Report from the House of Commons Select Committee on the Environment*, HMSO, London.

DOE (1996c) *House of Commons Environment Committee (1996) Housing Need, Second Report*, HoC, London.

DOE/DOT (1994a) *Planning Policy Guidance 13: Transport*, HMSO, London.

DOE/DOT (1994b) *PPG 13: A Guide to Better Practice: Reducing the Need to Travel through Land Use and Transport Planning: Planning Policy Guidance 13*, HMSO, London.

Douglas, M. (1987) *How Institutions Think*, Routledge, London.

Drewett, R. (1973) The developers' decisions processes, in: *The Containment of Urban England*, Vol. 2 (eds P. Hall, H. Gracey, R. Drewitt and R. Thomas), pp. 163–94, Allen and Unwin, London.

DTLR (2001a) *Land Use Change in England No 16*, Department of Transport, Local Government and the Regions, London.

DTLR (2001b) *Planning: Delivering a Fundamental Change*, Department of Transport, Local Government and the Regions, London.

DTLR (2001c) *Faster Fairer Planning for All*, Press Release 12 December, Department of Transport, Local Government and the Regions, London.

DTLR (2001d) *Reforming Planning Obligations: A Consultation Paper*, Department of Transport, Local Government and the Regions, London.

DTLR (2001e) *Compulsory Purchase and Compensation: Delivering a Fundamental Change*, Department of Transport, Local Government and the Regions, London.

DTZ Pieda (2000) *Spatial Patterns of Housing Development*, Scottish Homes, Edinburgh.

Duany, A., Plater-Zyberk, E. and Speek, J. (2000) *Suburban Nature: The Rise of Sprawl and the Decline of the American Dream*, North Point Press, New York.

Dyrberg, T (1997) *The Circular Structure of Power*, Verso, London.

ECOTEC (1993) *Reducing Transport Emissions through Planning*, HMSO, London.

EDAW (1997) *Living Places: Sustainable Homes and Sustainable Communities*, National Housing Forum, London.

Edwards, J. (1997) Urban policy: the victory of form over substance, *Urban Studies*, **34**, 825–43.

Eggertson, T. (1990) *Economic Behaviour and Institutions*, Cambridge University Press, Cambridge.

Ellin, N. (1996) *Postmodern Urbanism*, Princeton Architectural Press, New York.

Ellison, N. and Pierson, C. (1998) *Developments in British Social Policy*, Macmillan, Basingstoke.

Elson, M. (1999) Green belts: the need for re-appraisal, *Town and Country Planning*, **68**, 156–8.

Elson, M. and Nichol, L (2001) Gaps and wedges versus belts, *Planning*, **1405**, 10.

Elson, M., Walker, S. and MacDonald, R. (1993) *The Effectiveness of Green Belts*, HMSO, London.

English, J. (1998) Building for the masses, in: *Built to Last?* (eds J. Goodwin and C. Grant), pp. 91–100, Shelter, London.

Ennis, F (1996) Planning obligations and developers: costs and benefits, *Town Planning Review*, **67**, 145–60.

Environ (1996) *Local Sustainability*, Environ, Leicester.

Eppli, M. J. and Tu, C. C. (2000) *Valuing the New Urbanism*, Urban Land Institute, Washington.

Essex, S., Brown, A. and Bishop, K. (1999) Urban growth versus sustainability? The planners' conundrum, *Town and Country Planning*, **68**, 61–3.

Evans, A. (1982) Externalities, rent seeking and town planning, *Discussion Papers in Urban and Regional Economics, Series C, No. 10*, Department of Economics, University of Reading.

Evans, A. (1983) The determinants of the price of land, *Urban Studies*, **20**, 119–29.

Evans, A. (1988) No Room! No Room! The Costs of the British Town and Country Planning System, *Occasional Paper No. 79*, Institute of Economic Affairs, London.

Evans, A. (1991) 'Rabbit hutches on postage stamps': Planning, development and political economy, *Urban Studies*, **28**, 853–70.

Evans, A. (1996) The impact of land use planning and tax subsidies on the supply and price of housing in Britain: a comment, *Urban Studies*, **33**, 581–5.

Evans, A. (1999) The land market and government intervention, in: *Handbook of Regional and Urban Economics* (eds E. S. Mills and P. Cheshire), pp. 1638–67, Elsevier, North-Holland.

Evans, B. and Bate, R. (2000) *A Taxing Question: The Contribution of Economic Instruments to Planning Objectives*, Town and Country Planning Association, London.

Fabian Society (2000) *Paying for Progress: A New Politics of Tax for Public Spending*, Fabian Society, London.

Farthing, S. (1995) Landowner involvement in local plans: how patterns of involvement both reflect and conceal influence, *Journal of Property Research*, **12**, 41–61.

Field, B. and MacGregor, B. (1987) *Forecasting Techniques for Urban and Regional Planning*, Hutchinson, London.

Fischel, W. A. (1990) Four maxims for research on land use control, *Land Economics*, **66**, 229–36.

Ford, J. (1994) *Problematic Home Ownership: The Management, Experience and Consequences of Arrears and Possession in a Depressed Housing Market*, Joseph Rowntree Foundation, York Publishing Services, York and Loughborough University.

Ford, J., Burrows, R. and Nettleton, S. (2001) *Homeownership in a Risk Society: A Social Analysis of Mortgage Arrears and Possessions*, Policy Press, Bristol.

Forrest, R. and Murie, A. (1994) Homeownership in recession, *Housing Studies*, **9**, 55–74.

Forrest, R. and Murie, A. (1995) From privatisation to commodification: tenure conversion and new zones of transition in the city, *International Journal of Urban and Regional Research*, **19**, 407–22.

Forrest, R., Kennett, T. and Leather, P. (1997) *Homeowners on New Estates in the 1990s: New Problems on the Periphery?*, The Policy Press, Bristol.

Forrester, K. (1999) The bridge builder, *Planning*, **1320**, 17.

Freeman, J. (2000) *Freeman's Guide to the Property Industry*, Freeman Publishing, London.

Friends of the Earth (1998) *Tomorrow: A Peaceful Path to Urban Reform*, Friends of the Earth, London.

Fulford, C. (1996) The compact city and the market: the case of residential development, in: *The Compact City: A Sustainable Urban Form?* (eds M. Jenks, E. Burton and K. Williams), pp. 122–33, E & F N Spon, London.

Fulford, C. (1998) *The Costs of Reclaiming Derelict Sites*, Town and Country Planning Association, London.

Fyson, T. (1999) A new town for Cambridgeshire – a sustainable option, *Town and Country Planning*, **68**, 290–92.

Gentle, C., Dorling, D. and Cornfeld, J. (1994) Negative equity and British housing in the 1990s: cause and effect, *Urban Studies*, **31**, 181–200.

George Wimpey PLC (2001) *Proposed Acquisition of Alfred McAlpine Homes Holdings Limited*, George Wimpey PLC, London.

Gerald Eve (1992) *The Relationship between House Prices and Land Supply*, HMSO, London.

Gibb, K. (1999) Regional differentiation and the Scottish private housebuilding sector, *Housing Studies*, **14**, 43–56.

Gibb, K., Munro, M. and McGregor, A. (1995) *The Scottish Housebuilding Industry: Opportunity or Constraint*, Scottish Homes, Edinburgh.

Gibb, K., McGregor, A. and Munro, M. (1997) Housebuilding in recession: a regional case study, *Environment and Planning A*, **29**, 1739–58.

Gibb, K., Lever, W. and Kasparova, D. (2001) *The Future of UK Cities*, RICS, London.

Gibbs, D. C., Longhurst, J. and Braithwaite, C. (1998) 'Struggling with sustainability': weak and strong interpretations of sustainable development within local authority policy, *Environment and Planning A*, **30**, 1351–65, Pion Limited, London.

Gill, D. (1991) Planning gain: consequences for the developer and the land development process, *Scottish Planning Law and Practice*, **33**, 36–8.

Glancey, J. (1997) Home sweet home for the golden family: rising demand for housing is creating a building boom in the countryside, *The Independent*, 27 May.

Goodchild, B. (1992) Land allocation for housing: a review of practice and possibilities in England, *Housing Studies*, **7**, 45–55.

Goodchild, B. (1994) Housing design, urban form and sustainable development, *Town Planning Review*, **65**, 143–57.

Goodchild, B. (1997) *Housing and the Urban Environment*, Blackwell Science, Oxford.

Goodchild, B. and Karn, V. (1997) Standards, quality control and housebuilding in the UK, in: *Directions in Housing Policy: Towards Sustainable Housing Policies for the UK* (ed. P. Williams), pp. 156–74, Paul Chapman Publishing, London.

Goodchild, R. N. and Munton, R. (1985) *Development and the Landowner*, George Allen and Unwin, London.

Gordon, P. and Richardson, H. (1989) Gasoline consumption and cities – a reply, *Journal of the American Planning Association*, **55.3**, 376–9.

Government Office for the South East (1999) *Regional Planning Guidance for the South East of England: Report of the Panel into the Public Examination*, Government Office for the South East, Surrey.

Grant, M. (1998a) Commentary, in: *Reforming Land-use Planning: Property Rights Approaches* (ed. J. Corkindale), pp. 69–83, Institute of Economic Affairs, London.

Grant, M. (1998b) Removing the pain from planning gain, *Planning*, **1268**, 9.

Grayson, L. (2000) *The Housing Challenge: A Review of the Issues*, Planning Exchange, Glasgow.

Green, A., Owen, D., Champion, A., Goddard, A. and Coombes, M. (1986) What contribution can labour migration make to reducing unemployment? in: *Unemployment and Labour Market Policies* (ed. P. Hart), pp. 51–74, Aldershot, Gower.

Green Balance (1994) *The Housing Numbers Game*, Council for the Protection of Rural England, London.

Guy, S. and Henneberry, J. (2000) Understanding urban development processes: integrating the economic and the social in property research, *Urban Studies*, **37**, 2399–416.

Hadjimatheou, G. and Sarantis, N. (1998) Is UK deindustrialisation inevitable?, in: *Britain's Economic Performance* (eds T. Buxton, P. Chapman and P. Temple), pp. 527–46, Routledge, London.

Hall, D. (1999) Town expansion – constructive participation, *Town and Country Planning*, **68**, 170–72.

Hall, P. (1988) *Cities of Tomorrow*, Blackwell, Oxford.

Hall, P. (1993) *Urban and Regional Planning*, Routledge, London.

Hall, P. (1998) Planning in limbo, *Town and Country Planning*, **67**, 42–3.

Hall, P. (1999) *Sustainable Cities or Town Cramming?* Town and Country Planning Association, London.

Hall, P. (2001) How smart is smart growth? *Town and Country Planning*, **70**, 8–9.

Hall, P. and Pfeiffer, U. (2000) *Urban Future 21*, E & F N Spon, London.

Hall, P. and Taylor, R. (1996) Political science and the three new institutionalisms, *Political Studies*, **14**, 937–57.

Hall, P., Gracey, H., Drewitt, R. and Thomas, R. (1973) *The Containment of Urban England*, Allen and Unwin, London.

Hamilton, W. H. (1932) Institutions, in: *Encyclopaedia of the Social Sciences*, Vol. 8 (eds E. R. A. Seligman and A. Johnson), 84–9.

Hamnett, C. (1999) *Winners and Losers: Homeownership in Modern Britain*, UCL Press, London.

Hancock, K. (1993) Can pay? Won't pay? On economic principles of affordability, *Urban Studies*, **30**, 127–45.

Hancock, K. and Maclennan, D. (1989) *House Price Monitoring Systems and Housing Planning in Scotland: A Feasibility Study*, report to the Scottish Office, Centre for Housing Research, University of Glasgow.

Hancock, K., Jones, C., Munro, M. and Satsangi, M. with McGuckin, A. and Parkey, H. (1991) *Housing Costs and Subsidies in Glasgow: The Impact of Housing Subsidies in the Glasgow Travel-to-work-area*, Joseph Rowntree Foundation, York Publishing Services, York.

Harloe, M. (1975) *Swindon: A Town in Transition*, Heinemann, London.

Harloe, M. and Boddy, M. (1987) Swindon: a suitable place for expansion, *Planning Practice and Research*, **3**, 17–20.

Harrison, D. and Wintour, P. (1998) This tree is safe – as houses, *The Observer*, 25 January, 21–2.

Haskey, J. (1999) Divorce and remarriage in England and Wales, *Population Trends*, **95**, 34–40.

Hazell, T. (1996) Barratt on spree in southern area, *Estates Gazette*, **9602**, 73.

Healey, P. (1991) Models of the development process: a review, *Journal of Property Research*, **8**, 219–38.

Healey, P. (1992) An institutional model of the development process, *Journal of Property Research*, **9**, 33–44.

Healey, P. (1997) *Collaborative Planning: Shaping Places in Fragmented Societies*, Macmillan, Basingstoke.

Healey, P. (2001) Towards a more place-focused planning system in Britain, in: *The Governance of Place: Space and Planning Processes* (eds A. Madanipour, A. Hull and P. Healey), pp. 265–86, Ashgate, Aldershot.

Healey, P., McNamara, P., Elson, M. and Doak, J. (1988) *Land Use Planning and the Mediation of Urban Change*, Cambridge University Press, Cambridge.

Healey, P., Davoudi, S., O'Toole, M., Tavsanoglu, S. and Usher, D. (eds) (1992) *Rebuilding the City*, E & F N Spon, London.

Healey, P., Purdue, M. and Ennis, F. (1993) *Gains from Planning? Dealing with the Impacts of Development*, Joseph Rowntree Foundation and York Publishing Services, York.

Heap, D. and Ward, J. (1980) Planning bargaining – The pros and cons: or, how much can the system stand? *Journal of Planning and Environment Law*, 631–7.

Heferman, R. (2001) *Planning and New Labour: Political Change in Britain*, Palgrave, London.

Hellman, L. (1995) A century of development, *Building Design*, **1236**, 5.

Hetherington, P. (2000) Prescott green light for building boom, *The Guardian*, 8 March.

Hetherington, P. and May, T. (1998) Middle England's mad, bad dream in bricks and mortar, *The Guardian*, 27 January, 15.

Higgins, M. and Karski, A. (2000) The built environment and design, in: *An Introduction to Planning Practice* (eds P. Allmendinger, A. Prior and J. Raemaekers), pp. 247–84, John Wiley, London.

Hill, D. (2000) *Urban Policy and Politics in Britain*, Macmillan, Basingstoke.

Hodgson, G. (1988) *Economics and Institutions*, Polity Press, Cambridge.

Hodgson, G. (1989) Institutional economic theory: the old versus the new, *Review of Political Economy*, **1**, 249–69.

Hodgson, G. (1993) *The Economics of Institutions*, Edward Elgar, Aldershot.

Hodgson, G. (1997) The ubiquity of habits and rules, *Cambridge Journal of Economics*, **21**, 663–84.

Hodgson, G. (1998) *Evolution and Economics*, Edward Elgar, Cheltenham.

Hodgson, G. (1999) *Economics and Utopia*, Routledge, London.

Hodgson, G., Samuels, W. J. and Tool, M. E. (1994) *The Elgar Companion to Institutional and Evolutionary Economics*, Edward Elgar, Aldershot.

Holmans, A. (1995) *Housing Demand and Need in England 1991–2011*, Joseph Rowntree Foundation and York Publishing Services, York.

Holmans, A. (1996) Housing demand and need in England to 2011: the national picture, in: *The People – Where Will They Go?* (eds M. Breheny and P. Hall), pp. 7–15, Town and Country Planning Association, London.

Holmans, A. (1997) UK housing finance: past changes, the present predicament, and future sustainability, in: *Directions in Housing Policy: Towards Sustainable Planning Policies for the UK* (ed. P. Williams), pp. 175–98, Paul Chapman Publishing, London.

Holmans, A. (2001a) First-time buyers in the UK, *Housing Finance*, **49**, 27–35.

Holmans, A. (2001b) *Housing Demand and Need in England 1996–2016*, Town and Country Planning Association, London.

Holmans, A., Morrison, N. and Whitehead, C. (1998) *How Many Homes Will We Need? The Need for Affordable Homes in England*, Shelter, London.

Home, R. K. (1985) Forecasting housing land requirements, *Land Development Studies*, **2**, 19–34.

Hood, D. (1995) Scots rediscover new settlement tradition, *Planning*, **1144**, 20–21.

Hooper, A. (1980) Land for private housebuilding, *Journal of Planning Law*, 555–60.

Hooper, A. (1992) The construction of theory: a comment, *Journal of Property Research*, **9**, 45–8.

Hooper, A. and Nicol, C. (1999) The design and planning of residential development: standard house types in the speculative housebuilding industry, *Environment and Planning B: Planning and Design*, **26**, 793–805.

Hooper, A., Pinch, P. and Rogers, S. (1989) Housing land availability in the south east, in: *Growth and Change in a Core Region: The Case of South East England* (eds M. Breheny and P. Congdon), London Papers in Regional Science No. 20, Pion, London.

House Builders' Federation (1997) *New Homes: Because Britain Deserves Better*, House Builders' Federation, London.

House Builders' Federation (1999) *Urban Life: Breaking Down the Barriers to Brownfield Development*, House Builders' Federation, London.

House Builders' Federation (2001) *Planning for a Homeless Future*, Press Release 3 January, House Builders' Federation, London.

House of Commons Environment, Transport and Regional Affairs Committee (1998) *Housing: Tenth Report*, The Stationery Office, London.

House of Commons Environment, Transport and Regional Affairs Committee (1999) *Proposed Urban White Paper: Eleventh Report*, The Stationery Office, London.

Hugill, B. (1999) Why a rural fantasy will damage the city poor, *The Guardian*, 23 October.

Hulchanski, D. (1995) The concept of housing affordability, *Housing Studies*, **10**, 471–92.

Hull, A. (1997) Restructuring the debate on allocating land for housing growth, *Housing Studies*, **12**, 367–82.

Hull, A. (1998) The development plan as a vehicle to unlock development potential? *Cities* **15**, 327–35.

Imrie, R. and Thomas, H. (1993) The limits of property-led regeneration, *Environment and Planning C*, **11**, 87–102.

Imrie, R. and Thomas, H. (1997) Law, legal struggles and urban regeneration, *Urban Studies* **34**, 1401–18.

Inland Revenue Valuation Office (1999) *Property Market Report Spring 1999*, Estates Gazette, London.

Jackson, A., Morrison, N. and Royce, C. (1994) The supply of land for housing, *Discussion Paper No. 42*, Department of Land Economy, University of Cambridge.

Jacobs, M. (1999) Environmental modernisation: the New Labour agenda, *Fabian Pamphlet 591*, Fabian Society, London.

Jaffe, A. (1996) On the role of transactions costs and property rights in housing markets, *Housing Studies*, **11**, 425–35.

Jenks, M., Burton, E. and Williams, K. (1996) *The Compact City: A Sustainable Urban Form?*, E & F N Spon, London.

Johnston, B. (1999) Sites for investors, *Planning*, **1301**, 16.

Jones, C. and Armitage, B. (1990) Population change within area types: England and Wales, 1971–1988, *Population Trends*, **60**, 25–32.

Jones, C. A. (1979) Population decline in cities, in: *Urban Deprivation and the Inner City* (ed. C. Jones), pp. 23–36, Croom Helm, London.

Jones, C. A. and Leishman, C. (1998) *The Planning System, House Builders and the Supply of Land*, Proceedings of the Cutting Edge Conference, Royal Institution of Chartered Surveyors, London.

Jones, C. A. and Maclennan, D. (1987) Building societies and credit rationing: an empirical examination of redlining, *Urban Studies*, **24**, 205–16.

Jones, C. A. and Watkins, C. (1996) Urban regeneration and sustainable markets, *Urban Studies*, **33**, 1129–40.

Jones, C. A. and Watkins, C. (1999) Planning for the housing system, in: *Planning Beyond 2000* (eds P. Allmendinger and M. Chapman), pp. 89–105, John Wiley, Chichester.

Jordan, G. and Ashford, N. (1993) *Public Policy and the Impact of the New Right*, Pinter, London.

Jordan, G. and Maloney, W. (1997) *The Protest Business*, Manchester University Press, Manchester.

Joseph Rowntree Foundation (1994) *Inquiry into Planning for Housing*, Joseph Rowntree Foundation, York.

Kaiser, E. J. and Weiss, S. F. (1970) Public policy and the residential development process, *Journal of the American Institute of Planners*, **36**, 30–37.

Kasper, W. and Streit, M. (1999) *Institutional Economics*, Edward Elgar, Cheltenham.

Kavanagh, D. (1997) *The Reordering of British Politics*, Oxford University Press, Oxford.

Keating, M. (1988) *The City That Refused To Die*, Aberdeen University Press, Aberdeen.

Kemp, P. (1997a) Ideology, public policy and private rental housing since the war, in: *Directions in Housing Policy: Towards Sustainable Planning Policies for the UK* (ed. P. Williams), pp. 68–82, Paul Chapman Publishing, London.

Kemp, P. (1997b) Burying Rachman, in: *Built to Last?* (eds J. Goodwin and C. Grant), pp. 111–16, Shelter, London.

Kemp, P. (1999) Housing policy under New Labour, in: *New Labour, New Welfare State* (ed. M. Powell), pp. 123–47, Policy Press, Bristol.

Kennett, S. and Hall, P. (1981) The inner city in spatial perspective, in: *The Inner City in Context* (ed. P. Hall), pp. 71–87, Heinemann, London.

Keogh, G. (1985) The economics of planning gain, in: *Land Policy: Problems and Alternatives* (eds S. Barrett and P. Healey), pp. 203–28, Gower, Aldershot.

Keogh, G. (1994) Use and investment markets in British real estate, *Journal of Property Valuation and Investment*, **12.4**, 58–72.

Keogh, G. and D'Arcy, E. (1999) Property market efficiency: an institutional perspective, *Urban Studies*, **36**, 2401–14.

Keogh, G. and D'Arcy, E. (2000) Graaskamp, institutional economics and the real estate market, in: *Essays in Honor of James A. Graaskamp: Ten Years After* (eds J. DeLisle and E. Worzala), pp. 385–410, Kluwer Academic Press, Boston.

King, D. (1993) Demography and housebuilding needs: a critique of the 'demographic bulldozer' scenario, in: *Population Matters: The Local Dimension* (ed. T. Champion), pp. 101–18, Paul Chapman Publishing, London.

Kleinman, M. and Whitehead, C. (1996) *The Private Rented Sector*, National Federation of Housing Associations, London.

Kleinman, M., Aulakh, S., Holmans, A., Morrison, N., Whitehead, C. and Woodrow, J. (1999) *No Excuse Not To Build: Meeting Housing Need through the Existing Stock and the Planning Framework*, Shelter, London.

Kloosterman, R. C. and Musterd, S. (2001) The polycentric urban region: towards a research agenda, *Urban Studies*, **38**, 623–33.

Krabben, van der, E. and Lambooy, J. (1993) A theoretical framework for the functioning of the Dutch property market, *Urban Studies*, **30**, 1381–97.

Lambert, C. (1990) New housebuilding and the development industry in the Bristol area, *Working Paper No. 86*, School of Advanced Urban Studies, University of Bristol.

Lambert, C. and Boddy, M (1998) Planning for major urban expansion: a case study in the UK's M4 growth corridor, *Planning Practice and Research*, **13**, 371–88.

Lambooy, J. and Moulaert, F. (1996) The economic organisation of cities: an institutional perspective, *International Journal of Urban and Regional Research*, **20**, 217–37.

Law, H. and Mills, D. (2000) *The Effect of Land Value Taxation on Planning*, Land Value Taxation Campaign, Brighton.

Lawless, P. (1989) *Britain's Inner Cities*, Paul Chapman Publishing, London.

Lawson, T. (1997) *Economics and Reality*, Routledge, London.

Leedale, M. (2001) A very sticky issue of green gap constraint, *Planning*, **1413**, 8.

Le Grand, J. and Bartlett, W. (1993) *Quasi-markets and Social Policy*, Macmillan, Basingstoke.

Leishman, C. & Bramley, G. (2001) *A Local Housing Market Model with Spatial Interactions and Land-use Controls*, Discussion paper, Heriot-Watt University, Edinburgh.

Leishman, C. and Watkins, C. (2002) Estimating repeat sales house price indices for British cities, *Journal of Property Investment and Finance*, **20**, 36–58.

Leishman, C., Jones, C. and Fraser, W. (2000) The influence of uncertainty on house builder behaviour and residential land values, *Journal of Property Research*, **17**, 147–68.

Leopold, E. and Bishop, D. (1983) Design philosophy and practice in speculative housebuilding: Parts 1 and 2, *Construction Management and Economics*, **1**, 119–44 and 233–68.

Levett, R. (1998) *Monitoring, Measuring and Target Setting for Urban Housing Capacity*, Town and Country Planning Association, London.

Liberal Democrats (2000) Strategy for sustainability, *Policy Paper 41*, Liberal Democrats, London.

Lichfield, N. and Darin-Drabkin, D. (1980) *Land Policy in Planning*, George Allen and Unwin, London.

Lizieri, C. (1999) Making the investment?, *Town and Country Planning*, **68**, 265–7.

Llewelyn-Davies (1994) *Providing More Homes in Urban Areas*, SAUS Publications and Joseph Rowntree Foundation, Bristol.

Llewelyn-Davies (1996) *The Re-use of Brownfield Land for Housing: A Preliminary Study of Strathclyde*, Joseph Rowntree Foundation, London.

Llewelyn-Davies (2000) *Urban Design Compendium*, English Partnerships and the Housing Corporation, London.

Lock, D. (1991) Still nothing to gain by overcrowding, *Town and Country Planning*, **60**, 337–9.

Lowe, S. (1998) Homes and castles, in: *Built to Last* (eds J. Goodwin and C. Grant), pp. 1–8, Shelter, London.

Lowndes, V. (1996) Varieties of new institutionalism: a critical appraisal, *Public Administration*, **74**, 181–97.

Lowndes, V. (2001) Rescuing Aunt Sally: taking institutional theory seriously in urban politics, *Urban Studies*, **38**, 1953–71.

McFarquhar, A. (1999) *Planning Rape: Land Use Policy and Local Government Finance in the UK*, Adam Smith Institute, London.

Maclennan, D. (1982) *Housing Economics: An Applied Approach*, Longman, Harlow.

Maclennan, D. (1986) *The Demand for Housing: An Economic Perspective*, Scottish Office Development Department, Edinburgh.

Maclennan, D. (1992) *Housing Search and Choice in a Regional Housing System: New Housing in Strathclyde*, report to the Housing Research Federation, Centre for Housing Research, University of Glasgow, Glasgow.

Maclennan, D. (1994) *A Competitive UK Economy: The Challenges for Housing Policy*, Joseph Rowntree Foundation, York.

Maclennan, D. (1997) The UK housing market: up, down and where next?, in: *Directions in Housing Policy: Towards Sustainable Planning Policies for the UK* (ed. P. Williams), pp. 22–52, Paul Chapman Publishing, London.

Maclennan, D. and Gibb, K. (1993) Political economy, applied welfare economics and housing in the UK, in: *Current Issues in Welfare Economics* (eds N. Barr and D. Whynes), pp. 200–223, Macmillan, London.

Maclennan, D. and Pryce, G. (1998) *Missing Links: The Economy, Cities and Housing*, National Housing Federation, London.

Maclennan, D. and Tu, Y. (1996) Economic perspectives on the structure of local housing markets, *Housing Studies*, **11**, 387–406.

Maclennan, D. and Whitehead, C. (1996) Housing economics – an evolving agenda, *Housing Studies*, **11**, 341–4.

Maclennan, D., Munro, M. and Wood, G. (1987) Housing choice and the structure of urban housing markets, in: *Between State and Market Housing in the Post-industrial Era* (eds B. Turner, J. Kemeny and L. J. Lundquist), pp. 27–45, Almquist and Hicksell International, Gothenburg.

McMaster, R. and Watkins, C. (2000) The economics of urban land and housing: Richard T. Ely and the 'Land Economy' school reconsidered, *Aberdeen Papers in Land Economy, 00–10*, Department of Land Economy, University of Aberdeen.

Macnaghten, P. and Pinfield, G. (1999) Planning and sustainable development: prospects for social change, in: *Planning Beyond 2000* (eds P. Allmendinger and M. Chapman), pp. 17–32, John Wiley, Chichester.

Madanipour, A. (1996) *Design of Urban Space: An Inquiry into a Socio-Spatial Process*, John Wiley, Chichester.

Malpass, P. (1996) The unravelling of housing policy in Britain, *Housing Studies*, **11**, 459–70.

Malpass, P. (1999) Housing policy: does it have a future? *Policy and Politics*, **27**, 217–28.

Malpass, P. (2001) The uneven development of 'social rented housing': explaining the historically marginal position of housing associations in Britain, *Housing Studies*, **16**, 225–42.

Malpass, P. and Murie, A. (1999) *Housing Policy and Practice*, Macmillan, London.

Malpezzi, S (1996) Is theory outrunning measurement in real estate economics?, paper presented at the *SHAPE Conference*, London Business School.

Marsden, T., Murdoch, J., Lowe, P., Munton, R. and Flynn, A. (1993) *Constructing the Countryside*, UCL Press, London.

Meen, G. (1998) Modelling sustainable home ownership: demographics and economics, *Urban Studies*, **35**, 1919–34.

Meen, G. (2000) Housing cycles and efficiency, *Scottish Journal of Political Economy*, **47**, 114–40.

Meen, G. and Andrew, M. (1998) *Modelling Regional House Prices: A Review of the Literature*, Department of the Environment, Transport and the Regions, London.

Meen, G., Maclennan, D. and Stephens, M. (1997) Supply and sustainability: home ownership in Britain, in: *Housing Finance Review* (ed. S. Wilcox), pp. 16–22, Joseph Rowntree Foundation and York Publishing Services, York.

Meen, G., Gibb, K., Mackay, D. and White, M. (2001) *The Economic Role of New Housing*, National House Building Council, Amersham.

Meikle, J., Pattinson, M., Wheeler, D. and Zetter, J. (1991) Costs of residential development on greenfield sites, *The Planner*, **77.13**, 5–7.

Memery, C., Munro, M., Madigan, R. and Gibb, K. (1995) Reacting to the housing market slump, paper presented at the *ESRC Economic Beliefs and Behaviour Conference*, London.

Merrett, S. (1979) *State Housing in Britain*, Routledge and Kegan Paul, London.

Minton, A. (2000) Barratt cool on housing 'boom', *Financial Times*, 23 March.

Moir, J., Rice, D. and Watt, A. (1997) Visual amenity and housing in the countryside – Scottish local authority approaches, *Land Use Policy*, **14**, 325–30.

Monk, S. (1991) The speculative housebuilder: a review of empirical research, *Discussion Paper 31*, Department of Land Economy, University of Cambridge.

Monk, S. (2001) The role of the planning system in providing affordable housing: some issues and evidence, paper presented at the *Department of Land Economy Seminar*, University of Aberdeen.

Monk, S. and Whitehead, C. (1996) Land supply and housing: a case study, *Housing Studies*, **11**, 407–23.

Monk, S. and Whitehead, C. (1999) Evaluating the impact of planning controls in the UK – some implications for housing, *Land Economics*, **75**, 74–93.

Monk, S., Pearce, B. and Whitehead, C. (1996) Planning, land supply and house prices, *Environment and Planning A*, **28**, 495–511.

More, A., Goodlad, R., Maclennan, D., Munro, M. and Scott, S. (1993) *Local Market Analysis and Planning in Scottish Homes: A Best Practice Guide*, Scottish Homes, Edinburgh.

Mori, H. (1998) Land conversion at the urban fringe: a comparative study of Japan, Britain and the Netherlands, *Urban Studies*, **35**, 1541–58.

Muellbauer, J. (1990) The great British housing disaster, *Roof*, May/June, 16–20.

Munro, M. (1995) Homo-economics in the city: towards an urban socioeconomic research agenda, *Urban Studies*, **32**, 1609–21.

Murdoch, J. (2000) Space against time: competing rationalities in planning for housing, *Transactions of the Institute of British Geographers*, **25**, 503–19.

Murdoch, J., Abram, S. and Marsden, T. (2000) Technical expertise and public participation in planning for housing: 'Playing the numbers game', in: *The New Politics of Local Governance* (ed. G. Stoker), pp. 198–214, Macmillan, Basingstoke.

National Land Use Database (2000) *Final Estimates of Previously Developed Land in England: 1998*, Department of the Environment, Transport and the Regions, London.

Needham, B. (2000) Land taxation, development charges, and the effects on land-use, *Journal of Property Research*, **17**, 241–57.

Needham, B. and Verhage, R. (1998) Housing and land in Israel and the Netherlands: a comparison of their policies and their consequence for access to housing, *Town Planning Review*, **69**, 397–423.

Nelson, A. C. and Moore, T. (1993) Assessing urban growth management – the case of Portland, Oregon, the USA's largest growth boundary, *Land Use Policy*, **10**, 293–302.

Newby, H. (1985) *Green and Pleasant Land*, Hutchinson, London.

Newman, P. and Kenworthy, J. (1989) *Cities and Automobile Dependence: A Sourcebook*, Gower, Aldershot.

Newman, P. and Kenworthy, J. (1989) Gasoline consumption of US cities with a global survey, *Journal of the American Planning Association*, **55.1**, 24–37.

Newman, P. W. G. and Kenworthy, J. R. (1996) The land use–transport connection: an overview, *Land Use Policy*, **13**, 1–22.

Newman, P. and Kenworthy, J. (1999) *Sustainability and Cities: Overcoming Automobile Dependence*, Island Press, Washington, DC.

Newman, P. and Kenworthy, J. (2000) Sustainable urban form: the big picture, in: *Achieving Sustainable Urban Form* (eds K. Williams, E. Burton and M. Jenks), pp. 109–20, E & F N Spon, London.

Nicol, C. and Hooper, A. (1999) Contemporary change and the housebuilding industry: concentration and standardisation in production, *Housing Studies*, **14**, 57–76.

Niskanen, W. (1971) *Bureaucracy and Representative Government*, Aldine Atherton, Chicago.

Niven, R. (2001) Region drafts growth scenarios, *Planning*, **1423**, 10.

North, D. (1990) *Institutions, Institutional Change and Economic Performance*, Cambridge University Press, Cambridge.

Olson, M. (1965) *The Logic of Collective Action*, Harvard University Press, Cambridge.

O'Riordan, T. (1999) *Planning for Sustainable Development*, Town and Country Planning Association, London.

Owens, S. (1992) Energy, environmental sustainability and land-use planning, in: *Sustainable Development and Urban Form* (ed. M. Breheny), pp. 79–105, Pion, London.

Owens, S. (1994) Land, limits and sustainability, *Transactions from the Institute of British Geographers*, **19**, 439–56.

Oxley, M. (1998) *Increasing Urban Housing Development: Capacity and Constraints*, Proceedings of the Cutting Edge Conference, Royal Institution of Chartered Surveyors, London.

PA Cambridge Economic Consultants (1995) *Final Evaluation of the Enterprise Zones*, HMSO, London.

Parkinson, M. (1998) The United Kingdom, in: *National Urban Policies in the European Union* (eds L. van der Berg, E. Braun and J. van der Meer), pp. 402–33, Ashgate, Aldershot.

Parliamentary Office of Science and Technology (1998) *A Brown and Pleasant Land*, Parliamentary Office of Science and Technology, London.

Pawson, H. and Kearns, A. (1998) Difficult to let housing association stock in England: property management and context, *Housing Studies*, **13**, 391–414.

Peck, J. A. (1989) Reconceptualising the local labour market: space, segmentation and the state, *Progress in Human Geography*, **12**, 42–61.

Peiser, R. (2001) Decomposing urban sprawl, *Town Planning Review*, **72**, 275–98.

Pennington, M. (1998) Commentary, in: *Reforming Land-use Planning: Property Rights Approaches* (ed. J. Corkindale), pp. 84–8, Institute of Economic Affairs, London.

Pennington, M. (2000) *Planning and the Political Market: Public Choice and the Politics of Government Failure*, Athlone, London.

Peters, G. (1999) *Institutional Theory in Political Science: The New Institutionalism*, Pinter, London.

Planning (1998a) New settlement is backed by citizens, *Planning*, **1294**, 3.

Planning (1998b) Lack of land angers builder, *Planning*, **1259**, 1.

Planning (1999) Controversial plan for brownfield site, *Planning*, **1333**, 3.

Planning (2000a) Report advocates urban extensions, *Planning*, **1387**, 3.

Planning (2000b) Report urges fewer dwellings in centre, *Planning*, **1393**, 3.

Podogzinski, H. U. and Sass, T. R. (1991) Measuring the effects of municipal zoning regulations: a survey, *Urban Studies*, **28**, 597–621.

Popular Housing Forum (1998) *Kerb Appeal: The External Appearance and Site Appeal of New Houses*, Popular Housing Forum, Winchester.

Potter, S. (1987) British new town statistics 1985–87, *Town and Country Planning*, **56**, 292–7.

Power, A. and Mumford, K. (2000) *The Slow Death of Great Cities? Urban Abandonment or Urban Renaissance*, York Publishing Services for the Joseph Rowntree Foundation, York.

Poxon, J. (1994) *The enabling council: dream or reality?* Unpublished, Department of Town and Regional Planning, University of Sheffield, Sheffield.

Pratt, R. and Larkham, P. (1996) Who will care for compact cities? in: *The Compact City: A Sustainable Urban Form?* (eds M. Jenks, E. Burton and K. Williams), pp. 277–88, E & F N Spon, London.

Prescott, J. (2000) *Planning Policy Guidance Note No. 3: Housing – Statement by Deputy Prime Minister (7 March 2000)*, Department of the Environment, Transport and the Regions, London.

Prince's Foundation and English Partnerships (2000) *Sustainable Urban Extensions*, Prince's Foundation, London.

Property Advisory Group (1981) *Planning Gain*, Department of the Environment, London.

Pryce, G. (1999) Construction elasticities and land availability: a two stage least squares model of housing supply using the variable elasticity approach, *Urban Studies*, **36**, 2283–304.

Radley, S. P. (1996) The economic and social limits to increases in sustainable home ownership, *Housing Research Findings No. 189*, Joseph Rowntree Foundation, York.

Raggett, B. (1998) Paper presented to the *RTPI CPOs seminar*, C. B. Hillier Parker, London.

Raymond, K. (2000) The Kent Design Initiative: towards a sustainable future, in: *Achieving Sustainable Urban Form* (eds K. Williams, E. Burton and M. Jenks), pp. 258–65, E & F N Spon, London.

Razin, E. (1998) Policies to control urban sprawl: planning regulations or changes in the 'rules of the game', *Urban Studies*, **35**, 321–40.

Richardson, T. (1996) Foucaldian discourse: power and truth in urban and regional policy making, *European Planning Studies*, **4**, 279–92.

Roaf, R. and Rockwood, R. (2000) Building to sustainability standards, *Town and Country Planning*, **69**, 188–91.

Roakes, S. L. (1996) Reconsidering land value taxation – the golden key? *Land Use Policy*, **13**, 261–72.

Roberts, S. and Randolph, W. G (1983) Beyond decentralization: the evolution of population distribution in England and Wales, 1961–1981, *Geoforum*, **14**, 75–102.

Roger Tym and Partners (1991) *Housing Land Availability*, HMSO, London.

Rosenburg, L. and Watkins, C. (1999) Longitudinal monitoring of housing renewal in the urban core: reflections on the experience of Glasgow's Merchant City, *Urban Studies*, **36**, 1973–96.

Rowan-Robinson, J. and Durman, R. (1993) Planning policy and planning agreements, *Land Use Policy*, **10**, 197–204.

Royal Town Planning Institute (2001) *A New Vision for Planning*, Royal Town Planning Institute, London.

Rudlin, D. and Falk, N. (1999) *Building the 21st Century Home: The Sustainable Urban Neighbourhood*, Architectural Press, Oxford.

Rydin, Y. (1985) Residential development and the planning system: a study of the housing land system at local level, *Progress in Planning*, **24**, 7–69.

Rydin, Y. (1986) *Housing Land Policy*, Gower, Aldershot.

Rydin, Y. (1992) Environmental dimensions of residential development and the implications for local planning practice, *Journal of Environmental Planning and Management*, **35**, 43–61.

Rydin, Y. (2000a) Planning and a modernised environmental agenda, *Town and Country Planning*, **69**, 42–3.

Rydin, Y. (2000b) From indicators to outcomes? *Town and Country Planning*, **69**, 348–50.

Samuels, A. (1978) Planning agreements: their use and misuse, *Local Government Review*, 609–12 and 624–6.

Samuels, W. (1995) The present state of institutional economics, *Cambridge Journal of Economics*, **19**, 569–90.

Saunders, P. (1990) *A Nation of Homeowners*, Unwin Hart, London.

Scottish Office (1991) Siting and design of new housing in the countryside, *Planning Advice Note 36*, Scottish Office, Edinburgh.

Scottish Office (1996) Structure plans: housing land requirements, *Planning Advice Note 38*, Scottish Office, Edinburgh.

Scottish Office Environment Department (1994) Fitting new housing development into the landscape, *Planning Advice Note 44*, Scottish Office, Edinburgh.

Seidl, A. (1997) Colour blindness in the housing debate, *Estates Gazette*, **9711**, 58–61.

Shaw, C. and Haskey, J. (1999) New estimates and projections of the population cohabiting in England and Wales, *Population Trends*, **95**, 29–33.

Shucksmith, M. (1990) *Housebuilding in Britain's Countryside*, Routledge, London.

Shucksmith, M., Watkins, L. and Henderson, M. (1993) Attitudes towards residential development in the Scottish countryside, *Journal of Rural Studies*, **9**, 243–55.

Shucksmith, M., Phimister, E. and Vera-Toscano, E. (2001) Housing markets, regulation and social exclusion in rural Britain, paper presented at *XIX European Congress for Rural Sociology*, Dijon.

Simmie, J. (1974) *Citizens in Conflict: The Sociology of Town Planning*, Hutchinson, London.

Simpkins, E. (2001) Rise of the super builder, *Sunday Telegraph Business Section*, 5 August, 5.

Slater, A. M., Carmichael, K. and Flint, L. (1999) Affordable housing provision by legal agreement: a study of their use in Scotland, *Aberdeen Papers in Land Economy*, *99–08*, Department of Land Economy, University of Aberdeen.

Smit, J. (2002) The colour of money, *Building Supplement on Homes*, February, 17–18.

Smith, A., Williams, G. and Houlder, M. (1986) Community influence on local planning policy, *Progress in Planning*, **25**, 1–82.

Smyth, H. (1984) Land supply, housebuilders and government policy, *Working Paper 43*, School for Advanced Urban Studies, University of Bristol.

Social Trends (2001) *Social Trends*, HMSO, London.

Spicker, P. (1998) Victorian values, in: *Built to Last* (eds J. Goodwin and C. Grant), pp. 17–24, Shelter, London.

Stewart, A. (1995) Development special report, *Property Week*, 12 January, 30–34.

Stockdale, A. and Lloyd, G. (1998) Forgotten needs? The demographic and socio-economic impact of free-standing new settlements, *Housing Studies*, **13**, 43–58.

Strange, I. (1999) Urban sustainability, globalisation and the pursuit of the heritage aesthetic, *Planning Practice and Research*, **14**, 301–11.

Stretton, H. (1996) Density, efficiency and equality in Australian cities, in: *The Compact City: A Sustainable Urban Form?* (eds M. Jenks, E. Burton and K. Williams), pp. 40–52, E & F N Spon, London.

Studdert, P. (2001) The Cambridge experience, *Town and Country Planning*, **70**, 56–7.

SVDLS (2000) *Scottish Vacant and Derelict Land Survey*, Scottish Executive, Edinburgh.

Syms, P (1994) The funding of developments on derelict and contaminated sites, in: *Industrial Property: Policy and Economic Development* (eds R. Ball and A. C. Pratt), pp. 63–82, Routledge, London.

Syms, P. (1997) *Contaminated Land*, Blackwell Science, Oxford.

Syms, P. (2001) *Releasing Brownfields*, Joseph Rowntree Foundation, York.

Syms, P. and Knight, P. (2000) *Building Homes on Used Land*, RICS Books, London.

Tate, J. (1994) Sustainability: a case of back to basics? *Planning Practice and Research*, **9.4**, 367–79.

Teitz, M. B. (1999) Urban sprawl – the debate continues, *Town and Country Planning*, **68**, 353.

Tewdwr-Jones, M. (ed.) (1996) *British Planning Policy in Transition*, UCL Press, London.

Tewdwr-Jones, M. and Allmendinger, P. (1998) Deconstructing communicative rationality: a critique of Habermasian collaborative planning, *Environment and Planning A*, **30**, 1975–89.

Thomas, L. and Cousins, W. (1996) The compact city: a successful, desirable and achievable urban form? in: *The Compact City: A Sustainable Urban Form?* (eds M. Jenks, E. Burton and K. Williams), pp. 53–65, E & F N Spon, London.

Thompson-Fawcett, M. (2000) The contribution of urban villages to sustainable development, in: *Achieving Sustainable Urban Form* (eds K. Williams, E. Burton and M. Jenks), pp. 275–87, E & F N Spon, London.

Thornley, A. (1996) Planning policy and the market, in: *British Planning Policy in Transition* (ed. M. Tewdwr-Jones), pp. 189–203, UCL Press, London.

Tiesdell, S. and Allmendinger, P. (2001) Neighbourhood regeneration and New Labour's third way, *Environment and Planning C: Government and Policy*, **19**, 903–26.

Town and Country Planning Association (1997) Living within the social city region, *Town and Country Planning*, **66**, 80–82.

Troy, P. (1996) Urban consolidation and the family, in: *The Compact City: A Sustainable Urban Form?* (eds M. Jenks, E. Burton and K. Williams), pp. 155–65, E & F N Spon, London.

Tucker, L. R. (1978) Planning agreements: the twilight zone of *ultra vires*, *Journal of Planning and Environmental Law*, 806–809.

Turok, I. (1992) Property-led urban regeneration: panacea or placebo? *Environment and Planning A*, **24**, 361–79.

Turok, I. (2001) Countryside protection or economic revitalisation? *Town and Country Planning*, **70**, 16.

Turok, I. and Edge, N. (1999) *The Jobs Gap in Britain's Cities*, Policy Press, Bristol.

Tyler, P. (2001) *Turning our Urban Areas Around – Do Area Based Initiatives Work? A Review of the Evidence Base and Lessons for Future Policy*, paper presented to Belfast City Council, Belfast.

UK Government (1994) *Sustainable Development: the UK Strategy*, Cm 2426, HMSO, London.

UK Round Table on Sustainable Development (1997) *Housing and Urban Capacity*, UK Round Table on Sustainable Development, London.

Urban Land Institute (1999) *Smart Growth: Myth and Fact*, Urban Land Institute, Washington, DC.

Urban Task Force (1999) *Towards an Urban Renaissance*, E & F N Spon, London.

Vigar, G., Healey, P., Hull, A. and Davoudi, S. (2000) *Planning, Governance and Spatial Strategy in Britain: An Institutional Analysis*, Macmillan, Basingstoke.

Walton, W. (2000) Windfall sites for housing: an underestimated resource, *Urban Studies*, **37**, 391–409.

Warren Evans, R. (1997) Myths and hobgoblins, *Town and Country Planning*, **66**, 90–92.

Watkins, C. (2002) The definition and identification of housing submarkets, *Environment and Planning A*, **33**, 2235–53.

Weiss, M. A. (1989) Richard T Ely and the contribution of economic research to national housing policy, 1920–1940, *Urban Studies*, **26**, 115–26.

Weiss, S. F., Smith, J. E., Kaiser, E. J. and Kenny, K. B. (1966) *Residential Developer Decisions*, Center for Urban and Regional Studies, University of North Carolina.

Wellings, F. (2000) *Private Housebuilding Annual 2000*, Credit Lyonnais Securities Europe, London.

Wellings, F. (2001) *Private Housebuilding Annual 2001*, Credit Lyonnais Securities Europe, London.

Wenban-Smith, A. (1999) *Plan, Monitor and Manage: Making It Work*, Council for the Protection of Rural England, London.

Whitehead, C. (1993) Privatising housing: an assessment of UK experience, *Housing Policy Debate* **14**, 1.

Whitehead, C. (1997) Changing needs, changing incentives, in: *Directions in Housing Policy: Towards Sustainable Planning Policies for the UK* (ed. P. Williams), pp. 7–21, Paul Chapman Publishing, London.

Wilcox, S. (1997) *Housing Finance Review, 1996/97*, Joseph Rowntree Foundation, York.

Wilcox, S. (1999) *The Vexed Question of Affordability*, Scottish Homes, Edinburgh.

Wilcox, S. (2000) *Housing Finance Review, 1999/00*, Joseph Rowntree Foundation, York.

Wilding, S. and Raemaekers, J. (2000) Environmental compensation for greenfield development: is the devil in the detail? *Planning Practice and Research*, **15**, 211–31.

Williams, J. (2000) Tools for achieving sustainable housing strategies in rural Gloucestershire, *Planning Practice and Research*, **15**, 155–74.

Williams, K. (1999) Urban intensification policies in England: problems and contradictions, *Land Use Policy*, **16**, 167–78.

Williams, K., Burton, E. and Jenks, M. (1996) Achieving the compact city through intensification: an acceptable option?, in: *The Compact City: A Sustainable Urban Form?* (eds M. Jenks, E. Burton and K. Williams), pp. 83–96, E & F N Spon, London.

Williams, K., Burton, E. and Jenks, M. (2000) *Achieving Sustainable Urban Form*, E & F N Spon, London.

Williams, P. (ed.) (1997) *Directions in Housing Policy: Towards Sustainable Planning Policies for the UK*, Paul Chapman Publishing, London.

Williamson, O. (1975) *Markets and Hierarchies*, Free Press, New York.

Wingo, L. (1961) *Transportation and Land Use*, Resources for the Future, Washington.

Winter, P. (1994) Planning and sustainability: an examination of the role of the planning system as an instrument for the delivery of sustainable development, *Journal of Planning and Environmental Law*, 883–900.

Woodward, S. (1998) Is vacant land really vacant? *The Planner*, **74**, 14.

World Bank (1994) *World Development Report 1994*, Oxford University Press, New York.

Wyatt, M. D. (1994) A critical view of land value taxation as a progressive strategy for urban revitalization, rational land use and tax relief, *Review of Radical Political Economics*, **26**, 1–25.

Index

Real Estate Issues

Series Managing Editors
Stephen Brown   RICS Foundation
John Henneberry   Department of Town & Regional Planning,
    University of Sheffield
James Shilling   Department of Real Estate and Urban Land Economics,
    University of Wisconsin – Madison

Real Estate Issues is a book series presenting the latest thinking into how real estate markets operate. It is inclusive in nature, drawing both upon established techniques for real estate market analysis and on those from other academic disciplines. It embraces a comparative approach, allowing best practice to be put forward and tested for its applicability and relevance to the understanding of new situations. It does not impose solutions, but provides a means by which solutions can be found. *Real Estate Issues* does not make any presumptions as to the significance of real estate markets, but presents the real significance of the operation of these markets.

Books in this series

Guy & Henneberry *Development and Developers*
Adams & Watkins *Greenfields, Brownfields and Housing Development*
O'Sullivan & Gibb *Housing Economics*
Couch, Fraser & Percy *Urban Regeneration in Europe*
Stephens *Housing Finance and Owner-occupation*
Brown & Jaffe *Real Estate Investment*
Seabrooke & How *International Real Estate*
Allen & Barlow *Housing in Southern Europe*
Ball *Markets and Institutions in Real Estate and Construction*

RICS **FOUNDATION**

To Judith, Daniel and Eleanor Adams
who encouraged and supported David from start to finish
and to the memory of Margaret Ronald

Contents

Figures and Tables

Figures

Tables

Preface

> 'Why do they need to build outwards on to those green fields when there is so much vacant land within the city?'

Today, this is a common call, whether made on television, in the press or just in everyday conversation. It places technical concerns about planning, land use, housing policy and related issues firmly at the heart of public and political debate. Moreover, this controversy is not confined merely to the UK but is international in nature, with similar concerns now apparent in the USA, Continental Europe and much of the advanced world.

At one level, the question is easily answered: it is normally much easier to build on greenfield than brownfield land. But this simple response soon generates more searching questions such as 'easier for whom?', 'why?' and 'must this always be so?' The hunt for answers rapidly takes us to another and more complex level of analysis, where we begin to investigate the strategies and interests of diverse stakeholders, the process of decision-making in the political and business worlds and the conflicting ways in which land is valued financially and as a source of cultural and environmental identity. If we are not careful, we are soon lost in all this complexity and have no more effective answer than the simplicity of our initial response.

This book is intended for all those who have asked that initial question but will not be satisfied with the simple answer. It seeks to unravel how choices and processes in both the public and private sectors interconnect and help frame those contentious debates about urban growth, housing development, decentralisation and regeneration. We argue that sustainable compact cities can be achieved only if the process of development is better managed and the products of development are of higher quality, and suggest that this has important implications for both private investment and public policy.

Although written from an academic perspective, the book is meant to appeal to a much broader range of policy-makers, interest groups, professionals, developers and commentators concerned with urban and regional policy in general and housing development in particular. Academically, it should serve as a valuable advanced text for researchers and students of fields such as housing policy, land economy, land management, property development, urban planning and urban studies who already have some basic knowledge about planning and political systems. Above all, we would hope that politicians and their professional advisers at national, regional and local levels might read this book and conclude that apparently simple questions do not always deserve simple answers!

David Adams and Craig Watkins
Aberdeen, March 2002

Acknowledgements

We wish to acknowledge the contribution of all those who have helped bring about this book, while absolving them from any responsibility for what has now emerged. Thomas Munjoma gathered information at the start of the project, while Joanne Dunse assisted with editorial work at the end. Both Thomas and Joanne proved dedicated and meticulous in the tasks they undertook for us and we are grateful both to them and to the RICS Foundation who supported the project financially.

Alan Hooper acted as an external commentator on all the draft chapters and his comments, as always, proved perceptive, detailed and constructive. We are particularly grateful for the time he devoted to this task, often at short notice, although he bears no responsibility for how we interpreted his many valuable suggestions.

We also benefited from the expert comments of Fred Wellings on Chapter 5 and from the detailed analysis of vacant and derelict land in Scotland especially undertaken for us by Esther Roughsedge of the Scottish Executive and reproduced in Chapter 8.

We are grateful for permission from the following sources to reproduce copyright and illustrative material: The Planning Exchange (Tables 7.2 and 7.3), Joseph Rowntree Foundation (Fig. 2.1), Steve Tiesdell (Figs 2.3, 7.1, 7.5, 8.7 and 8.8), ITPS Limited (Fig. 3.1), Pion Limited (Figs 3.2 and 7.4), The Town and Country Planning Association (Fig. 3.3), Countryside Properties plc (Figs 3.7, 3.12, 7.2 and 8.4), Island Press (Fig. 3.8), HMSO (Fig. 3.9), Liverpool University Press (Fig. 4.1), Copthorn Homes (Fig. 5.3), North Country Homes Group (Fig. 5.4), Octagon Developments Ltd (Fig. 5.5), Walton Homes (Fig. 7.3), Fairclough Homes (Fig. 8.5), Persimmon Homes and Matthew Streten Photography Ltd (Fig. 10.1) and finally to Alison Sandison for her assistance in reproducing Figs 8.1, 8.2, 8.3, 9.1, 9.2 and 9.3.

The University of Aberdeen granted us both research leave in 2001, and we much appreciated the space this period provided to plan and commence the book. We also wish to acknowledge the contributions of those colleagues who covered our management and teaching responsibilities during this time and who remained supportive in offering valuable comments as the book neared completion. In this context, we have particularly appreciated the academic friendship of Phil Allmendinger and Steve Tiesdell, our colleagues in the Department of Land Economy, who have encouraged our